An Introduction to Experimental Economics

An Introduction to Experimental Economics

GAUTAM GUPTA

Orient BlackSwan

AN INTRODUCTION TO EXPERIMENTAL ECONOMICS

ORIENT BLACKSWAN PRIVATE LIMITED

Registered Office
3-6-752 Himayatnagar, Hyderabad 500 029 (Telangana), INDIA
e-mail: centraloffice@orientblackswan.com

Other Offices
Bengaluru, Bhopal, Chennai, Ernakulam
Guwahati, Hyderabad, Jaipur, Kolkata, Lucknow
Mumbai, New Delhi, Noida, Patna, Vijayawada

First published by Orient Blackswan Private Limited 2016

ISBN 978 81 250 6079 6

Typeset in
Adobe Caslon Pro 10.5/12.5
by Manmohan Kumar, Delhi

Printed in India at
Rakmo Press, Greater Noida

Published by
Orient Blackswan Private Limited
1/24 Asaf Ali Road
New Delhi 110 002
e-mail: delhi@orientblackswan.com

To my wonderful family
Ma, Nila, Toto and Ananya

Contents

Tables, Boxes and Figures

TABLES

BOXES

FIGURES

Acknowledgements

I had ventured into experimental economics quite by accident and I have to thank Olof Johansson-Stenman and Fredrik Carlsson, my colleagues in Göteborg University, Sweden, for initiating me into this exciting field. This book is largely drawn from the course material of a masters course in experimental economics that I offer at Jadavpur University, supplemented by my own research, and I thank the students of this course, particularly the batch of 2013 for commenting on an earlier draft of the book. I thank my former research student Santanu Mitra (Women's Polytechnic, Kolkata) for collaborating with me in writing Chapter Seven.

Many people have given me helpful suggestions and tips about experiments, particularly on design issues. I thank Pushkar Maitra (Monash University, Melbourne), Ananish Chaudhuri (University of Auckland), Utteyo Das Gupta (Franklin & Marshall College, Pennsylvania), Arvind Ramalingam (University of East Anglia), Ritwik Banerjee (Aarhus University), Arnab Mitra (Portland State University), Neeraj Hatekar (University of Mumbai). I would also like to thank Pushkar for helping me set up the lab in Jadavpur University where many of these experiments were conducted. I also thank research scholars Savita Kulkarni (University of Mumbai) and Sanjukta Basu (Gokhale Institute of Economics and Politics, Pune). I sincerely thank Abhishek Das (Jadavpur University. Kolkata) for helping me with the research for this book. I also thank Shubhashrita Basu (Womens' Christian College, Kolkata) for compiling the bibliography of the book.

Much of the experiments were funded by the Centre for Advanced Studies, Department of Economics, Jadavpur University as well as the University with Potential for Excellence (UGC) Programme, Social Science component; I thank Ajitava Raychaudhuri (Jadavpur

University) who is Coordinator and Joint Coordinator of these two programmes respectively. Some of my earlier work has been funded by Swedish International Development Agency (SIDA), Monash University and the World Bank for which I thank them.

I thank Urs Fischbacher (z-Tree), Ananish Chaudhuri, University of Chicago Press, Econometric Society (*Econometrica*) for permission to reproduce copyrighted material without charge and Princeton University Press for allowing permission to use some copyrighted material. Finally, I thank the two anonymous reviewers for many helpful comments and suggestions and the publication team at Orient BlackSwan, especially Mimi Choudhury and Roopa Sharma, for their patience and understanding.

Publisher's Acknowledgements

For permission to reproduce copyrighted material in this volume, the publisher wishes to make the following acknowledgements.

Ananish Chaudhuri for permission to use data from Figures 2.4, 3.2 and 3.3 of Ananish Chaudhuri, *Experiments in Economics: Playing Fair with Money* (Oxford: Routledge, 2009) for Tables 2.3 and 2.5 of this volume. © Ananish Chaudhuri

The Econometric Society for the following permission clearances.

To render Figures 1 and 2 of R. McKelvey and T. Palfrey, 'An Experimental Study of the Centipede Game', *Econometrica* 61 (1991): 547–73, as Table 2.6 in this volume. © The Econometric Society

To render data from M. Allais, 'Le Comportement de l'Homme Rationnel devant le Risque: Critique des Postulats et Axiomesde l'Ecole Americaine', *Econometrica* 21 (1953): 503–46, as Table 4.1 in this volume. © The Econometric Society

Urs Fischbacher for permission to print screenshots of various stages of a program on z-Tree appearing as figures 7.2, 7.3, 7.4, 7.5, 7.6, 7.7 and 7.8 in this volume.

Santanu Mitra for permission to carry his essay, co-authored with Gautam Gupta, 'Introduction to Programming using z-Tree' as Chapter Seven in this volume.

University of Chicago Press for the following two permission clearances.

To carry Table 1 of E. Hoffmann and M. L. Spitzer, 'The Coase Theorem: Some Experimental Test', *Journal of Law and*

Economics 25 (1982): 73–98, as Table 2.7 in this volume. © University of Chicago Press

To carry Table 1 of Gerald Marwell and Ruth E. Ames, 'Experiments on the Provision of Public Goods: I. Resources, Interest, Group Size, and the Free-Rider Problem', *American Journal of Sociology* 84 (1979): 1335–60, as Table 3.2 in this volume. © University of Chicago Press

Princeton University Press for the following two permission clearances.

To carry Figure 1.1, Table 2.6, Figures 8.1 and 8.2 of Douglas D. Davis and Charles A. Holt, *Experimental Economics* (Princeton: Princeton University Press, 1993), as Tables 2.1 and 2.3, Table 2.2, Figures 4.1 and 4.2 respectively in this volume. © Princeton University Press. Permission conveyed through Copyright Clearance Center, Inc.

one

Introduction

Even though the conduct of experiments in economics with human subjects began in the 1930s this method did not gain wide acceptability in the discipline till the 1980s or even the 1990s. The process essentially involves gathering some persons, usually students, in a room, presenting them with an artefactual situation in which the persons are assigned roles, and getting them to take quantifiable decisions with monetary incentives. The data thus gathered is analysed to produce results. The reason why experiments in economics required this long to gain acceptability has to do with the methodologies initially used in economics to explore the subject. To understand this, let us take a look at the past.

The emergence of the discipline of economics is usually associated with the publication of *Wealth of Nations* by Adam Smith in 1776[1]. This book and subsequent books on economics by other early thinkers such as Ricardo (1817), Bentham (1781), Mill (1848), Say (Thweatt 2000) and Marx (1867) mainly used introspection to develop economic theory. They usually began by describing an artefactual economic situation and logically argued what the decision-making agent is likely to do. Their books are dotted with examples, real or imaginary, that support the propositions they have set forth. There is some use of aggregate level secondary data to explore some theoretical concerns.

[1] The book titled *An Inquiry into the Nature and Causes of the Wealth of Nations* was one of the earliest books in economics to have had a profound influence on subsequent early economic theory. Though considered to be a first, mention should be made of some economic ideas in ancient texts of various civilisations—such as Kautilya's Arthasastra (Mabbett 1964)—as well as writings on mercantilism, bullionism and physiocracy in the seventeenth and eighteenth centuries. For a complete discussion of these ideas, see Schumpeter (1954).

Thus introspection became the key tool that led to the development of economic theory. Economists observed the world around them and thought about economic situations and transactions. They conjectured what economic agents must be thinking and what such agents are likely to do. This was then formalised into a theory. Later, during the neo-classical revolution economists such as Marshall (1890), Walras (1874) and Pareto (1896–97) resorted to building models. Models served to explore economic situations more logically and propositions could be formalised more elegantly. Gradually, economists began to make use of mathematics in their models. First, only analytical geometrical diagrams were used to explain the working of a model. Later, the use of algebra, particularly differential and integral calculus, differential and difference equations became quite popular. Other mathematical tools and techniques were also used. A time soon came when a model would be considered unacceptable unless expressed mainly in the language of mathematics.

But introspection alone could not have elevated economics to the level of a social science. It became necessary to seek real life validation of existing theories. This was mainly done by using *secondary* data. Secondary data is data that is collected by some agency, other than the investigator, and for some purpose other than the present investigation. For example, when a client conducts any transaction with a bank, the bank keeps a record of that transaction for their own benefit. So every deposit, withdrawal or loan and loan repayment is recorded. Such data are routinely aggregated at the regional and national level by the headquarters of a bank to monitor its own activities. Now if a researcher can persuade all the banks in the country to release this data, certain hypotheses related to savings and investment behaviour of the people of the country could be estimated and tested.

A major concern in social sciences about collection of data is that the process of collection must be such that the act of observing (i.e. data collection) must not alter the observation itself. Now when bank data is generated, the person taking a loan is not even aware that that data will be used for economic investigation. Hence she will conduct her business with the bank in the manner she considers best for herself. Thus such *happenstance* data from naturally occurring economic processes can be thought to be reliable and without contamination. This type of data, when available, can be safely used for verifying economic hypotheses.

Such data are routinely collected and made available to researchers by Census authorities, National Sample Survey Organisation, Reserve Bank of India, Centre for Monitoring Indian Economy and various government departments.

In many cases, data appropriate for testing a particular hypothesis may not at all be available or not available in the form required. In such cases the investigator must collect *primary* data, usually through a questionnaire-based survey. Suppose one is interested to study the economics of health as practiced by people in a city. First, some households will need to be selected through randomisation after appropriate stratification. Then a household level survey will have to be conducted using a suitable questionnaire which has been rigorously piloted and field-tested. Such data suffers from two kinds of problems. First, there may be questions in the questionnaire that respondents are unwilling to answer or unwilling to answer truthfully. For example, in a health profile survey respondents may not give truthful answers to questions related to HIV/AIDS or about sexually transmitted diseases (STDs) due to social stigma. In rural India, people severely underreport agricultural income and land holdings in the belief that somehow the government will get to know these numbers and impose a tax on these. This falsification of data is a direct result of the fact that the household being observed is acutely aware of the fact that it is being observed. Then, one has to devise ways in which these questions can be asked so that they yield correct answers. Second, most questionnaire-based surveys rely on the ability of the respondent to recall past events. So, if there are questions about children's health—e.g., how many times each child has been taken ill, how many doctors visits, expenditure on medicines, workdays missed due to child's illness—some wrong answers may be given by a respondent because she simply does not remember but is embarrassed before the investigator to say so. In spite of these problems, questionnaire-based field surveys often need to be conducted as it yields data otherwise not available and in the format required by the investigator.

Until a few decades ago, this would exhaust the list of methods researchers could use to advance the pool of knowledge in economics. Economics was entirely considered a non-experimental subject. In their celebrated textbook *Economics*, Samuelson and Nordhaus (1985: 8) wrote: 'One possible way of figuring out economic laws

... is by controlled experiments. Economists (unfortunately) cannot perform the controlled experiments of chemists or biologists because they cannot control other important factors. Like astronomers or meteorologists they generally must be largely content to observe.' It is ironic that this was being written when experiments with human subjects had already become a reality in economics.

EARLY BEGINNINGS IN EXPERIMENTS

Up until the 1980s there was much reluctance and skepticism expressed about the validity of the use of experiments in investigating economic problems by some stalwart economists who rejected outright the possibility of using experimental methods. History will record that Thurstone (1931) reported an experiment where he had used this method to construct an individual's indifference curves[2]. This was done by asking subjects to make hypothetical choices between commodity bundles consisting of hats and coats, hats and shoes or shoes and coats. Each subject was asked to make such hypothetical choices a very large number of times. For example, in the choice involving the bundle of hats and shoes, subjects were asked to choose between 8 hats and 8 shoes versus 6 hats and 9 shoes, and so on, a large number of times. By reporting the detailed data for one individual subject he showed that it was possible to estimate a curve that fit the data quite closely and that indifference curves were indeed convex to the origin.

W. Allen Wallis and Milton Friedman (1942) wrote a lengthy critique of Thurstone, where they rejected the idea of using experiments to investigate economic problems. They mainly objected to experiments on the ground that they were ill-specified and based on hypothetical choices. They wrote, 'It is questionable whether a subject in so artificial an experimental situation could know what choices he would make in an economic situation. Not knowing, it is almost inevitable that he would, in entire good faith, systematize his answers in such a way

[2] Though Thusrstone (1931) is generally thought to be the first experiment in economics, Alvin Roth reports in the *Handbook of Experimental Economics* (Roth 1995) that the Bernoulli cousins, Daniel and Nicolas, performed experiments on their famous St Petersburg Paradox in 1738.

as to produce plausible but spurious results.' This is a fine example of serious objections expressed by renowned economists about the use of experiments in economics.

Experiments in economics differ from experiments in the physical sciences in one very crucial way, which raises some serious philosophical questions. In the physical sciences, the entity being observed is an inanimate object (a sub-atomic particle, a chemical compound, a beam of light). The instruments of observation are also inanimate and man-made (an electronic microscope, a spectrophotometer) and the observer is a human being. In economic experiments both the observed and the observer are human beings with an artefactual, contrived situation acting as the instrument of observation.

Rousseas and Hart (1951) reported, in response to the Wallis-Friedman critique, an experiment about construction of indifference curves. They required subjects to choose from options of breakfast menus consisting of some number of eggs and some number of strips of bacon. Each subject made a single choice and choices made by different subjects were pooled to form indifference curves. This was done by combining the choices that were similar. In subsequent literature, the practice of testing theories of individual behaviour using data collected from groups of subjects was considered to be incorrect.

In the mean time von Neumann and Morgenstern (1944) had published their book *Theory of Games and Economic Behavior*. This book which espoused, among other things the Expected Utility (EU) theory[3] made way for using a very powerful tool to investigate individual choices. Individual choices were experimentally tested under the general ambit of the EU theory by many researchers. These include Preston and Baratta (1948), Mosteller and Nogee (1951), Allais (1953) and Davidson and Marschak (1959) among others. The general trend of these investigations involved having subjects participate in a game with opportunities to take or refuse certain gambles or lotteries. These lotteries entailed the use of real monetary rewards and analyses were conducted on the information derived from these decisions to construct utility curves for each subject. The result could then be used to make predictions about future behaviour which could also be tested for accuracy. However, it should be noted that today much more is

[3] For a simple exposition of this theory, see Chapter 4.

known about systematic violation of EU theory, which can be observed through experiments. Perhaps the most famous of these is the Allais paradox, which has been discussed in detail in Chapter Four.

Another area in which von Neumann and Morgenstern (1944) had a lasting impact is interactive games, usually between two players that involve strategic decision making. Dresher and Flood got subjects to play such a game in Rand Corporation in 1950 (Flood 1952, 1958). This game would later come to be known as the prisoners' dilemma game. This game involved a hundred repetitions of simultaneous choices being made by a Row player and a Column player with the payoff matrix known to both. The idea was to check if they found the Nash equilibrium. They reported that the actual outcome was neither complete defection that is the Nash equilibrium nor complete cooperation that is the social optimum. The prisoners' dilemma games and related games are discussed in detail in Chapter Two.

Public goods games involving the voluntary contribution mechanism with the associated free riding, too, are a subject matter of a strong line of experiments. These can be seen as *n* person prisoners' dilemma games and are discussed in Chapter Three.

Finally, organisation of markets to study if predicted price outcomes are actually realised has been the subject matter of some early experiments. Edward H. Chamberlin (1948) conducted one of the earliest such experiments and reported the results. Chamberlin created an experimental market with subjects being designated buyers and sellers. He informed each buyer of the price below which he could profitably buy and each seller the price above which she could profitably sell. Buyers and sellers were then allowed to renegotiate with each other in a decentralised market situation. He reported the results of his experiments with a hypothetical good for 46 markets and showed that in forty-two of these the actual transacted volume was above the competitive equilibrium volume.

ADVANTAGES OF EXPERIMENTS

The main advantage of conducting laboratory experiments in any discipline is control and replicability. Control refers to the fact that ambient conditions in which the experiment is conducted can be so controlled that the object of study is not influenced by factors extraneous to the experiment. Replicability refers to the ability of other investigators to reproduce the experiment, thereby verifying the findings independently. In fact, lack of replicability is a serious problem with happenstance data from naturally occurring processes, where the data is recorded in a unique and non-replicated spatial and temporal background in which other unobserved factors are constantly changing.

Experiments in economics begin by describing an artefactual situation in the classroom or the laboratory before a gathered group of human subjects, usually university students. The artefactual or stylised situation must closely mimic the real life situation that is the object of the investigation. A set of clear and precise instructions are given to the subjects. The subjects must be given a clear and well-defined role in the situation. Thus the researcher knows precisely the set of information that the subjects have when taking decisions. This is the first aspect of experimental control. Now a stimulus is delivered to the subjects within the given situation and a response by the subjects needs to occur which must be recorded. It must be ensured that the researcher is able to establish a unique one-to-one connection between the stimulus and the response in the sense that there is no ambiguity about the fact that a particular response has definitely occurred due only to the stimulus that has been delivered.

Experimental control is further maintained by appropriate conditions in the room or lab, such as prevention of interruption or disturbance from outside and often no communication between subjects. This excludes the entire class of artefactual field experiments, the conditions for which are separately discussed in Chapter Five. Replicability is also ensured through reading out instructions that have been previously written down. Examples are presented both by reading out and with visual aids. Within these conditions control represents the capacity to manipulate laboratory conditions so that behaviour can be observed under several alternative conditions and these can be used to evaluate alternative theories. As mentioned earlier, replicability is one major advantage of experimental data as opposed to naturally occurring happenstance data. Suppose one were to obtain data for value and volume of imports and exports and major factors that influence trade for a period of ten years between two countries. Now, many other unrecorded factors will have changed in those ten years around the world that affect trade between these two countries. Hence, the econometric and statistical analysis that leads to results remains unique to that particular data set.

It is often the case, that there are some variations in the stimuli that is delivered. Each such variation is called a treatment. Thus the researcher is able to distinguish how each variation generates a different response compared to some baseline. Here, a different set of subjects are assigned to each treatment. This process is discussed in further detail in Chapter Six.

If analyses based on secondary or primary data are termed *passive* observation, the recording of experimental response arising out of the delivered stimulus is a process of *active* observation. The key to this is that the subjects are fully aware that they are being observed. Yet, the fact that they know that they are being observed must not be allowed to alter their behaviour. This alteration of behaviour is more likely to happen when the subjects are university students and the experimenter is a professor in the same university. For example, in a public goods game (more on this game in Chapter Three) a student subject may really wish to contribute little or nothing, but may feel that the experimenter will then think that this student has a poor moral character and therefore decides to contribute a handsome amount.[4]

There are really two ways to control this tendency. First, strong monetary incentives tied to the outcome of the experiment must be used. It may be noted that in the early days of experimental economics, monetary incentives were hardly used. Often hypothetical payments were used as in the famous Kahneman and Tvresky (1979) study. In some other studies, student subjects were rewarded with few extra points in examinations. Now of course, these are strictly prohibited. Only real money (with a show up fee) can be used for experimental results to be considered scientific, which can be taken seriously. The logic of this is that the direction that a strong financial incentive takes is clear, since more is always better. This may not be the case with other incentives. Further, monetary incentives can be precisely recorded with a measurable unit of account. Second, various blind protocols can be used to ensure that the investigator is unable to identify a particular decision with a particular subject, and the subjects are aware of this

[4] This is known in the literature as the experimenter effect.

(this is explained in Chapter Six). This goes a long way in ensuring the fact that though subjects are aware that they are being observed it does not alter their behaviour.

The use of experiments has its fair share of problems. First, many problems are not amenable to experiments. For example, it is nearly impossible to design experiments to test models that seek to explain GDP growth rates or govern Central Bank policy. Second, the experiment being conducted must have strong real life parallelism with the problem being investigated, and this is sometimes difficult to achieve, even when a stylised experiment can be designed. This severely reduces the effectiveness of the experiment to address the problem at hand. Finally, there is the issue of finding an appropriate pool of subjects. Up until the 1980s, and even early 1990s, the received wisdom was that the subject pool did not matter as long as they were human beings. Therefore, the most frequently used pool of subjects used were university students, the only reason being that this is the one pool of subjects readily available to the experimenters who are mostly university professors. However, there were two objections to using university students. First, it is seen that experimental economists regularly publish papers that make broad claims about economic decision-making processes based upon experiments conducted on a very narrow section of humanity, namely western, educated, industrialised, rich and democratic (WEIRD) persons where the American undergraduate belong.[5] The implicit assumption is that there is little variation in economic behaviour across human populations or that these standard subjects are representative of the entire species as a whole. It would seem that lived experience would make a difference in the way a person thinks and behaves. Therefore, student subjects in the same cultural milieu would likely behave differently from corporate CEOs, farmers, industrial workers or unemployed youth.

Another related issue is that of differences in cultures. Again, the initial implicit assumption was that culture did not matter. Then came the study by a team led by Alvin Roth (Roth, Prasnikar, et al. 1991). They recruited student subjects in four countries, USA, Yugoslavia, Japan and Israel. So now we see subjects similar to one another, as all

[5] For a more comprehensive critique of the wide literature that uses such a narrow subject pool see Henrich, Heine and Norenzayan (2009).

are students, but culturally different. The results from the ultimatum game they played show that while there are similarities, there are also important differences.

It is now quite common to run experiments using subjects from different countries and cultures. So that important socio-cultural differences and their impact on economic decision making can be picked up and compared. For example, Gneezy, Leonard and List (2009) conduct a controlled experiment to study if there are gender differences in selecting into competitive environments. They conducted the experiments with Maasai subjects in Tanzania, where the society is highly patriarchal and Khasi subjects in India, where the society is matrilineal. This study found that Maasai men opt to compete more than Maasai women but with Khasi subjects the opposite was true. Such multicultural experiments are described in Chapter Five. Further, it has now become quite important to run experiments with subjects other than students. One sees more and more experiments where the subjects are persons who are likely to have a lived experience in the area where the real life problem is located. This makes it more necessary to run experiments in the field. This brings with it its own share of hazards. These, too, are described in Chapter Five.

SOME RECENT APPLICATIONS OF EXPERIMENTS IN ECONOMICS

Once it is acknowledged that the nature of the subject pool matters in explaining decisions and outcomes in an experiment, a whole set of new opportunities opens up. Various kinds of heterogeneities can be built into the subject pool to see how these impact decisions and outcomes. In other words, if there are two or more distinct groups within the subject pool, then experiments can be used to check how behaviour differs across such groups. For example, a two-stage game could be played with a woman making the first move and a man making the second move, and again with a man making the first move and a woman as the second mover to test a certain hypothesis about behavioural differences based on gender. This, of course, must be compared with a few control sessions, where the genders of the first and second mover are not disclosed to one another. Likewise, one could divide the subject pool by income class into rich and poor (around some arbitrary income level) and have one of each group partner in a two-stage game, alternating the start between rich and poor players, to check if the rich or the poor behave differently when all else is same. Turning to relations between religious communities where the population is mixed and such relations have a sensitive edge, one could have Hindus and Muslims play a 2-stage game, with each alternating as first mover, to see if the lived experience of existing in a mixed community makes for differences in behaviour across religious communities. Such possibilities are endless and provide ample scope to study the impact of various socio-cultural identities on economic decision making. In all such cases, it is necessary that such results be statistically pitted against data gathered from a few control sessions, where the group identities of the subjects are not disclosed to other subjects. These recent uses of experiments where the subject pool is divided by gender, religion, caste or lived experiences are discussed in Chapter Five.

Another recent advance of experimental economics is the interdisciplinary field of neuroeconomics. It combines research methods in neuroscience, experimental and behavioural economics, cognitive and social psychology to study human decision making, the ability to process multiple alternatives and choose an optimal course of action. The main areas in which neuroeconomics ventured into are decision making under uncertainty, loss aversion, intertemporal choice and social decision making. As this is a sub-discipline in its own right, neuroeconomics is not discussed in this book.

EXPERIMENTS OUTSIDE A COMPUTER LABORATORY

In recent times it has become more or less customary to run experimental sessions in a computer laboratory. This has the advantage that experimental sessions can be run in a relatively shorter time so that subjects' patience is not taxed, and a rather larger data set can be generated in that time. The recording of decisions and outcomes are also easier and efficient. However, there are situations when it is either not possible or not desirable to run sessions in a lab. The above example of introducing group identities into experimental sessions is a case in point. It is then necessary to conduct experiments in the field. Field experiments, as they are now called, are often (though not always) hand-run in locations near where the chosen subject pool lives, which may be a village, a slum or an environmentally sensitive area. Secure locations must be identified to run field experiments to ensure complete experimental control.

A fairly recent and novel addition to the variety of experiments being conducted all over the world are natural field experiments[6]. These are experiments that make use of a phenomenon that takes place on its own, that is, without the intervention of the experimenters. The experimenter must have foreknowledge that such an event is about to happen. What the experimenter does is she skilfully manipulates any one aspect of the event (compared to some control where no manipulation has been done) so that the difference in outcome over the control can be uniquely linked to that one manipulated factor. Field experiments of various types and natural field experiments are elaborately discussed in Chapter Five[7].

Finally, it has become almost mandatory to provide monetary rewards to subjects for experimental results to be considered scientific in economics. Yet, it is possible to run experiments where no monetary reward, real or imaginary, are promised or given. Typically these are decision processes which do not have outcomes that can be measured in monetary terms, so no expectation of a monetary reward arises in the mind of a subject. These are hand-run under an artefactual circumstance with student or other subjects in a classroom format. A decision sheet, much like a survey questionnaire is used. For non-monetised experiments to be considered scientific, the subject pool must be large. This is so such that any random or outlying decisions present in the data set due to absence of monetary incentives can cancel each other out. A couple of examples of non-monetised experiments are described in Chapter Five.

[6] There is some terminological confusion here. Natural field experiments were earlier called field experiments. This was when artefactual field experiments as we know them today did not exist. But with the advent of artefactual field experiments, these were renamed as natural field experiments. Hence in some earlier papers in the 1990s, natural field experiments are termed field experiments.

[7] For a comprehensive discussion of all kinds of field experiments see Harrison and List (2004).

USES OF EXPERIMENTS IN ECONOMICS

Experiments have found useful application in a wide range of areas in economics. More applications are happening on a daily basis. These areas include, but are not limited to, coordination, bargaining behaviour, strategic choice, auction markets, public goods, macro-economic predictions, overlapping generation environments, contracts and agreements, various issues in industrial organisation, asset markets, individual decision and choice under uncertainty. It is useful to classify the myriad uses into some broad categories for better understanding of this technique. Following Alvin Roth in the *Handbook of Experimental Economics* (Roth 1995), three broad categories are listed below. These categories are created on the basis of what an experiment is motivated by and who the experimenter wishes to communicate with.

i. *Speaking to Theorists*: This category of experiments is intended to test the predictions of well-developed economic theories of long standing. Incidentally, it is the case that in the process of testing, unpredicted outcomes have been frequently noticed. When such unpredicted outcomes are observed quite regularly, then a need is felt to return to the drawing board and revise existing theory.
ii. *Searching for Facts*: This class of experiments mainly address issues and variables about whose behaviour existing theories may have very little to say. Often these experiments carry innovations over earlier experiments by varying some condition to isolate the effect of a single stimulus. After many repetitions and variations, certain regularity may be observed in the movement of the variables under study. This then leads to the creation of new theories.
iii. *'Whispering in the Ear of Princes'*: This class of experiments are usually conducted to measure the effectiveness of a certain policy regime or to rank alternative policy instruments by how effective they are. At present, when policy alternatives exist, policymakers and bureaucrats often choose one using a combination of intuition, hunch and guess. Sometimes such a policy works and sometimes it does not, and money, time and effort are wasted. Experiments offer a relatively inexpensive way to test for policy effectiveness and to rank alternative policy regimes and institutional frameworks.

THE PHILOSOPHY OF EXPERIMENTAL ECONOMICS

It would be amiss to end the introduction to this book without a discussion on the philosophical underpinning of experimental economics. Philosophers interested in the philosophy of science have mainly looked at epistemology in the natural sciences because they are supposed to be the most advanced disciplines with respect to both their methodology and their results. The questions frequently asked are: How should genuine scientific knowledge be generated? How do scientists avoid falling into error? What does scientific knowledge consist of? Is it the why or the how of a process that we are investigating?

More recently there has been some interest in looking at experimental economics with the same set of questions.[8] This opens up the possibility of investigating an important problem of scientific inference: the problem of external validity or how to generalise experimental results to non-laboratory settings.

Philosophy of science often makes use of models. These models aim at capturing the process of scientific reasoning. They are idealised and as such do not represent the practical reasoning followed by a science in all its details. Rather, they try to capture some essential aspects and deliberately simplify in order to represent a problem elegantly. Moreover, they often have a hybrid descriptive-normative status in that they posit ways in which scientific reasoning should take place while identifying our most common cognitive mistakes.

Experimental economics is mostly grounded in the well-known Hypothetico-Deductive model (HD model). This model is in the well-grounded empiricist tradition, according to which empirical evidence is the primary source of validation of the theories that explain the natural and social worlds. The HD model is a proposed description of scientific method. According to the HD model, scientific enquiry proceeds by formulating a hypothesis in a manner that can be falsified with the help of a test using observable data. A test that concludes contrary to the predictions of the hypothesis is interpreted as falsification of the hypothesis. Likewise, a test that does not conclude contrary to the predictions of the hypothesis is seen as corroboration. It is now

[8] For a more exhaustive discussion of the philosophy of science of experimental economics, see Guala (2005).

possible to compare the explanatory power of competing hypothesis by testing how strictly observable data corroborates the predictions of these hypotheses.

Box 1.1 Models of Scientific Enquiry in the Philosophy of Science

Philosophy of science is a branch of philosophy concerned with the basis, methods and implications of scientific theories. This branch of philosophy tries to identify what should be regarded as science, the purpose of scientific theories and the reliability of such theories. Most centrally, it explores the relationship between science and truth. In this sense, philosophy of science shares borders with metaphysics, ontology and epistemology. Many central problems in this body of knowledge remain unresolved. Can science reveal the truth about unobservable phenomena? Can scientific reasoning be justified at all?

Philosophy of science dates back to Aristotle but the current trends emanate from the mid-twentieth century, in the wake of a movement termed *logical positivism*. This movement tries to formulate criteria to ensure the meaningfulness of philosophical statements and ways of objectively assessing such statements. Some thinkers wish to ground science in axiomatic assumptions. However, the vast majority of theorists in this branch of philosophy use a *coherentist* approach which considers a theory validated if it makes sense of observations as part of a coherent whole.

In the discussions on the philosophy of science, the following concepts assume importance:

Epistemology: Branch of philosophy that deals with what knowledge is, how we accept some things as true and how we justify this acceptance.

Empiricism: Set of philosophical approaches to building knowledge that emphasises the importance of observable evidence from the natural world.

Induction: Method of reasoning in which a generalisation is considered to be true based on individual examples that fit that generalisation.

Deduction: Method of reasoning where a conclusion is logically reached beginning with some premises or fundamentals.

(Box 1.1 contd...)

(...Box 1.1 contd)

Occam's razor: This concept claims that when all other things are equal, a simpler explanation is to be preferred to a more complex one. This concept is often used to rank theories in terms of their acceptability.

Demarcation: The problem of distinguishing between science and non-science. This is a contentious issue in the philosophy of science. Some areas of speculation that often masquerade as science are referred to as pseudoscience, fringe science or junk science. Examples are astrology, numerology or creation science. Demarcation is used to distinguish between these and science. Physicist Richard Feynman used the term 'cargo cult science' for cases where researchers claim that they are doing science because their activities have the outward appearance of science but lack the ability to be rigorously evaluated. Philosophers have however not been unanimous about the method of demarcation.

Falsification: A concept suggested by Karl Popper (1946), that scientific evidence can only be used to rule out ideas, not to support them. Popper held that scientific ideas can only be tested through falsification, never through a search for supporting evidence.

There are problems of looking at the predictions of a hypothesis and testing it with observable data. For example, such predictions could be probabilistic in nature. One can predict that a certain medicine will effect a cure in 70 per cent cases. Tests in this case must be repeated a large number of times to support this conjecture.

Further, evidence contrary to the hypothesis also raises some philosophical issues. Such evidence is used for falsification of the hypothesis. Now, it is always possible to prevent the falsification of the hypothesis. This is because every falsifying observation is always embedded in a theoretical background, and by suitably modifying the theoretical background the falsifying observation can be altered to bring it in line with the predictions of the hypothesis.

In conclusion, it can be said that experimental economics is, at present, a happening investigative method. This is to mean that it has overcome the initial resistance of the profession and the reluctance by researchers to use it, which was clearly evident up to the 1970s. The profession has also converged on an acceptable protocol that is to be followed by investigators in order for the study to be accepted as scientifically done. Yet, many issues remain unresolved and continuous experimentation and learning with an open mind must continue for the present for experimental economics to gain the credibility and respectability of experimental physics or experimental chemistry. Those readers of this book who are already engaged in research in experimental economics or those who plan to do so in the future can rightfully claim to have been part on an ongoing and exciting experiment.

Note on the Organisation of the Volume

Though experimental economics has proliferated into many areas of economics, I find the three main areas which use experimental economics extensively are: a) games involving strategic decisions where there are typically two players and the decision of one player is contingent upon how she expects the other player to behave, b) public goods games with small groups and a group fund designed to test the existence of the free rider problem through a voluntary contributions mechanism, and c) games involving a choice between two or more lotteries that seek to explain decision making under conditions of uncertainty. Accordingly, the next three chapters discuss these three themes. Each of these chapters discusses underlying theory, issues with experimental design and a discussion of results of well-known experiments already conducted. Chapter 5 contains discussion on more recent advances in experimental economics that go beyond 'traditional' experimental economics. To begin with we discuss experiments outside the computer laboratory, even outside the university. Typically these will also make use of non-student subjects. Further there are experiments involving cultural groups such as gender or religious identity, experiments that are conducted in several countries to compare between different cultural contexts. There is a discussion of natural experiments that make use of an event that would have happened in any case. Finally, we discuss experiments where monetary reward is not used. Much of my own research informs this chapter. Chapter 6 contains issues of methodology and a protocol that is to be followed for the experiment to be considered scientific. The last chapter discusses how to use z-Tree, a software for running experiments in a laboratory, which should be of practical use should the reader decide to conduct experiments.

two

Experiments with Games of Strategic Choices

The discipline of economics possibly began with the publication of Adam Smith's *Wealth of Nations*[1] where he first propounded his theory of the 'Invisible Hand'. At the basis of this much quoted and powerful theoretical construct was the definition of rationality in terms of an individual's self-interest. 'It is not from the benevolence of the butcher, the brewer or the baker, that we expect our dinner, but from their regard to their own interest. We address ourselves, not to their humanity but to their self-love, and never talk to them of our own necessities but of their advantages' (Smith 1981/1776: 26–27) Thus, rationality came to be defined in terms of the self-interest of the economic agent. In other words, an agent is considered to be rational only if she acts in self-interest. In turn, expression of self interest came to be described as such decisions and actions she takes that she thinks is best for her. These decisions and actions are contingent upon the circumstances in which an individual finds herself (which are themselves outcomes of earlier decisions) and the information about various alternative outcomes she has at that point of time. This motivation, coupled with the existence of a competitive economic system, leads to an equilibrium that is good for all concerned. The broadest possible generalisation of this concept subsequently led to the Walras-Pareto paradigm. In summary, Walras (2013/1874) showed that if competitive conditions existed in all markets, then by a process of competitive bidding between buyers

[1] This book, popularly referred to as *Wealth of Nations* bears the title *An Inquiry into the Nature and Cause of the Wealth of Nations*, and along with its companion volume *The Theory of Moral Sentiments* (1759) marks the beginning of modern economics.

and sellers under full information, all markets would be in equilibrium and all markets would clear. In other words, all buyers would be able to buy the quantities they intended to buy and all sellers would be able to sell the quantities they intended to sell at the prevailing price, in all markets simultaneously. Walras termed this General Equilibrium.

The paradigm was taken forward by Pareto (1896) with the so-called first and second theorems of welfare economics. In the first theorem it was claimed that every Walrasian general equilibrium was Pareto optimal in the sense that all gains from trade had been realised and it was not possible to improve the condition of any one member of society without hurting the condition of at least one other member. The second theorem, often erroneously termed the converse of the first theorem, makes a far stronger claim. It says that every Pareto optimal solution for the economy can be realised as an outcome of a Walrasian general equilibrium. Thus if one were prepared to accept the Pareto definition of welfare maximisation for society, all that is required is full information and a competitive economy, provided there are no externalities in production or consumption. This would be sufficient to ensure that all improvements in any one person's life, without diminishing the utility of any other person, have been achieved[2]. This led to the fundamental neo-classical philosophy that competition is a good thing. It enhances efficiency, improves productivity and growth and leads to an overall social optimum. This philosophy dominated the literature for decades.

John Nash[3] changed all that. In 1950 he was a graduate student of mathematics in Princeton University. Being mentally ill, he would undergo longish periods when he did no research. This led to a situation where he risked losing his funding. He was given one last chance by the department to show some evidence of productive research. Desperate, he came up with the paper that made the *prisoners dilemma* famous[4].

[2] Both Walrasian general equilibrium and Pareto optimality require that market for all commodities exist and there is no externality in production or consumption.

[3] John Forbes Nash, Jr (1928–2015) was a PhD from Princeton University. He shared the Nobel Prize in Economics in 1994. He is the subject of Hollywood film *A Beautiful Mind* which is based on a biography with the same title.

[4] The stylised story of two prisoners was originally due to Merril Flood and Melvin Dresher, researchers at RAND Corporation in 1950. In the same year, Albert W. Tucker gave it a game form with prison sentences. The equilibrium, of course, is due to Nash.

It contradicted the concept of the benevolent role of competition in society and flew in the face of 150 years of classical and neo-classical economics. In an equilibrium, that came to be named after him, Nash demonstrated that with full information, competitive behaviour could, in fact, lead away from the social optimum.

To demonstrate this, Nash used a stylised story[5]. There were two criminals who had jointly committed a crime. The police officer investigating the crime was able to identify the two individuals responsible for the crime but was unable to find any proof that would stand up to scrutiny in a court of law. He realised that it would be pointless to attempt prosecution of these criminals in such a situation. His only hope was to secure a confession from any one of the two criminals, which would also implicate the other. So he adopted the following strategy. He brought both the criminals in for questioning and put them in separate rooms, so that they could not communicate. Each knew that the other had been brought in. Now he made an offer to each criminal and told each of them that the same offer has been made to the other. The offer is that if one criminal confesses, thereby implicating the other in the crime, then the one confessing would be sent to jail for 1 year only while the other criminal would go to jail for 7 years. If, however, both confessed, then there would be no reason to show leniency and both would go to jail for 5 years. By implication, if both refused to confess, then we have the original situation back again, where both would be charged with a lesser crime only and get a sentence of 2 years each.

The possible outcomes of the game is represented in Table 2.1,[6] in a format that is termed a *payoff matrix*. Nash had termed the two players as *prisoners* and we denote them here as *P1* and *P2*. There are two strategies available to each prisoner, to confess (*C*) or not to confess (N). This results in four cells numbered 1 to 4 clockwise. In each cell, there are two numbers separated by a comma. Each number is the number of years spent in jail; where the first number refers to the jail term for *P1* and the second number refers to the jail term for *P2*. We

[5] This example closely follows Davis and Holt (1993: 7–8).

[6] For important observations on Tables 2.1 and 2.2, the author is grateful to the students of the course experimental economics in the third semester of their MA in economics programme at Jadavpur University during the year 2013–14.

put a negative sign before the jail terms indicating that going to jail is bad for the prisoners.

Table 2.1 Payoff Matrix in a Standard Prisoner's Dilemma Game

		P2			
		C		N	
P1	C	−5,−5	①	−1,−7	②
	N	−7,−1	④	−2,−2	③

Source: Republished with permission of Princeton University Press, from Davis and Holt (1993: 8); permission conveyed through Copyright Clearance Center, Inc.

Consider cell 1. This outcome is reached when both prisoners confess. Both get prison terms of 5 years. In cell 2, *P1* confesses but *P2* does not. Hence *P1* goes to jail for 1 year only while *P2* gets 7 years. Converse is the outcome in cell 4. Finally, cell 3 is reached when both prisoners do not confess, and consequently both are charged with a lesser crime and go to jail for 2 years each. Clearly, in a society of only the two prisoners, social optimum will be reached in cell 3. The question now is: Can this outcome be reached? Nash had shown that this outcome will not be reached, and that too because of self-interest and the underlying competitive environment. How does this work? First consider *P1*. Ideally he would like to go to jail for 1 year only, even if it means confessing and sending his partner in crime to jail for 7 years. He can never be sure that *P2* will not confess, so for him *N* cannot be optimal strategy, as cell 3 may never be reached. Therefore, in an effort to reach cell 2 he will confess. Now consider *P2*. His actions will be symmetrical with *P1*. Again, as he too is not sure that *P1* will not confess, he realises that cell 3 may never be reached. Alternatively, in an effort to reach cell 4, *P2* will confess. The combination of the actions of the two prisoners will take this two-prisoner-society to cell 1, which is the Nash equilibrium (Nash 1950).

In the above, there is competition between the two prisoners to confess ahead of the other. It is clearly shown that not only will society be unable to reach the social optimum; the two prisoners will actually end up in cell 1, which is the worst possible outcome for society. The prisoners' dilemma game demonstrates that competition is not necessarily good for society; in fact, competitive behaviour can drive society to inferior outcomes characterised by Nash equilibrium.

We see many real life examples of competitive behaviour or the inability to trust others leading to such collective behaviour that result in disastrous outcomes. The *kumbh mela* was held from 14 January to 10 March 2013 on the banks of the river Ganges in the historic city of Allahabad, India. This is the largest gathering of Hindus in India. The high point of the gathering is a holy dip in the river, which has to be performed at certain auspicious times during the *mela*. On 10 February 2013, the Allahabad railway station was bursting at the seams with an extremely large gathering of people, eager to return home after completing the *mauni amavasya snan*, the holy dip and prayers. Special trains were arranged regularly for the purpose. Yet, a stampede occurred while people rushed to board a train. Thirty-six persons were killed (*TNN* 2013). Clearly, if people had behaved in an orderly manner, queued up to board trains, moved with caution and care, these lives would not have been lost. But the belief that one will be left behind if one did not rush and scramble led to this tragedy. Tragedies of this kind are egalitarian; anyone in the gathering could be the next victim. Yet, the regularity with which such accidents keep occurring point to the fact that people have an inherent belief about the behaviour of others that shapes their own behaviour. People believe that others will compete hard for a place, and that makes them also compete equally hard, leading to a disaster. If, instead, there was general belief that order will be maintained, this could possibly have led to a situation where everyone behaved in an orderly manner, and disasters avoided.

PRISONER'S DILEMMA IN EXPERIMENTS

Contrary to the obvious, that a prisoners dilemma situation will necessarily result in a Nash equilibrium, is empirically difficult to verify. As discussed in the earlier chapter, this belongs to that class of problems where real life data is almost impossible to collect. This paves the way for the playing of a game with a contrived situation between a pair of players, each with two alternative choices, to see what outcome is arrived at.

Consider a situation where there are only two neighbourhood grocery shops, which operate during working hours on weekdays only. Now both owners are contemplating extending their business hours to the weekend[7]. In a full information model both know that the other is contemplating such a move. The weekend business constitutes a new market for both players, so extending shop hours to the weekend may be thought of as a decision to enter a new market. To begin with, assume that if both shops retain their original hours (i.e., do not enter the new market) the customers are equally divided between the two shops and each earn a profit of *P*. Now, if one shop opens in the weekend while the other remains closed, the one that extends to the weekend additionally earns extra profit *R*. This is new business from customers who had found it impossible to shop during working hours on weekdays and hence had to shop far away. Additionally, the shop that extends to the weekend is able to attract customers away from the shop that does not, and this transfer business results in extra profits of *L*. Consequently the shop that does not extend to the weekend loses *L* from the original *P*. Finally, extending to the weekend involves an extra fixed cost *C*. You may think of this as the salary of an extra employee who needs to be hired to keep the shop open in the weekends. If both players decide to keep their respective shops open in the weekends then the profits from new business *R* is split equally between the two shops. Note that if both shops keep open on weekends, both retain their original customers and there is no loss or gain from transfer business *L*[8].

Now to summarise, if both players stay open only on weekdays (*N*) both earn *P*. If one shop extents to the weekend (*E*) and the other does not (*N*) the one that extends earns $P + R + L - C$ and the one that does not now earns $P - L$. Finally, if both shops decide to extend to the weekend (*E*) then both earn $P + (R/2) - C$. To create an example, we put values for these, such as $P = 800$, $R = 1300$, $L = 500$ and $C = 1100$. This leads to the following payoff matrix presented in Table 2.2.

[7] This example is based on Davis and Holt (1993: 92–95).

[8] It may be recalled that grocery shops in London would be closed during weekends up until the 1960s. These shops were owned entirely by British owners. Later, a few shops began to remain open during weekends. These were mainly owned by the migrant Asian community desperate to find a foothold in the business. This competition eventually forced all grocery shops to remain open in the weekends.

Table 2.2 Payoff Matrix for an Entry Game

		P2	
		N	*E*
P1	*N*	800,800	300,1500
	E	1500,300	350,350

Source: Republished with permission of Princeton University Press, from Davis and Holt (1993: 95); permission conveyed through Copyright Clearance Center, Inc.

Notice that the cooperative solution here is (*N*,*N*) resulting in each player earning a profit of 800. However, the incentive to deviate from this cooperative solution lies in the fact that each player can unilaterally increase her profit from 800 to 1500 by extending business hours to the weekend. This primarily happens because of new business that appears leading to extra profits *R* but also because some customers transfer their purchases leading to additional profits *L*. There is also extra cost of staying open in the weekend to the extent of fixed cost *C*. The shop that does not extend to the weekend loses *L* from the original *P*, but does not incur *C*. However as both players perceive this; it will appear to be in the best interest of each player to decide to extend to the weekend resulting in each ending up earning $P + (R/2) - C$ where each earns the lowest amount among all possible situations, and this is the Nash equilibrium of the game.

It is now straightforward to design an experiment around this game. This is precisely what was done by Cooper, Douglas, et al. (1991). There were 21 student subjects and each subject was paired with a different subject in a sequence of 20 matchings. Thus each subject would be paired with any one other player only once. This was explained to the students to avoid possible retaliation for an earlier round. The payoffs were given in terms of lottery tickets and these were used later to decide if the subject could earn a rewards of $1 after each matching. This has the desired effect of inducing risk-neutral behaviour. The data garnered from this experiment is shown in Table 2.3.

As shown in Table 2.2, the theoretical prediction is that the Nash equilibrium (*E*,*E*) is the inevitable outcome of the game, but both players are better off under strategy pair (*N*,*N*) which cannot be reached.

Table 2.3 Percentage of Cooperative Choices made in 20 Matchings

Matchings	Percent of Cooperative Choice (*N*,*N*)
1 to 5	43
6 to 10	33
11 to 15	25
16 to 20	20

Source: Republished with permission of Princeton University Press, from Davis and Holt (1993: 95); permission conveyed through Copyright Clearance Center, Inc.

Experimental results from Cooper, Douglas, et al. (1991) however suggest otherwise. It shows that intelligent players when explained the structure of the payoffs do in fact trust their partners and stick to strategy choice *N* for a substantial percentage of times. Experimental evidence further suggests that as multiple rounds are played and some expectations are not fulfilled, there is a certain erosion of this trust. Thus the cooperative strategy pair (*N*,*N*) percentage is initially high but comes down in later rounds. However, the important result is that in a simple prisoners' dilemma game with a single Nash equilibrium, the inevitable outcome is not necessarily the Nash equilibrium and the social optimum may be reached approximately between 25 and 50 per cent of the times.

The prisoners' dilemma game has been played by economists and psychologists many hundreds of times with many variations. In one variation, most typically played, the same pair of players is made to choose from a payoff matrix over multiple rounds. This essentially captures the behaviour of a pair of duopolists who are forced to interact with each other over several market periods. Supposing there are two strategies available to each duopolist, setting product price high (*H*) or low (*L*). In the one-period version, the Nash equilibrium is (*L*,*L*). The socially optimal outcome (*H*,*H*) is typically not reached. But if the game is played over multiple rounds, with the same pair of subjects, we are likely to see more (*H*,*H*) outcomes. In fact, each player will hesitate to deviate from this strategy for fear of a retaliatory punishment in the next period, resulting in lower payoff for both players. Therefore strategy choice pair (*H*,*H*) could continue as long as there is some positive probability that the game would continue for one more period. If the number of rounds is not known in advance, this strategy choice could very well continue indefinitely. However, if the number of periods is known it is likely that there will be deviation from the cooperative solution in the last period. This brings up the issue of *backward induction* which will be discussed when we talk about the Centipede game a few sections below.

THE ULTIMATUM GAME: ALTRUISM OR FAIRNESS

Many economic situations, where only two parties are trying to reach an agreement, involve some form of bargaining. Typically, wage negotiations between a firm's management and its workers' union can take this form. Bargaining may extend to the field of electoral politics as well. In a pre-election coalition between two or more political parties, bargaining may involve the share of seats each party would be allowed to contest. Depending on the election results, this share will potentially reflect the proportion of seats each party may have in Parliament after the election is over.

Many bargaining situations lead to an impasse with neither side agreeing to the offer made by the other. In such situations, the agent

Figure 2.1 The Ultimatum Game

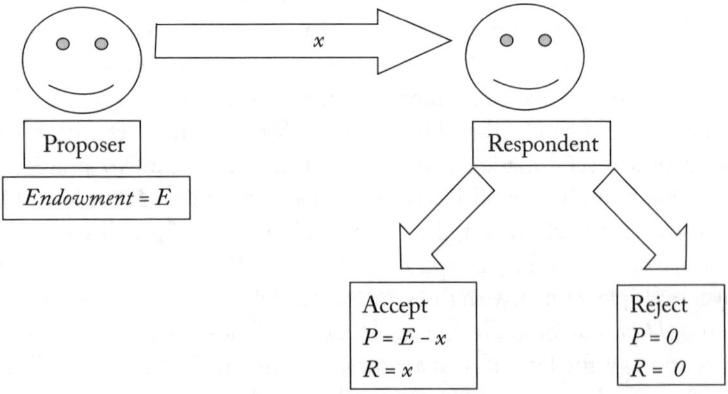

Source: Drawn by the author for this publication.

with the greater bargaining power may make a take-it-or-leave-it offer, essentially thereby serving an ultimatum. It is often the case that the other contracting party will accept this ultimatum offer from the stronger party, and both sides are able to obtain their respective shares of the total pie. Alternatively, the other party may reject this ultimatum offer and can ensure that the stronger party also gets nothing. For example, the workers of a firm may go on strike for higher wages and reject every offer of wages made by the firm. Thus the strike is so prolonged that the firm goes bankrupt. This is what is sought to be captured by the Ultimatum Game (UG).

In a straightforward extension of the prisoners' dilemma game, the UG is played between two players, a Proposer (*P*) and a Respondent (*R*). Now there is a certain sum of money (called endowment), say Rs 100, placed at the discretion of the Proposer. The Proposer is asked to propose a division of this amount between herself and her anonymously paired Respondent. So if the Proposer chooses to give Rs x to the Respondent ($0 \leq x \leq 100$) then the Proposer will get to keep ($100 - x$). But the money will not be distributed at this stage. Rather, this proposal in the nature of an offer from the Proposer will be communicated to the Respondent and the Respondent will be asked to either accept or reject the offer. It is explained to the players that if the Respondent accepts the offer, the money will actually be given out as proposed by the Proposer. If the respondent rejects the offer, both players get nothing.

Now the assumption here is that both players are rational in the sense that they are self-interested only, and both players know that the other player is self-interested. Hence both players care only about their own payoff. So what would be the theoretical prediction of a rational offer by the Proposer, and what would be a rational response by the Respondent? Clearly, the objective of a rational Proposer would be to maximise her own payoff subject to eliciting an *accept* from the Respondent. This is achieved by the Proposer offering a small but positive amount to the Respondent and keeping a very large share for herself. This will be accepted by a self-interested Respondent as a rejection by the Respondent will imply that the Respondent will not get even that small positive amount. This is often captured by way of example with the limiting case where the Proposer offers a Proposer:Respondent split of 99:01 and the Respondent accepts. Why would the Respondent accept? If the Respondent did not accept she would not get even the one rupee that she now gets as she accepts the offer. Recall that the assumption of rationality in the strict sense of self-interested behaviour implies that a player only cares about her own payoff irrespective of what happens to others. As the Proposer knows this about the Respondent, the Proposer has no reason to offer any higher amount to the Respondent.

So it came to pass that for many years the UG remained a theoretical construct, to be taught in game theory classes, where the students would learn about self-interested strategic decisions, take copious notes, reproduce the same 99-01 result in examinations and secure good points.

All this changed with the intervention of three people, Werner Guth, Rolf Schmittberger and Bernd Schwarze, economists at the University of Cologne (Guth, Schmittberger and Schwarze 1982). In fact, the contribution of Guth and his colleagues had far reaching consequences. Earlier experiments conducted on the basis of relevant economic theory had largely tended to confirm the theoretical predictions. But experiments on the UG challenged the theoretical predictions head on. Results from these experiments served two very important purposes. First, they demonstrated the importance of using experimental methods in verifying theory. And, second, they underscored the importance of returning to the drawing board to continuously expand the boundaries of theory to make theory more capable of explaining observed phenomena.

Guth and his colleagues were interested in studying the behaviour of agents in bargaining situations where the bargaining situation involved one agent making an ultimatum type offer. Their objective was to study the decisions of the recipients of such offers and whether such decision could be anticipated by the agent making the offer. They recruited 42 post graduate students who were put in 21 anonymous pairs of one Proposer and one Respondent each. The proposers were allotted a sum of money ranging from 4 to 10 marks. Namely, each value from 4 marks to 10 marks was allotted to 3 Proposers each. Each Proposer had to make an offer suggesting a split of the endowment between herself and her paired Respondent. The offer was communicated to the corresponding Respondent in writing and the Respondent had to then say in writing if she would accept or reject the offer. The same condition applied as before. If the Respondent accepted the offer both

Proposer and Respondent would get the money as proposed, but if the Respondent rejected the offer both got nothing. The results of the Guth, Schmittberger and Schwarze (1982) study are striking. First, unlike theoretical predictions, there were very few offers giving a very low amount for the Respondent. Second, relatively more generous offers were also rejected. Both facts suggest that there is more at play here as the motive behind the decision-making than mere self-interest.

Let us look more closely at the results of the experiment on the UG conducted by Guth, et al. As different Proposers started with different amounts, the offers mentioned below will be in percentages for comparability. Seven out of 21 Proposers offered half the starting amount to the Respondents. None of these offers were rejected. Seventeen of the 21 Proposers offered 20 per cent or more of their initial endowment to the Respondents. Only one such offer was rejected. There were only two offers in which the Proposers sought to keep the entire endowment for themselves and offered zero to the Respondent. One such offer was rejected, which is an expected result as the Respondent would have got zero anyway, whether she accepted or rejected the offer. The zero offer that was accepted is a surprising result and can only be put down to kindness on the part of the Respondent.

Guth and his colleagues were surprised by the fact that the results of the experiment were in utter variance with the theoretical predictions. They felt that it was perhaps possible that the student subjects had failed to grasp the implications of their decisions and were confused about the rules of the game. In order to check this out, they brought in the same 42 student subjects and got them to play the same game as before. Again there were 21 pairs and Proposers remained Proposers. The only difference could be that they may have been paired with a different Respondent and their initial endowment may have been different. Since the subjects had played the game once before they were now expected to have a better understanding of the game.

The results of this repeat experiment were even more surprising. The number of offers wanting to give half the starting amount to the Respondent came down from 7 to 3. Again, none of these offers were rejected. The number of Proposers who offered 20 per cent or more of their endowment to the Respondent rose slightly from 17 to 18. Four such offers were rejected. There was only one offer where the Proposer sought to keep the entire endowment and offered zero to the Respondent. This offer was rejected. In both the experiments, there were very few offers that sought to give very little or nothing to the Respondents and this clearly contradicted the theoretical prediction.

It is now time to consider what factors may be causing this departure from theoretical predictions. At the time when Guth, et al. conducted these experiments, the dominant thinking in economics was that economic agents behave rationally in the sense that they are self-interested enough to care only about maximising their own payoffs, or rather maximising their utility which automatically follows if payoffs have been maximised; that any other considerations may have a bearing on the decision or strategy of an economic agent found no takers in economic theory.

The UGs conducted by Guth, et al. clearly demonstrate that economic agents are not only driven by a desire to maximise their own payoff. So what could be driving these results? First, consider the Proposer. A rational Proposer would wish to maximise the amount she gets to keep out of her initial endowment provided she is able to obtain an acceptance from the Respondent. So she would need to speculate what amount would be just enough, which when offered to the Respondent would make the latter accept the offer. Turn now to the Respondent. It is important how she perceives the offer. If she were to care only for her own monetary payoff, then only a very small offer would be sufficient. If she rejects the offer she gets nothing. The UG experiments by Guth, et al. show that this is not the case. Both Proposers and Respondents behave in a manner that bring into consideration factors other than pure self-interestedness. So what factors are these?

The literature fields two candidates. These are: (i) Altruism and (ii) Fairness. First, let us consider *altruism*. Economists have long neglected the role played by altruism as a motive behind economic decisions[9]. This neglect had been defended for long on the grounds that altruism as a motive accounts for a miniscule percentage of economic transactions. It is now recognised that charitable giving by individuals worldwide constitutes a total fund that runs into trillions of dollars.

[9] At present there is a fairly large volume of literature exploring altruism. For an excellent survey of this literature see Kolm and Ythier (2006), especially chapter 8, i.e. Fehr and Schimdt (2006), for a survey of experimental work in the field.

It is interesting to explore what motivates altruism in monetary form or in the form of charitable giving. Most individuals would like to think of themselves in a positive light. So you like to think of yourself as possessing some positive attributes like goodness, kindness, sense of humour, etc. To the contrary, we all know of some individuals who are always criticising others or making disparaging remarks about people. These are people with a very low self-esteem or a very low opinion of themselves and need to constantly run others down in order to compare themselves favourably with others. Fortunately, such persons are not large in number; else life would have been very tedious. Instead, most people like to think of themselves as good, kind, funny or charming. In this sense it is important for people to think of themselves as a kind person. Now, it is not enough just to think of oneself as kind, but undertake such actions from time to time which appear to be kind actions in one's own eyes. It is not that others are observing you. Your actions may be unobservable to others. But certainly, you will be observing yourself. These actions must appear kind in your own eyes, only then can you think of yourself as a nice and kind person. Thus, this need to be and remain nice or kind may prompt the Proposer to make a more equitable offer, something closer to 50:50 rather than a 99:01. It follows that a Respondent who thinks of herself as a fair person will then expect a fair (equitable) offer, and when such an offer is made, it will be accepted.

Box 2.1 A Note on Altruism

Altruism may be defined as behaviour which is other-regarding. This means that a person takes such decisions that are likely to benefit some other person and is usually costly to the decision maker.

There are several forms this altruism may take:

Pure altruism: This is the kind of altruism where the *only* intention of the person taking the decision or the action is to bestow some benefit on some other person. There is absolutely no self-interest involved in the sense that agents gain utility from welfare of other persons.

Impure altruism: Following Andreoni (1990) we can define impure altruism as the decision or action of an economic agent whose *main*

(Box 2.1 contd...)

(...Box 2.1 contd)

motive is to bestow some benefit on some other person, but a secondary motive is to derive some personal benefit for herself through the aforesaid action. Now, what possible personal benefit could there be? Andreoni introduced the concept of *warm glow*. This is the feel-good feeling you may have when you have made a monetary donation to a charitable cause. You may make the donation in such a way that it is likely to be publicly announced. Then all your friends will take notice and they will know what a nice person you are. So in the aftermath of a flood or an earthquake you may send money not to the Prime Minister's Relief Fund, where it is unlikely to be noticed by your friends, but rather to the relief fund being collected by a major newspaper so that your name appears in print. Now, there is a possibility that some of your friends will see it. Thus your utility function may be written as:

$$U = U(x,w)$$

where U is your level of utility, which is a function of x a vector of consumption commodities, and w which is the level of warm glow. It is easy to see that it is well nigh impossible to have pure altruism any more. All altruism have now become of the impure form, because the very act of giving to a charity is likely to induce in you a warm glow, even when others do not get to know about it. Warm glow now behaves exactly like a market commodity, for which you have to spend money and which brings you utility directly.

Parental altruism: This is defined as a decision or action designated to bestow a benefit on another person who is socially close to you such as your offspring. You buy ice-cream for your child and that makes the child happy. Seeing the happiness of your child makes you happy and gives you utility. Parental altruism may be extended to any other person close to you, such as a parent, a partner, a sibling or a close friend. Here the child's utility function is directly incorporated inside your own utility function. So if U^P and U^C are utilities of the parent and the child respectively, and x and y are two commodities, then $U^P = U^P [x,y,U^C(x,y)]$ with the usual budget constraint. This implies that you have to forego the consumption of some amount of x or y in order to provide some x or y to your child which gives utility to the child which in turn gives you utility.

(Box 2.1 contd...)

(...Box 2.1 contd)

Reciprocal altruism: These are decisions and actions that reciprocate how others treat you. So you meet good behaviour with good behaviour and bad behaviour with bad behaviour. In both cases some costs may be incurred by you, which you are willing to bear in order to remain reciprocally altruistic. This is the form of altruism that is most frequently socially practiced. This form of altruism, therefore, can bestow both benefit and harm to another person and is always costly to the decision maker. Rabin (1993) referred to this as *fairness*.

The second motive behind generous Proposer offers that deviate from theoretical predictions is *fairness*[10]. First, look at it from the point of view of the Respondent. If she were to receive an offer from the Proposer, where the Proposer aims to keep most of the initial endowment and give only a small amount to her (99:01, as the theory predicted) the Respondent may very well perceive this as an unfair offer representing bad behaviour on the part of the Proposer. Being prone to fairness, she will then respond by rejecting the offer. This will mean, of course, that the Respondent will lose the small amount that was on offer and this will bring disutility. But this disutility will be more than compensated from the utility brought on from the satisfaction of seeing the Proposer lose a much bigger amount. Now, the Proposer knows this. She, therefore, offers a much higher amount to the Respondent; an amount that the Proposer believes will be perceived as a fair offer by the Respondent and would evince an acceptance from the Respondent. This would partly explain the kind of offers that Guth, et al. saw in the two sets of games they had conducted.

The problem remains that the Guth, et al. results are a bundling of altruism and fairness and we do not know yet how much of the offer made by the Proposer to the Respondent is due to the Proposer's sense of altruism and how much is due to the Proposer's apprehension about fairness-prone behaviour by the Respondent. It would certainly

[10] Fairness has now been incorporated into economic theory by Rabin (1993). Fairness is also referred to as reciprocal altruism where you respond to nice and kind behaviour by being nice and kind and to mean and nasty behaviour by being mean and nasty, even at some cost to yourself.

be interesting to unbundle the two effects. This is discussed later in this chapter.

Before leaving the UG it is important to discuss a couple of practical matters. First, how should the game be conducted? It can be run in a computer lab that is suitably organised or it can be hand-run in a room. If it is run in a lab, the screens of the Proposers and the Respondents have to be created in z-Tree first. This is discussed in Chapter Seven. If it is to be hand-run, then a sheet of paper needs to be used that looks like Box 2.2 below.

Box 2.2 Decision Sheet in an Ultimatum Game

Ultimatum Game
Proposer-Respondent pair number___
Endowment to the Proposer = Rs 100

Proposer to propose a division of this amount between Proposer and Respondent

Proposer Keeps: ___________
(Choose a number between 0 and 100)
Respondent Gets; ___________
Remember that the two numbers must add up to 100

Decision of the Respondent: (Tick one)
Accept/Reject

Proposers and Respondents are decided by draw of lots and put in pairs and then held in separate adjoining rooms to maintain anonymity from each other. After the initial instructions are given where the game is explained to the participants with examples, the decision sheet is given to a Proposer. She fills out the part meant for her. Then the sheet is collected and given to the paired Respondent who then records her decision to accept or reject. The sheet is then returned to the experimenter. The earnings are paid out according to the decisions recorded.

In the standard UG the matching between the Proposer and the Respondent is kept anonymous. That is, the Proposer knows that she is matched with a Respondent and vice versa but does not know who that person is. This is done to ensure that either Proposer or Respondent is not influenced by how the other person looks or the person's age or gender. If the experiment is conducted in a lab with multiple pairs, anonymity is automatically achieved as long as the identity of the pairs is not announced by the experimenter. This is because any one player sitting at a particular terminal knows that she is matched with some other person in the lab but does not know who that person is.

If the experiment is hand-run, anonymity may be achieved in the following way. Think of two adjacent rooms named here as a blue room and a red room. Ten subjects each are brought in and asked to sit in chairs numbered 1 to 10 in each room. Then number 1 in the blue room will be paired with number 1 in the red room, number 2 in the blue room would be paired with number 2 in the red room and so on. Subjects are told that there are 10 persons in the other room and each person in this room has been randomly paired with one person in the other room. Now, a coin is tossed to decide which room will contain the proposers, and then the subjects in the other room will be respondents. Now, identical instructions are given in both rooms and explained with the help of graphics and examples. The UG is played with the help of an instrument such as the decision sheet described above which is given to the Proposer first. After she has filled out her part, it can be given to the paired Respondent. Once she has recorded her decision, it is returned to the experimenter.

So far we have discussed anonymity between Proposer and Respondent. We may also have to safeguard against experimenter effect. This effect occurs when the participant actually wishes to take some decision p but changes it to some other decision q because she wishes the experimenter to know that she has decided on q rather than p. For example, a Proposer may actually wish to give very little to the Respondent but is embarrassed to say so in front of the experimenter and ends up offering a higher amount. This may be particularly true when the subjects are students and the experimenter is a faculty member at the same institute. To remove this experimenter effect, a double-blind system is used. Here the experimenter obtains the results but does not know which subject has taken a particular decision. The subjects must be clearly explained the double-blind process and they must come to believe that the process is truly double blind. This is difficult to execute when the game is played in a computer laboratory. This is because most software requires the terminals to be numbered sequentially in order to record the data being generated. In the hand-run mode this is easily achieved. One needs to have a table with a paper tray on it placed in the corridor immediately outside the blue and red rooms. Let now the game instrument in the form of a decision sheet be handed out to the ten Proposers. These should be identical sheets and should not be marked or numbered in any way. After all the offers are recorded, Proposer 1 is required to go and place her sheet, face down, on the paper tray outside the room. Respondent 1 is required to collect it. Next, Proposer 2 goes out and places her sheet and Respondent 2 collects it, and so on. Finally all respondents are required to place the completed sheet in the paper tray outside the room, one by one. Two research assistants may be asked to supervise the process in the two rooms and ensure silence. The payments are to be made immediately after the Respondents decision is received. The main experimenter may leave the rooms during this process. Alternatively, one may also use a pigeon-hole box set such as are commonly used in university departments to deposit hard copy mail to each faculty member. The holes must be numbered and must all have unique locks and keys. Now the Proposers can be assigned numbers randomly in such a manner that the experimenter does not know which Proposer picked which number. Once the decision sheets are handed out, the Proposers record their decisions and deposit them in the numbered box corresponding to the number she is assigned. Similarly, the Respondents can open the numbered boxes corresponding to the number each is assigned and record their reactions to the Proposers' decisions. The experimenter can now collect the decision sheets and make the payments. The payments will have to be made in two steps. First the payment corresponding to the Proposers will be placed in the numbered boxes. The Proposers are asked to collect the payments. Next, the payments for the Respondents will be placed in the same numbered boxes and the Respondents asked to use the same keys to open the corresponding numbered boxes and collect the payment. The whole process should be supervised by a research assistant with the experimenter not being present after the instructions for the game is delivered. The process of recording one's decision and the manner of collection of payment should be explained in advance to the subjects so that they are convinced that the experimenter will not be able to identify which subject took a particular decision. Only then will the subjects be free of experimenter bias.

The high popularity and usefulness of UG has resulted in the game being played with many variations and with different objectives in mind. Blount (1995) conducted the UG in its standard form, but added two more treatments. In one the actual split between the Proposer and the Respondent was decided by a disinterested 'third party' who stood to neither gain nor lose anything from the decision. In the other the split was decided by chance, that is by the spinning of a roulette wheel. The attempt was to see if unfair offers would be rejected even when not made by the person who may gain from it. Falk, Fehr and Fischbacher (2003) played four versions where the initial endowment was 10 units or points. In each version, instead of the Proposer having the freedom to choose any split of the 10 points, the Proposers were allowed to choose one of two predetermined splits. The first choice was the same in all four versions—a 08:02 split between Proposer and Respondent. The second choice varied between 02:08, 05:05, 08:02 and 10:00 splits between Proposer and Respondent. Expectedly, Respondents were not only concerned about the absolute value of their payoffs but rather showed a preference for more equitable offers. They mostly accepted those offers where, given the two choices before the Proposer, the more equitable offer has been made.

Hoffman, McCabe and Smith (1996a) asked if the initial endowment was high, perhaps a Proposer could offer a small amount to the Respondent, but still get the Respondent to accept the offer. This is because the offer would be a small per cent of the higher initial endowment but still higher in absolute value than the offer made to the Respondent out of a smaller endowment. If this result was found, it would have come closer to the initial theoretical prediction. The initial endowment was $10 with 24 paired players and $100 with 27 paired players. $100 is certainly a non-trivial amount, especially to student subjects, and if a Proposer offered $10 out of this, it would only be 10 per cent of the endowment but much higher in absolute value than what the Respondent would receive in 05:05 split in a version where the initial endowment was $10. If Respondents cared mainly about their own payoffs, such offers would be accepted. This did not turn out to be the case. The offers in both the $10 and $100 versions of the game were close to 50:50 splits. Another innovation by the same authors was to hand out a trivia quiz before the game and announce the scores. Then, make the high scorers Proposers and low scorers Respondents. This would provide a sense of entitlement to the Proposers as if they had earned the money. This would entail lower offers to the Respondents as Proposers feel that they have earned the money by performing well in a quiz and therefore have the right to keep more. This turned out to be the case in this study. There are many more versions and treatment of the UG exploring many other aspects of bargaining.

CHECKING FOR ALTRUISM: THE DICTATOR GAME

It has been discussed above that apart from pure self-interest, UG offers are affected by a sense of altruism on the part of the Proposer as well as an anticipation of fairness-prone behaviour from the Respondent by the Proposer. What we see in the experiments is a bundled result of both factors and it would be nice to unbundle the two causes. It is with this intention that Forsythe, Horowitz, et al. (1994) conducted the UG and another game called the Dictator Game (DG). In DG, the set up is exactly the same as UG. Again there is a Proposer and a Respondent. An initial endowment is given to the Proposer. Again, the Proposer has to suggest a split of the initial endowment between herself and the Respondent. The only difference is that the Respondent has to accept the offer. The Respondent does not have the option of rejecting this offer. Therefore the money will be split in the manner offered by the Proposer. In this sense the Proposer is a dictator.

What happens here is that any behavioural motivation on the part of the Proposer in anticipation of fairness-prone behaviour by the Respondent is taken out. In other words, the Proposer need not suffer from any fear of rejection by the Respondent. What now guides the behaviour of the Proposer, apart from self-interest, is the desire to be altruistic to the Respondent. Conventional economic theory, that puts all faith in self-interested behaviour by economic agents, would suggest that under these conditions Proposers would simply keep the entire initial endowment for themselves and give nothing to the Respondent. What did Forsythe, et al. see? The results are summarised in Table 2.4. In their UG the modal offer was a 50:50 split, which was offered by 55 per cent of the Proposers. Next, another

20 per cent Proposers offered 40 per cent of the endowment to their matched Respondent. So between these two groups three quarters of the Proposers were covered. Another 20 per cent of Proposers offered to give away 20 per cent of the endowment and a further 5 per cent offered to keep only 40 percent.

Table 2.4 Results of Ultimatum and Dictator Games conducted by Forsythe, Horowitz, et al. (1994)

Percentage of Proposers Offering	0%	10%	20%	30%	40%	50%	60%
UG%	0	0	20	0	20	55	5
DG%	45	0	30	5	5	10	5

Source: Adapted from Figure 2.4 in Chaudhuri (2009: 52), by permission of Ananish Chaudhuri.

Turning next to the DG we can clearly see that offers fall sharply. Now that there is no threat of rejection by the Respondent, 45 per cent Proposers plan to keep the entire endowment. This, in fact, is the modal offer. Another 30 per cent Proposers plan to give away only 20 per cent of the endowment. Very few Proposers make higher offers to the Respondent.

Thus the Forsythe, et al. results seem to suggest that anticipation of fairness-prone behaviour from the Respondent, that is the threat of rejection resulting in losing all, is a more powerful motivator than a genuine desire to act altruistically and seems to power the decision of most Proposers.

MOTIVATING FAIRNESS: THE TRUST GAME

One is often not fully aware of the role played by *trust* as well as *trustworthiness* in everyday life. Both in economic transactions and social interactions trust actually plays a major role. Consider, for example, that a product or a service is for sale. The seller makes a claim about the quality of the product. More often than not, it is either impossible to verify this claim or prohibitively costly to do so.

A carpenter makes a claim about the quality of wood used in the making of a cabinet (termite resistant) or a house painter claims a payment based on the number of hours worked. It would be practically impossible to verify both and more often than not, we are used to making such payments on trust. This is trust at the individual level. Sociologist Anthony Giddens (1990) wrote about the importance of trust on 'Expert Systems' in modern societies. He gives the example of driving through a busy intersection. We blindly trust the functioning of the signalling system. We believe that the signalling system has been properly designed and implemented so that it will not turn green in both directions at the same time. When you walk into a building or use a bridge you have not yourself verified the fitness of the design and construction of the building or the bridge but trust the underlying certification process to have ensured the reliability of the same so that you do not expect the building or the bridge to collapse when you are inside or on it.

It becomes important to be able to measure how much one person in a particular society is ready to trust another person. Likewise, it is also important to see how much a person, who has been trusted, honours that trust. There is enough empirical evidence to suggest that societies which are more trusting, grow at a higher rate (Zak and Knack 2001). This is because such societies are able to save on much unproductive transaction costs such as costs incurred in gathering information about a potential business partner, costs for creating contracts or court and legal costs.[11]

As before, we return to the UG and the fact that UG offers represent a bundling of altruistic behaviour by the Proposer and anticipation of fairness-expecting behaviour from the Respondent by the Proposer. Unbundling of the two effects can be achieved by having subjects play a UG followed by a DG and comparing the results.

However, fairness (or reciprocity) can be measured and calibrated directly. This is done with the help of a Trust Game (TG). This is shown in Figure 2.2. First proposed by Joyce Berg, John Dickhaut and Kevin McCabe (1995) it was called an Investment Game. There are two

[11] Paul J. Zak and Stephen Knack (2001) developed a theoretical model where they show that low-trust environments reduce investments and lowers the growth rate of the economy. Such societies may get caught in a poverty trap.

Figure 2.2 The Trust Game

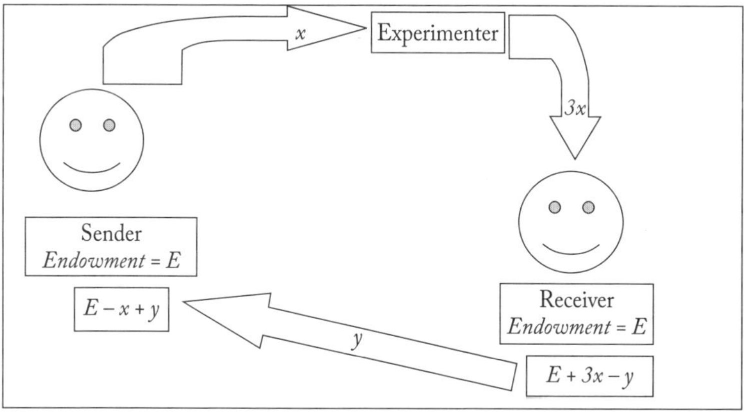

Source: Drawn by the author for this publication.

players called Sender and Receiver. A Sender and a Receiver constitute a matched pair. As in the UG, Senders and Receivers are held in separate rooms to maintain anonymity. Both Sender and her paired Receiver are each given the same initial endowment (E), say Rs 100. This is done to avoid any decisions that may be affected by distributional consequences. Next, the Sender is asked to decide on a sum of money x which she would like to send to the Receiver, i.e. $0 \leq x \leq 100$. It is explained that she gets to keep for herself any amount she does not send. If the Sender decides to send nothing at all, the game ends and both players get to keep their initial endowment, in this case Rs 100. Any positive amount that the Sender decides to send is sent through the experimenter, who first multiplies it by some positive integer m (= 3, say) and then gives the money to the Receiver. If m = 3, then if the Sender sends Rs 50 to the Receiver the Receiver gets Rs 150. Now the Receiver is asked to return some money y to the Sender, $0 \leq y \leq (100 + 3x)$. It is explained to the Receiver that whatever money she does not send back, she gets to keep. Once, the Receiver has taken a decision, the game ends.

If the game is played in a computer laboratory, then it will need to be programmed in z-Tree, which is discussed in Chapter Seven. If the game is hand-run an instrument in the form of a Decision Sheet is to be used. This will look as in Box 2.3.

Box 2.3 Decision Sheet in a Trust Game

Trust Game

Sender-Receiver Pair Number______

Sender has Rs 100
Receiver has Rs 100

Sender would like to give ________ to the Receiver
(to be filled in by Sender)

Receiver now receives __________
(to be filled in by Experimenter)

Receiver would like to send back ______ to the Sender
(to be filled in by Receiver)

What does theory have to say about how the Sender and the Receiver are likely to behave? Under assumption of simple self-interested behaviour by both Sender and Receiver, we use backward induction to understand what is likely to happen. Backward induction is the logic of looking at the end of the game first, figure out what may happen there and given that outcome look at the stage before that, and so on. Here, the Receiver makes the last move. If she is self interested, she would like to maximise her own payoff. She has no reason to send any money back, she can then take home the entire Rs $100 + 3x$. That is $y = 0$. But the Sender knows this, therefore the Sender would not send any money in the first place (i.e., $x=0$). Each would go home with the initial endowment of Rs 100. This is the sub-game perfect Nash equilibrium of the TG.

Notice that there are two forces working on the Sender. On the one hand the Sender is not sure if the Receiver will send any money back, so it is better for the Sender to send nothing in the first place. On the other hand, the Sender would like to increase her own payoff, and this can only be done by making the money grow. The money will grow only if the Sender sends money to the Receiver. To maximise returns to both Sender and Receiver, the Sender should send her *entire endowment* to the Receiver and the Receiver should then return half of what she now has. This is the socially efficient solution.

Notice also that the relationship between the Sender and Receiver is very similar to that of a bank and a borrower. The money sent by the Sender is like the bank lending to a borrower and the money returned by the Receiver is like the borrower repaying the principal and interest to the bank. The bank earns interest only by lending to borrowers, but lending also entails the risk of non-repayment of principal and interest. This is why in its original avatar in Berg, Dickhaut and McCabe (1995), this game was called the Investment Game.

Instead of assuming simple self-interested behaviour on the part of the Sender and the Receiver, let us consider a situation where the Sender decides to trust the Receiver completely. The Sender then sends the entire initial endowment of Rs 100 to the Receiver. The percentage of the initial endowment sent to the Receiver then can serve as a measure of trust. Now, this Rs 100 is multiplied by 3 by the experimenter and handed over to the Receiver. The Receiver now gets Rs 300. She already has her initial endowment of Rs 100. So she has Rs 400 in all. Next, consider a situation where the Receiver decides to fully reciprocate the trust of the Sender. She sends back to the Sender half the amount of what she now has, that is Rs. 200. This can serve as a measure of trustworthiness. So both Sender and Receiver can go home with Rs 200 each. This is an equilibrium under Full Trust with Full Reciprocity (FTFR). Cleary both players are better off under an FTFR equilibrium than under Nash equilibrium.

Let us look at the results of the Berg, Dickhaut and McCabe (1995) study, which had 32 pairs of student subjects and where a double-blind protocol was used. Both Sender and Receiver begin with an endowment of \$10. Two things become immediately clear in Table 2.5. First, the theoretical prediction that the Sender will send nothing, as this is the sub-game perfect Nash equilibrium arrived at via backward induction, was executed by only two of the 32 (6.25 per cent) Senders. So it can be safely concluded that trust of an anonymous partner is much higher in practice than suggested by theory. In fact, we find that 5 out of 32 (about 15 per cent) Senders trusted the anonymously paired Receiver completely and sent the entire endowment, which is socially efficient and 20 out of 32 Senders (62.5 per cent) sent back half or more of their initial endowment. Second, much of this trust is not fully reciprocated. In fact, much of the reposed trust is minimally reciprocated or not at all. Consider first the 5 Senders who sent the entire \$10. So 5 receivers got \$30. Each had \$10 to begin with. So these 5 receivers had \$40 each.

Only one such receiver sent half of this amount back, that is $20 and two more sent at least half of what they received from the Sender via the experimenter, that is $15. Going down the table we will see 8 more Receivers (25 per cent) sent back at least half or more of the amount they had received from the Sender via the experimenter. So, there is evidence to show that people are more trusting than they are trustworthy.

Table 2.5 Results of the Trust Game by Berg, Dickhaut and McCabe (1995)

Amount Sent ($)	Number of Senders	Amount Received by Receiver ($)	Amount Returned ($)	Number of Receivers
10	5	30	20	1
		30	15	2
		30	1	1
		30	0	1
8	1	24	3	1
7	3	21	6	1
			1	2
6	5	18	12	1
			8	1
			3	1
			1	1
			0	1
5	6	15	15	1
			11	1
			7	1
			5	2
			0	1
4	2	12	1	2
3	4	9	6	1
			5	1
			1	1
			0	1
2	2	6	4	1
			0	1
1	2	3	1	1
			0	1
0	2	0	0	2

Source: Adapted from Figures 3.2 and 3.3 in Chaudhuri (2009: 91), by permission of Ananish Chaudhuri.

One possibility here is that while the game was explained to the players with examples by Berg, et al., the Senders having no experience of playing such a game in the past were confused about what to really expect from the Receivers. Hence their trusting behaviour. The Receivers, being the last movers faced no uncertainty and made good by returning only small amounts or nothing at all. To check for this, Berg, et al. ran the TG a second time with one variation. For convenience let us call the above game the No History treatment. They now recruited 56 new players who were split into 28 anonymous pairs of Senders and Receivers. All conditions of the Trust Game remained exactly the same as in the previous session. The one change made was that all the participants in the second session, termed here as the With History treatment, were provided a summary of the decisions taken by the 32 pairs in the No History treatment.

The purpose of the second session goes like this. Say the Senders in the first treatment, having no experience in playing a TG, did not quite know what to expect from the Receivers. Even though it was explained to them that the Receivers would take the last decision and the game would end thereafter, they may not have fully realised that the Receivers really had no monetary incentive to return any money. The second treatment seeks to correct this. When given the decisions taken by others in an earlier treatment, there is now experience by proxy; the players now know what may generally be expected to happen. If this conjecture is true, then the amounts sent by Senders in the With History treatment should be lower than amounts sent in the No History treatment.

However, there is an alternative way in which the participants of the With History treatment could view the results from the No History session. Instead of looking at the downside risk of sending high amounts, the participants in the With History session could choose to emulate the decisions of the more trusting and trustworthy pairs. For instance, they could choose to make an example out of the pair where the Sender sent the entire initial endowment of $10, whereby the Receiver got $30. But the Receiver already had $10, so she had $40 in all and thereafter sent back $20 from this. If such would be the response of the subjects in the With History treatment, we should see both amounts sent by Senders and amounts sent back by Receivers go up in this treatment compared to the earlier treatment.

What actually happened in the With History treatment by Berg, et al.? Players in the With History treatment, on average showed more trust and trustworthiness than the No History session. Of the 28 Senders, only 3 sent zero amounts. Senders who sent \$5 got back \$7 on average. Senders who sent \$10 got back \$13 on average. Thus both Senders and Receivers were better off in the With History session than the No History session.

Other examples of Ultimatum, Dictator and Trust games conducted with wider subject pools are discussed in Chapter Five. It is now acknowledged that if societies are able to generate and protect norms of trust they are able to generate a better social optimum (See Box 2.4).

Box 2.4 A Story about Trust and Social History

*An Arabian Folktale**

Once upon a time in the drylands of Arabia there were two close friends, Hanif and Iqbal. They had grown up together and lived in the same village. By profession, they were traders and had to travel long distances to ply their trade. In one such journey, Hanif purchased a stallion and brought it back. It was a stallion like no one had seen before. Its size, its mane, its deportment and its speed was the cynosure of all eyes. Iqbal took a fancy to the animal and was desperate to own it. He asked Hanif to sell him the horse. He even offered to pay Hanif a handsome price for the stallion. Hanif himself was in love with the horse and refused to sell it under any circumstances. But Iqbal would not give up; he continued to pester Hanif to sell him the horse.

One day, tired with Iqbal's pestering, Hanif said, 'If you can ride the stallion for twenty paces, I will gift you the horse. You don't have to pay anything.' Iqbal was overjoyed. He ran to the horse and climbed on to it. But try as much as he did, he could not move the horse at all. So loyal was the horse to its master, that it obeyed no command from anyone else. Iqbal failed to win Hanif's offer.

Iqbal was furious. He swore to get even, using trickery if necessary. He disguised himself as an old man and lay on the side of a road, groaning, where he knew Hanif would be passing by on his stallion.

(Box 2.4 contd...)

(...Box 2.4 contd)

Sure enough, a short while later Hanif arrived. Noticing the old man by the side of the road and clearly in pain, Hanif stopped and dismounted. He asked the old man what the matter was. Iqbal replied, 'I was riding a horse, which turned out to be a wicked one. He threw me off and ran away. I am injured and cannot move. Please help me.' Hanif picked Iqbal up and placed him on his own horse. After going a little distance, Iqbal shouted, 'Oh Allah! What have I done!' He added that he once had a daughter who died young. Her only memory is a *panja* (a handprint) which he always wears in a small bag on his neck. It seems that when he had fallen from the horse it must have come unstuck. Iqbal requested Hanif to retrieve this bag. As Hanif got down from the horse, Iqbal sat upright on the horse and rode away. The horse must have thought that the new rider has the master's approval to ride and hence obeyed Iqbal's commands.

Hanif was completely shocked. Now, Iqbal rode back to Hanif, threw off his disguise and laughed out loud. He said, 'My friend, I have now done what you had challenged me to do. I have been able to ride on your horse. Now you have to give him to me.' Hanif was saddened by the trickery of his friend. He said, 'I will give you my horse, but you must promise never to tell this story.' 'Why not' asked Iqbal. Hanif replied, 'Because when someone hears this story, he will never again stop on a desert road to help a fellow traveller.'

*As told to the author by Dr Kinsuk Sen.

There is a lesson to be learnt here about the definition of rationality that has been followed where self-interestedness plays a key role. We have already discussed results where subjects in experiments have clearly demonstrated that they have not acted in a self-interested manner but have come out better off. These last results in the Berg, et al. TG further show that human subjects are capable of drawing out positive lessons from an experience which is a mixed bag of positive and negative outcomes. By only focusing on the positive outcomes and emulating these they are capable of actually changing the aggregate outcome in society. This does call for an expanded definition of rationality that goes beyond mere short-term self-interestedness.

RATIONALITY AND BACKWARD INDUCTION: THE CENTIPEDE GAME

Now we will look at a multi-stage game which is a straightforward extension of the TG. First, however, we will need to be familiar with some concepts. Let us consider a multi-stage game with two players. In order to understand how equilibrium in such a game may be discovered, one needs to review an important concept introduced by Selten (1965), that of a subgame. A subgame in a multi-stage game is a part of the main game that, by itself can be construed as a game. So a subgame must have a well defined initial node and must contain all the parts of the main game that can be reached through actions taken at this node in the main game. The concept of subgame perfection implies a strategy in the original game that specifies a complete set of actions in each subgame. An important and related concept is the rationality based on backward induction. In a multi-stage game the rationality of backward induction implies that the optimal decision in the final stage of the game is worked out first. Next, the last but one stage is taken up and optimal decision at that stage is worked out with the knowledge of the decision in the final stage. Next, the last but two stage is taken up and analysed in a similar way and so on till the first stage of the game. This method of analysing decisions in each stage of a multi-stage game can be applied only when the main game has a fixed number of stages.

As an illustrative example let us consider an extension of the TG which is the Centipede Game. The Centipede Game is an extensive form game played between two players, for convenience termed here as Red player and Blue player, who get alternating opportunities to end the game, receiving a favourable payoff for herself. However, if they choose to continue, the payoff gets increased at every stage. Thus, like the prisoners' dilemma this game presents a social dilemma, that is, a conflict between maximisation of self-interest and mutual benefits. In this game, first conceived by Rosenthal (1982), subjects can mutually earn a large payoff by playing cooperatively, even though, backward induction suggests that the first player should choose to defect in the very first round, resulting in a very low payoff for both players. Experiments with this game have shown that the subjects reveal partial cooperation and results have been inconsistent with the traditional game-theoretic analysis of backward induction and this has raised much controversy about the application of backward induction in deriving solutions to social interactions (McKelvey and Palfrey 1991).

The payoff structure in any one round in the Centipede Game conducted by McKelvey and Palfrey (1991) is shown in Table 2.6. Suppose a Red player gets to start the game. She has two options:

i. Either to take 40 cents and terminate the game, in which case her partner (a blue player) receives 10 cents, or
ii. To pass the game to her partner

If Red chooses to continue the game to the second stage by choosing Pass her partner (Blue player) gets the opportunity to choose whether to continue the game or terminate it. If Blue chooses to take the offer she gets 80 cents and the partner (Red) gets 20 cents. Alternatively, Blue can pass and the decision passes on to Red. In this way, the opportunity to choose whether to take or pass keeps on alternating till the end of the fourth stage.

Here it may be noted that the payoff of the decision maker (0.40, 0.80, 1.60, 3.20, 6.40) as well as that of the passive partner (0.10, 0.20, 0.40, 0.80, 1.60) keeps on doubling at the end of each stage, till the fourth stage. At the fourth stage, if the Blue player decides to take, she gets \$3.20 and her partner, the Red player gets 80 cents. However, if she decides to pass then the Red player gets \$6.40 and Blue player gets \$1.60.

It can be seen from Table 2.6 that the decision maker in the fourth stage is the Blue player. If she passes at this stage her earning is \$1.60 but if she accepts the offer (i.e., she takes) she can earn \$3.20. Hence she should always accept at this stage. But the Red player knows this. Given this knowledge, the Red player should take in the third stage while Red is still the decision maker. But the Blue player knows this. Given this knowledge, the Blue player will take in the second stage, and so on till the first stage. So, given the rationality of backward induction, every round of this game should get terminated in the first stage itself. At least that is the theoretical prediction.

As we see in Table 2.6, in the row marked outcome percentage, this is not the observed result. Only 8 per cent of the number of games played were terminated in the first stage. Maximum terminations took place in the second stage (41 per cent) closely followed by terminations in the third stage (38 per cent). So, it is neither true that subjects use backward induction fully (if they did, the game would have terminated always in the first stage) nor that they do not use backward induction at all (the game would then have gone on to the fourth stage).

Table 2.6 The Payoff Structure and Flow of the Game

Stages	**1**	**2**	**3**	**4**	
Decision maker	**RED**	**BLUE**	**RED**	**BLUE**	
Payoff	Pass ➔ Take ↓	Pass ➔ Take ↓	Pass ➔ Take ↓	Pass ➔ Take ↓	↘
RED	0.40	0.20	1.60	0.80	6.40
BLUE	0.10	0.80	0.40	3.20	1.60
Outcome Percentage	8%	41%	38%	10%	2%
Status	Game Ends	Game Ends	Game Ends	Game Ends	Game Ends

Source: McKelvey and Palfrey (1991). Reprinted by permission of The Econometric Society.

Thus some trust exists between the anonymous players. Note that in the game described above there were 10 Red and 10 Blue players and they were kept anonymous to each other. There were 10 rounds where each Red player was matched each time with a different Blue player. The results reported above are from the sixth to the tenth round, earlier rounds being treated as trial rounds meant to give experience to the players so that no confusion was there and the players knew what to expect. McKelvey and Palfrey offered the explanation that some players were altruistic and preferred to pass in early stages of the game. Even though altruistic players were few, their very presence made the probability of passing in the early stages high.

THE COASE THEOREM AND BARGAINING SOLUTIONS

An externality in production or consumption occurs when during such activity an unintended by-product is generated which either benefits or harms others. If the unintended outcome is beneficial to others it is termed a positive externality but if it harms others it is a negative externality. For the present, we will consider only negative externalities. If a factory is producing steel, it will also produce smoke, which is an unintended by-product, which harms human health. This would constitute a negative externality. The presence of such externalities engenders market failures in the sense that the market typically over-produces a negative externality compared to the social optimum. This calls for the role of an external regulator such as the government.

The Central Pollution Control Board (CPCB) is such an external regulator. Established by legislation passed in the Parliament, it has legal powers to prescribe limits to pollution, police and monitor pollutant generating activities and apprehend and prosecute such polluters. An alternative approach that is in use in many countries is to impose a unit tax on the pollution level. Now the polluter has the option of either using pollution abatement technology to clean up or pay a tax on pollutant level generated. Given the level of pollution, the producer will do whatever is cheaper[12].

A third and a certainly more novel approach was proposed by Ronald Coase (1960) who won the Nobel Prize in Economics in 1991 for the same. In what eventually came to be known as the Coase theorem, he held that the problem of an externality could solve itself provided strict property rights could be assigned over the medium in which the externality exists. This would allow complete right of one or the other parties—either polluter or pollutee—to dispose pollutants or retain the medium clean. They could then bargain with each other and settle for a side-payment as compensation that would bring the level of pollutants to the socially optimal level. Of course, there were some restricting conditions such as there can be only two contracting parties, complete assignment of property rights and absence of transaction costs.

Consider the case illustrated in the Figure 2.3 above. There is a stream flowing north to south. There is a chemical factory upstream and a township downstream. Let the chemical factory be represented by its owner and the township by its mayor. Now, the chemical factory would

[12] For a comprehensive discussion on setting of standards, imposition of tax and the conditions under which each is appropriate see Pindyck and Rubinfeld (2013).

Figure 2.3 Coase Theorem at Work

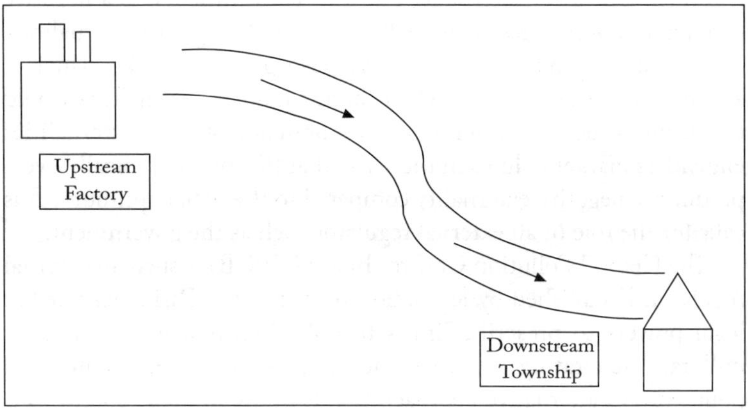

Source: Drawn by the author for this publication.

like to discharge effluents into the stream and the township would like to use the stream water for drinking and domestic use. Clearly, if the chemical factory is allowed to dispose effluents into the stream then the water cannot be suitable for domestic use and if the water is to be used for domestic purposes then the chemical factory cannot be allowed to dump effluents into the stream. Coase theorem would claim that the problem can be solved by assigning property rights over the stream. It does not matter who gets the property rights, either the factory or the town. For example, let the property rights be given to the factory. Now the owner of the factory has full rights to discharge effluents in the stream. Then the mayor of the town would approach the factory owner with an offer of payment against the commitment by the factory not to discharge effluents in the stream. What is the maximum amount the town would offer? It would not be greater that the cost of getting clean water for domestic use from somewhere else. What is the minimum amount the factory would accept? It would not accept anything less than what it would cost the factory to dispose off its effluents in some alternative location. In this way the range of the compensation can be calculated. Conversely, let the stream be given over to the township. Now the owner of the chemical factory would offer compensation to the town in exchange for the right to dispose its effluents in the river. And again, the range of this compensation can be found considering outside options of the town and the factory. This is the essence of the Coase bargaining solution.

Hoffman and Spitzer (1982, 1985) decided to test in a laboratory, the capacity of economic agents to strike efficient bargains. For this, they had subjects put in pairs of A and B players. Roles of A and B were assigned by lottery and the pairings, unlike in the past were not anonymous. Either A or B would be designated as the Controller by the toss of a coin. This is equivalent to having the property rights over the stream. Now there is some hypothetical activity that can happen at levels 0 to 6. Against each level there is a payoff both for A and B. This is given in Table 2.7 below.

Table 2.7 Payoff Structure in a Coase Bargaining Game

Activity Level	0	1	2	3	4	5	6
A's Payoff	0	4	6	8	9	10	11
B's Payoff	12	10	6	4	2	1	0
Total payoff	12	14	12	12	11	11	11

Source: Hoffman and Spitzer (1982). Reproduced by permission of The University of Chicago Press.

The subjects were explained the rules of the game and the payoffs but the total payoff was not shown. Now the Controller has property rights and hence gets to choose the level of the activity. The player who is not the Controller can attempt to get the Controller to change his decision by offering her a part or all of her own earnings. For example, let A be the Controller in a particular game. A declares her intention to choose activity level 6. Now B can make the following offer: If you change your decision from Activity level 6 to Activity Level 2, I will give you 5 units from my earnings. If an agreement is reached, both A and B must enter the agreed figures in an agreement form and sign. Accordingly, the players are paid by a monitor who collects the agreement forms.

Clearly, if A or B is the Controller (11,0) or (0,12) would be the disagreement payoffs. This is what results when there is no agreement. Depending on who is the Controller, that player will not accept an outcome that offers her less than these disagreement outcome amounts.

In the Hoffman and Spitzer studies, there were two treatments. In the first, described above, both A and B players were told the payoff of both players; in the second they were only told their own payoff against each activity level.

The results of the study was quite curious. In the first, full information treatment, of the 12 pairs, 11 pairs were able to agree on activity level 1 where joint payoff is maximum. In 5 of these 11 pairs, side payments had to be made such that the joint earning was split equally giving the Controller 4 or 5 units less than the disagreement payoff. In the other 7 pairs, the Controller retained an amount exactly equal to the disagreement payoffs through side payments. In the partial information treatment where subjects know their own payoffs only against each activity level, again out of 12 pairs, 11 pairs agreed on activity level 1 which maximises joint payoffs and in 6 of these pairs they opted for equal splits of the joint payoff through side payments and in 4 pairs the Controller retained exactly her disagreement payoff through side payments.

The results show that in two-sided bargaining situation, with well defined property rights, players mostly are in fact able to come to a mutually agreed solution, where joint payoff is maximised. Curiously, in many cases this solution is achieved without payment of compensation or side payments by the player who does not have the property right.

In this chapter, we have discussed strategic choice. There are economic situations where what I may decide to do will depend on what I expect you to do. Likewise, what you will decide to do will symmetrically depend on what you believe I will do. These games of strategic choices can be one shot, as in prisoners' dilemma, Ultimatum, Dictator or Trust Games or they may be multi-stage with scope for repeated interaction such as the Centipede Game. Again, these games may be played maintaining anonymity between players as is usual for the Ultimatum or Trust Games or they may be played with open and face-to-face communication as with the Coase Bargaining game. A very important element of such games is the knowledge of the strategy set of your partner and your contingent decision for every element of the strategy set of your partner. In other words, you will need to know all the options that your partner has and then work out your best response for each of your partner's choices. Further, it is important to know if the game is one shot or multi-period, and if repeated then repeated over how many periods. There are games with infinite horizons, that is, the game will come to an end at some point in the future but that point is not known in advance. Trust and belief play important roles in such games.

We have seen, contrary to theoretical predictions, much experimental evidence throws up results that defy conventional logic and rationality in economics. It is important to conduct these experiments carefully so that results, even if counter-intuitive, stand up to scrutiny. It is only then that, instead of quarrelling with the results, we can go back to the drawing board of theory and begin to modify our understanding of human behaviour.

three

Experiments with Public Goods

The early developments in neo-classical economics largely happened around a class of goods that we now call private goods. These are all the goods that we buy from the market and the consumption of which make up the arguments in our utility function. There are well-established markets for each such good where the roles of buyers and sellers are well-defined. Under competitive conditions, each such market is able to discover a price at which equilibrium occurs. The simultaneous occurrence of such equilibriums in all commodity markets is Walrasian general equilibrium.

However, there are a class of goods, called public goods that have remarkably different properties in consumption, that make private firms unwilling to supply them in the market. This is because, for this class of goods, prices cannot be used to exclude consumers. Why this happens is explained below. Consequently, the markets of such commodities cannot be included in a Walrasian general equilibrium. To begin the discussion more formally we define a pure public good. This is really a theoretical abstraction that is adopted to provide a benchmark case against which more realistic cases of public goods may be discussed and compared. A pure public good has two unique properties in consumption. These are:

i. *Non-excludability*: If the public good exists, it is impossible to exclude anyone from consuming it.
ii. *Non-rivalry*: Many persons can consume the public good simultaneously. In other words, the consumption of the good by one person does not reduce the quantity available for consumption by the next person.

As a direct consequence, it can be shown that once the public good is created the marginal cost of providing it to an additional consumer is zero. An almost ideal example (and there are not many) of a *pure* public good is national defence. The army, the navy and the air force exist to protect the country against external threats and aggression. Thereby all persons living within the geographical boundary of the country are equally protected. In that sense, the consumption of defence services is non-rival. Also, it is not possible not to provide this service to any person living within the geographical boundary of the country; hence defence service is non-excludable.

This is in contrast to a pure private good whose consumption is perfectly rival and completely excludable. Consider, for example, a wristwatch that you are wearing. Its consumption is perfectly rival in the sense that because you have it I cannot have it. I can go to a shop and buy a wristwatch which is exactly like yours, but I cannot have the one that you have bought because you already have it. Further, all those who cannot pay the price of this watch are automatically excluded from consuming it. This exclusion is also costless.

Now consider the provision of a pure public good. It is easy to see that due to non-excludability in consumption, the marginal cost of providing a pure public good to an extra consumer is zero. As long as the pure public good is created, one more consumer can be added on to the list of existing consumers at no extra cost. Also, the addition of this one extra consumer to the pool of existing consumers in no way diminishes the consumption of this pure public good to the consumers who were consuming this good before the extra consumer was added. This is due to non-rivalry in consumption; implying that existing consumers should have no objection to this new consumer being added to the consumer pool, as their consumption is not affected in any way by this additional consumer.

It should be recognised that a *pure* public good is extremely hard to come by in real life. Even classical examples of a pure public good, such as television broadcasts lose their pure nature when satellite technology and signal scrambling is introduced. This is because in the bulk of examples of public goods, consumption assumes rivalry at some point, or some institutional mechanism can be evolved which makes exclusion possible. Let us look at a couple of examples. A journey by a train or a bus is often seen as an example of non-rival consumption, but if the train or bus becomes so crowded that one more person can get in only if someone gets off, then consumption becomes rival. In fact, congestion at some point is the main reason why many public goods lose their *pure* character. A road or a bridge are handy examples of public goods with non-excludable consumption but becomes excludable when a toll booth is established. Thus the pure nature of the public good is lost and these are termed impure public goods.

In fact, if we think of a range of types of goods with a pure private good at one end and a pure public good at the other, there are two more types that fall in between.

Table 3.1 Taxonomy of Private and Public Goods

	Rival	Non-Rival
Excludable	Pure private good	Club goods
Non-Excludable	Common property resources	Pure public good

In particular, mention must be made of common property resources or common pool resources which are often not private property but managed by a community. Examples are local forest or a watershed. Now, if fuel-wood is collected from a local forest such consumption is non-excludable within the community that manages it but is rival in consumption. In fact, it is not uncommon for members of such communities to face periodic shortages of fuel-wood due to overconsumption by others. Fishing in the deep sea is prone to unclear property rights. If such fishing is done with trawlers and reaches large scale proportions then such natural resources can become rival but remain non-excludable due to the absence of property rights.

Club goods are goods or services produced by a group of persons for their own consumption. Typical example is a social club offering leisure services such as sports or dining facilities. Such facilities are non-rival within members of the club but excludable since entry of new members can be restricted by existing members. It should be noted that club goods are typically prone to congestion whereupon their consumption may become rival. All such goods have been the subject matter of experiments in economics.

The Free Rider Problem in Public Goods

The above described features of a public good give rise to the free rider problem. This situation arises, not because consumers have zero willingness-to-pay for the pure public good but because they are unwilling to reveal it. One can think of willingness-to-pay for a good as the price of that good that a consumer is agreeable to pay in order to consume that good. Consider the hypothetical example where the government of the day is attempting to provide defence services to its people not through taxation but through voluntary contributions by the citizens of the country. It has been declared that voluntary contributions for provision of defence services must be sent in by all citizens by a certain date and the size of the army will be decided by the amount of contributions thus received. The presumption by the government here is that all individuals will have some positive willingness-to-pay for defence services and if all should come forward and contribute amounts that are consistent with a person's own willingness-to-pay, then the sum of these amounts will provide the army.

Now think of any one individual consumer of defence services in the country. She may have some positive amount in mind that corresponds to her own willingness-to-pay for this pure public good. But being self-interested, she may be unwilling to reveal it. Why does this happen? This consumer may think thus: The government is asking people to contribute for the provision of defence services. I certainly need and want that defence services be provided. And I am certainly willing to pay some money for it. But do I need to? Not really. Because there are millions of people out there who will surely pay some money for the provision of defence services. Hence an army will certainly be there. Once it is there, I too will be covered. There is no other way. And certainly no one will mind the fact that I am being covered, even though I did not pay, because the fact that I am being covered by defence services will not diminish the coverage of any other person who has paid.

This is the origin of the free rider problem. It is easy to see that the line of thought by one consumer described above can be extended to *all* consumers in the economy. The implication of this is that no money will be contributed by anyone against the call for voluntary contributions for the provision of defence services. Thus, the public good will not be provided at all.

Box 3.1 A Story about Free Riding

A Pond of Milk: An Indian Folktale

Once upon a time, there was a king. The king was not a nice person and liked to torture his subjects in many ways. Once he had a dream where he came to know that great benefits would come to him if he were to take three dips in a pond of milk. So, he ordered his minister to create a pond of milk.

A plot of land was identified within the palace grounds and a large hole was quickly dug. But where to find so much milk to fill the pond? The minister was troubled. He decided to send his public announcer with a royal order to the area where all the *yadav*s (cowherds) lived and had their cowsheds. The public announcer delivered the royal order. Every yadav was ordered to carry one pitcher of milk to the palace ground and pour it into the hole that had been dug. This they had to do within the night so that by morning the pond of milk would be ready.

The minister watched all night. He saw a long line of yadavs, with pitchers in their hands covered by a cloth come to the hole in the ground and pour into it. He was very pleased that his plan was working. He was happy that the king would find the pond of milk ready when he awoke the next morning.

It is easy to guess what happens next. When the sun rose in the morning, everyone in the palace was shocked to find an ordinary pond, a pond of water. Do you see what has happened here? Each and every yadav thought everyone else will pour milk so no one will be wiser if he pours a pitcher of water. But if everyone does the same thing, there will only be a pond of water.

A related question in economics is, can there be a market for a public good? Clearly, no. This is because the market is an institutional arrangement in which producers and consumers participate *voluntarily*. But for this class of goods, private firms would not be able to use prices to exclude non-customers. To see this clearly, suppose a firm plans to produce and sell a pure public good. Such a firm will be unable to find any buyers for its product because all such buyers, being self interested and mindful of the non-rival and non-excludable nature of consumption of a pure public good, will be unwilling to reveal their willingness-to-pay for the public good. Thus the market for a pure public good will not exist and the public good would not be provided at all.

Neo-classical economics—which is critically dependent on the Walras-Pareto paradigm involving a competitive economy leading to Walrasian general equilibrium leading to Pareto optimality—faced a grave crisis once the non-rival and non-excludable nature of consumption of a pure public good was noticed and discussed. Certainly the universality of the Walrasian general equilibrium faced a severe challenge because it was unable to include a pure public good among the array of goods and services that could be provided through such an equilibrium simply because the market for such a good would not exist and hence the good would not be provided at all.

The person who rescued neo-classical economics from this crisis was Paul A. Samuelson. He did this by introducing a new player into the system: a *Social Planner*[1]. This is a hypothetical, omniscient and omnipotent person, who has all information about the preference ordering of all members of the society and all production plans and costs of all public and private goods. Now consider an economy with n consumers ($i = 1 \ldots n$) and two goods, one a private good X and the other a pure public good G. Using his omniscience the Social Planner comes to know the marginal rates of substitution (MRS) of X for G of all consumers. In the same way the social planner also knows the marginal rate of transformation (MRT) of X for G.[2] Thus he is able to

[1] In this context, mention should be made of the work of two other researchers who made important contributions to the public goods literature before Samuelson (1954). First, Lindahl (1958/1919) described optimal provision of a public good where the level at which it is provided is determined by the amount collected when each individual pays according to her marginal benefit derived from the public good. Second, Pigou (1931) stated that each individual derived benefit or utility from the consumption of a public good. At the same time the payment of taxes to finance these public goods resulted in a disutility. The optimal level at which the public good should be provided can be found by equating the marginal utility of public goods with the marginal disutility of tax payments.

[2] MRS is simply the slope of the indifference curve between two commodities and is equal to the ratio of a very small decrease in one commodity to the corresponding (very small) increase in the other commodity so that the consumer is on the same indifference curve. It measures how much of one commodity the

find the efficient level of provision of the pure public good by solving the following condition;

$$\Sigma_i MRS_{X,G} = MRT_{X,G} \tag{3.1}$$

The Social Planner now knows the efficient level at which each public good is to be provided and this level accurately reflects the preference pattern of society in terms of consumption of the public good G and the private good X. The institutional solution, according to Samuelson is for the government to provide the public good at the level suggested by the Social Planner and the provision of the public good is to be paid for by taxation.

Notice that the optimality condition in equation 3.1 above is exactly the same as required by Walrasian general equilibrium. In that sense, the provision of the public good is akin to the provision of a private good by the market. Except, in this case, the optimal level has not been found through market interactions between buyers and sellers but imposed from above.

THE VOLUNTARY CONTRIBUTIONS MECHANISM

The free-rider problem has been examined in various experimental contexts, and as expected, it was found that institutional and environmental factors affect the extent to which people free-ride. In the vast majority of cases, the free rider problem has been put to the test through an experimental set up of the Public Goods Game, generally known as the voluntary contribution mechanism (VCM). Here follows a description of such an experimental set up in its most elementary design. A number of subjects are recruited and made to sit in isolated

---

consumer is willing to give up in exchange for more of the other commodity so that utility level is unchanged.

A production possibility set measures the set of outputs that are feasible given the amount of inputs and the current level of technology. This set for two outputs is bounded by the two axes and a curve that is concave to the origin. The MRT is the slope of this curve at any one point. It measures how much of one output must society give up at the margin to gain a small increase in the other output, such that all inputs are fully used.

or anonymous locations. In this simple design any verbal or non-verbal communication among the participants is not allowed. Next, each participant is given an initial endowment of Rs *e*. It is explained to the participants that there is a group fund (also called a public account) to which they will be asked to contribute and that the group fund is now empty. Each participant is asked to decide on an amount, such as Rs x, where $0 \leq x \leq e$, which she would like to contribute to the group fund. Any amount she chooses not to contribute, that is $e - x$ is hers to keep, which she will be able to take away at the end of the game.

The total amount collected in the group fund will be multiplied by some integer factor m and then distributed equally to the members of the group. Hence the total earnings of a participant will be in two parts. The first part is the part of her endowment that she did not contribute to the group fund, i.e., $e - x$. The second part is the equal share she got from the group fund after all participants have contributed and the total was multiplied by m by the experimenter. The sum of these two amounts is her earnings (or profit, as it is sometimes called).

The earnings of a participant is formalised as follows: Let there be n participants indexed $i = 1$ to n. The initial endowment for all participants is the same and is equal to e. Each participant contributes x_i amount to the group fund, which is multiplied by m and divided equally among the n participants in the group. Thus, the earnings of the ith participant R_i is given by:

$$R_i = (e - x_i) + \frac{m}{n}\left(\Sigma_{i \neq j} x_j + x_i\right) \tag{3.2}$$

Here the term in the first parenthesis is the amount player i does not contribute to the group fund and the second term is the amount she gets as an equal share of the amount collected in the group fund after it is multiplied by m. It is easy to see that the relationship between the earnings of player i will be negatively related to the contribution made by player i to the group fund, as long as $n > m$ (which is generally the case). Notice that:

$$\frac{\partial R_i}{\partial x_i} = -1 + \frac{m}{n} \text{ or } \frac{\partial R_i}{\partial x_i} < 0 \text{ for } m < n \tag{3.3}$$

This means that the marginal return to player i from an extra unit contribution to the group fund is negative. In other words, the more you contribute, the less you earn. Obviously, no self interested individual would want to contribute anything to the group fund. Accordingly, the collection in the group fund should be zero. This is the theoretical essence of the free rider problem and is the n person Nash equilibrium of the public goods game, where each player earns only her endowment e.

On the other hand it can clearly be seen that the social optimum where the earnings of each and every participant is maximised is reached when all players contribute their entire endowment e to the group fund. In that case there is no earning from the amount withheld from the group fund (hence, $e - x = 0$), but the entire sum of endowments is multiplied by m and each player goes home with m times her endowment. If all participants contribute their entire endowment to the group fund, then the amount collected in the group fund is $n.e$ and when this is multiplied by m and divided equally to all participants, each gets $m.e$ which is clearly greater than e for all $m > 1$. Hence this is the social optimum.

An explanation needs to be provided about the reasons for having a multiplicative factor such as m by which the group fund is multiplied before equal distribution to the participants. The use of this factor is to bring the situation in the lab as closely parallel to the real world. In VCM, the experimenter is asking subjects to contribute some part of their endowment towards creation of a public good, making clear at the same time that such contributions can be any amount from zero to e. In the real world if such contribution is collected a public good would have been created. Presumably, those who contributed (and those who did not) would receive the benefits of this public good for a long time and such benefits would be much more than the value of the amounts contributed. Now, in a VCM experiment it is impossible to actually create a public good on the spot whose benefits will immediately accrue to the participants. As a close second-best solution a multiplicative factor is used and the amount collected is multiplied. When an equal share of this is given to all the participants, a real life parallel is artificially created. This happens in two ways. First, contributors and non-contributors receive equal shares reflecting the non-excludable nature of the public good. Second, the multiplicative factor ensures that those who contributed get back more than what they contributed (in most cases).[3] This again is the case with public goods which is paid for once but its benefits continue to accrue over a long period of time, and are generally more valuable than the cost of the public good.

The theoretical prediction in a VCM experiment is that no money will be collected in the group fund due to the presence of the free rider problem. When such experiments are actually conducted this theoretical prediction is not borne out. It is seen that participants do contribute handsome amounts to the group fund. There may be a few individuals who contribute low amounts (or even zero) to the group fund, but there has never been an actual experiment conducted where the total amount collected in the group fund from all participants has been zero. These results are discussed in the following sections.

Before turning to the results of Public Goods Game (VCM) experiments there are some practical issues pertaining to the conduct of such experiments that needs to be addressed. First is the issue of maintaining anonymity between subjects, so that any one subject may not know or guess how another is behaving. This can be achieved in several ways. One way is if all subjects are sitting facing a computer terminal in a laboratory. But if a computer laboratory is not being used and the game is being hand-run, it is still possible to divide the subjects into equal sized anonymous groups such that each participant knows the group she is in but does not know who the other members of her group are. In any case, participants must be told not to talk at all during the game and if any participant has questions or doubts during the instruction stage, she should raise her hand and the experimenter should approach that participant and provide clarifications.

Let us take an example. Say, 20 participants have been recruited and they have been divided into 4 groups of 5 participants each and the groups are called A, B, C and D. To maintain anonymity between participants, each participant receives a decision sheet which tells her

[3] For instance, consider a 5-member group each with an endowment of Rs 50. One member contributes the entire Rs 50 but the other 4 contribute nothing. With a multiplicative factor of 2 there will now be Rs 100 in the group fund. Those who did not contribute will get Rs 50 + Rs 20 = Rs 70, but the member who contributed all will get only Rs 20. In situations where there is a lot of free riding contributing members may get less than what they contributed.

the group she is in (A, B, C or D) but does not know who the other members of her group are. Let each participant be given an initial endowment of Rs 50. Now there are 4 group funds for the four groups and the 5 members of each group are asked to contribute any amount from Rs 0 to Rs 50 to their respective group fund.

Second, we look at the issue of how the contributions are to be actually collected. It is possible to play this game with real currency money from the beginning. In that case, it must be ensured that enough change is handed out so that contribution of any amount is possible. For example if Rs 50 is the initial endowment and only integer amount contributions are permitted, then one Rs 20 note, two Rs 10 notes and coins worth Rs 5, Rs 2 and Re 1 should be provided to make all manner of contributions possible. This will be followed by each participant physically going out of the room, one at a time, onto the corridor where she will find four locked boxes, marked A, B, C or D, one for each group with a slit on top on a table. Empty envelopes should be provided. She will put her contribution in an envelope and drop the envelope in the box through the slit and return to her seat with the money she has not contributed. Next, once the participants have made their contributions the boxes are brought in, opened before the groups and the money counted.

In practice this may be cumbersome and time consuming, especially when multiple rounds are planned. Yet the contributions made by each participant must be kept anonymous from other participants to prevent herding behaviour.[4] If the game is played in a computer laboratory, the concerned z-Tree page will have to be configured. This is discussed in Chapter Seven. If the game is to be hand-run a decision sheet for each participant may be used. This should be prepared in advance and is to be distributed at the beginning of each round. The decision sheet is shown in Box 3.2.

In the computer laboratory or in the hand-run version, the decisions (sheets) are collected for each group, added and announced. Now the amounts in the group funds are to be multiplied by a multiplicative factor, earlier called m. In the present example, let $m = 3$. When equally

[4] Herding behaviour is seen when an economic agent is confused or undecided about a decision and therefore decides to do what she thinks most other people are doing.

Box 3.2 Decision Sheet for a Public Goods Game

Public Goods Game
Voluntary Contribution Mechanism

Decision Sheet
Participant Number_____________
This is Round Number___________
You are in Group _____ in this Round
Your endowment is Rs ____
You want to allocate to the Group Fund Rs ____
Remember you can allocate any amount from Rs 0 up to Rs 50 to the group fund. Any amount you do not contribute is yours to keep.

divided, each subject in a group gets $\frac{m}{n}$ part of the group fund and this is called the marginal per capita return (MPCR).

Third, we address the issue of how the earnings are to be actually paid out. In a multiple round game, again, it may be cumbersome and time consuming to actually pay the money after each round. Rather, the following may be announced and a record kept after each round: a) the amount being collected in the group fund of each group, b) what that amount becomes when multiplied by 3 for each group, and c) what is the individual share of each member of a particular group. Each participant may be given a sheet where she records the amounts she is keeping in each round (which she already knows) and the amount collected in the group fund (which is announced) so that she can calculate her earnings from each round after multiplying the group fund by 3 and dividing by 5 and adding this amount to the amount she did not contribute. The total amount earned by a participant over all the rounds may then be added up and paid out at the end of the session.

Let us see what may actually happen in our example. Remember there are 20 participants and they are divided in 4 groups of 5 participants each. Let us look at one such group. Clearly it is socially optimum for all 5 participants to contribute their entire endowment of Rs 50 to the group fund. This is how the earnings of each participant are maximised. In this case, if all 5 participants contribute the entire endowment of Rs 50, then Rs 250 is collected. Multiplied by the multiplicative factor of 3 this would become Rs 750 and each participant would earn Rs 150. This is the maximum return each could earn from one round.

But this outcome, according to theory, is unlikely to occur, due to the presence of free riding. This is because each participant is unlikely to expect that others too would contribute the entire Rs 50. Consider a free-riding player who contributes nothing, while other 4 participants in the group contribute Rs 50 each. Now there is Rs 200 in the group fund which becomes Rs 600 after multiplication by 3. So each of those who contributed Rs 50 now earn Rs 120 while the free-riding subject who contributed nothing earns Rs 120 + Rs 50 = Rs 170.

RESULTS FROM THE FIRST EXPERIMENT WITH PUBLIC GOODS

We now turn to a discussion of what has actually happened when a simple public goods game was played with VCM. The first such attempt to run a simple public goods game to test if the provision of a public good is possible through a VCM was by Marwell and Ames (1979).[5] Marwell and Ames were sociologists at the University of Wisconsin. They were the first to initiate systematic experimental research on the determinants of provision of public goods through voluntary contributions, in order to address 'a fundamental sociological question: when will a collectivity act to maximize its collective interest even though such behavior conflicts with a course of action that

[5] Even though Marwell and Ames (1979) was the first experiment to test the VCM through a game that later became the template for the public goods game, mention should be made of Bohm (1972) and Dawes, McTavish and Shaklee (1977). Bohm conducted an experiment to measure the demand for a public good, a television programme. Dawes, et al. conducted an experiment to study reactions of subjects placed under an abstract social dilemma. Both used monetary payoffs and their experiments have remarkable similarities with public goods games. These are not being discussed in detail here so as not to distract from the main thread of discussion. For a detailed discussion of these works see Ledyard (1995).

would maximize the short-term interests of each individual separately' (1979: 1335).

The subjects of this study were 256 high school students aged between 15 and 17. The experiment in this case was conducted in the subject's normal setting. First, the consent of the subject was obtained by a telephone call. Next, a detailed instruction sheet was mailed to the subject. This was followed by another phone call where the experimenter went over all the points of the instruction sheet and answered subjects' queries and doubts, to ensure that the subjects knew what they were required to do. An appointment was made for another telephone call for the next day (or soon after) and on this occasion the subjects were required to decide on their contributions to the public fund. During the entire period, the subjects remained in their normal environment and they were not brought in to a central location.

It should be mentioned here that in these early days of experiments, researchers were not too concerned about maintaining experimental control and hence Marwell and Ames did not think it important to bring the students into a room or a lab. At present, this would be unthinkable. This is because there is every possibility that some (if not all) subjects would consult someone after receiving the instructions but before deciding on contributions. Thus we have no way of telling who is actually taking the decisions and on what basis. This is especially true of young people of that age who would normally live with parents. So, prudential practice at present requires subjects to be brought into a room or a lab and anonymity and lack of communication between members of a group are to be maintained, unless the experiment itself requires the violation of anonymity or needs communication between members.

The subjects were divided into groups of 4 such that 64 groups were formed. Since there were 8 treatment conditions each treatment condition had 8 groups each. Within each group of 4 subjects there were two male and two female subjects. Each subject was given an endowment of a number of tokens, from which she could keep some for herself (private account) which would be redeemed at the end of the game at 1 cent per token, or allocate to a public fund whose redemption value was variable and depended on the total contribution received in the public fund. Each subject was given a table (as shown in Table 3.2) to explain the return from the contributions collected in the public fund.

Table 3.2 Payoff Chart used in Marwell and Ames (1979)

	How Much Money You Get		
Total Number of Tokens Invested in the Group Exchange by All Group Members	Total Money Earned by the Group ($)	Blue Player (2.25 cent of each group dollar)	Green Player (0.9 cent of each group dollar)
0–1,999	0	0	0
2,000–3,999	14.00	0.32	0.13
4,000–5,999	32.00	0.72	0.29
6,000–7,999	54.00	1.22	0.49
8,000–9,999	320.00	7.20	2.93
10,000–11,999	350.00	7.88	3.21
12,000–13,999	390.00	8.78	3.57
14,000–15,999	420.00	9.45	3.85
16,000–17,999	440.00	9.90	4.03
18,000	450.00	10.13	4.12

Source: Marwell and Ames (1979: 1344). Reproduced by permission of The University of Chicago Press.

This is a payoff table for a large group of 80 subjects with unequal endowment and unequal return. The first column shows tokens collected in the public fund. The second column shows dollar equivalent of each level of token collection. As can be readily seen the dollar redemption value rises with larger and larger collection. This provides positive incentives towards contribution to the public fund. Returns to individuals for each token conversion are at two different rates. Players are assigned colours blue or green and the rate of redemption for tokens to blue players are high, that is 2.25 cent per dollar collected in the public fund while the redemption rate for green players is low, that is 0.9 cents per dollar collected in the public fund.

Notice a unique feature of the payoff table, that a moderately high level of total group contribution, namely 7,999 tokens at the rate of 1 cent per token, the marginal return was about 6 cents while at all other levels the marginal return was less than 1 cent. This level corresponds to the so called 'provision point' that is the level of public fund at which the public good begins to be provided.

In this study, group size varied between small (4 persons) or large (80 persons). A small group had a total of 900 tokens and a large group of 80 had a total of 18,000 tokens. In fact, a deception was practiced by the researchers in the sense that there were no 80 person groups. All groups were 4 person groups. But half the players were told that they were in an 80 person group with the other 76 persons sitting elsewhere. Since players did not need to interact with each other they had no way of knowing that they were really in a 4 person group.

The results of the study by Marwell and Ames found lack of support for the strong free rider hypothesis. About 57 per cent of available resources were invested in the public fund. Further, rate of contribution was less when initial endowments were unequal.

One last point is about the deception about group size. It was possible to deceive the student subjects since they remained in their natural environments and interacted by phone. But if they were deceived about being in a group of 80, it is tempting to deceive them about being in a group of 4. In modern experimental economics, there is wide consensus that no deception should be practiced at all. This, in spite of the fact, that experimental psychologists and sociologists routinely conduct experiments that contain some deception. The consensus in economics comes from the notion that if all experimental economists avoid any deception, then over time economic experiments will begin to enjoy higher credibility and trust from the subject pool.

VARIATIONS OF THE PUBLIC GOOD GAME

Now that we have covered the basic public goods game involving the VCM it is time to turn to possible variations of the game that several researchers have introduced. Recall that these will all appear as treatments in the basic public goods game and are designed to investigate why certain results appear the way they do and what drives these results. First, we present the discussion in general terms, without referring to particular studies, for better understanding of these treatments. This will be followed by discussion of specific studies and what those results show.

A general finding of all public goods games hitherto played show two results:

i. The free rider problem, as predicted by theory, does not exist. There is no record of any public good experiment where all participants contributed nothing. This throws new light on our understanding of rational human behaviour, akin to the lessons learnt from the Ultimatum Game and the Trust Game in Chapter Two. That is to say, rationality does not rest on self-interest alone but includes some element of altruism as well as trust.

ii. If the public good game is played over several rounds, most experiments show a decay in average contributions over rounds. There could be two competing causes for this. First, even though the game is explained to the participants adequately with examples, etc., when they begin the game subjects really have no idea about what to expect from others. So they begin by contributing high. But experience over the first few rounds show that they are better off contributing low or not contributing at all. This is when the decay in contributions begins and this continues till the end of the game. Those who strongly hold that the free rider problem must exist use this fact of decaying contributions over rounds as evidence in support of their claim. They hold that subjects begin by contributing high because they have no prior experience of playing the public goods game, but as the subjects go along over rounds; they figure out that free riding is a better strategy. Hence the decay begins and supporters of free-riding hold that if the game would have been played over sufficiently large number of rounds, contributions would in fact drop to zero.

Second, however, there is an alternative explanation to the above. It is intuitive to expect that in any pool of subjects there will be some who are more altruistic and trusting and some who are less so. Let us define high contributors as those who contribute above the average of the group and low contributors as those contributing below the average. It is fair to expect that those who are more altruistic and trusting will begin by contributing high while the others will contribute low to begin with. Now each subject knows her own contribution and is told the total amount collected in the public fund. Hence she can calculate the average contribution of the group. If she is a high contributor, she figures that some or most others must be low contributors for the average to be where it is. She is likely to react by lowering her contribution in the next round. On the other hand, if she is a low contributor having contributed below the average, she will have gained more from this decision than others and is likely to continue this pattern of contributions. So, in subsequent rounds, high contributors are likely to reduce contributions while low contributors continue to contribute low, resulting in a decay in total and average contributions.

We now turn to the variations of the public goods game mentioned earlier. These variations fall into the following broad categories:

Group size

The size of the group is a matter of concern. Subjects have a perception of others' actions when group size is small; at least they believe they do. As group size is increased, this perception about what others might do weakens. This may lead to lowering of contributions, where this response can be thought of as opting for non-risky behaviour in the face of imponderables. Generally, small groups consist of 4 subjects. But groups can also be as large as 80 subjects (as in Marwell and Ames [1979], though not in reality). It is possible to start with a small group and gradually add subjects over rounds. This way the effect of group size on average contributions can be studied. There is one confounding factor though. The subjects playing from earlier rounds have more experience than subjects who were brought in later. So it becomes difficult to pinpoint the reason for explaining the results. It is better to create cohorts of varying group sizes, say 4, 8, 12, 16 and 20 and make each cohort play a fixed number of rounds and then compare the average across rounds for each cohort.

Gender, caste and religion

Basic social characteristics of the subject pool may also matter. To begin with, let us look at gender. If one believes that woman are more altruistic and trusting than men (and many studies—such as Solnick [2001]—have found this to be true in other contexts) it is worth checking this out through a public goods game. The subject recruitment should be done in advance and then groups formed and intimated to the subjects in advance so that different cohorts report for the experiments at different times. In this case group size should be kept the same across cohorts. One could have some all women groups, some all men groups and some mixed groups. At the end of the delivery of instructions, examples and quiz, it should be specifically mentioned that all subjects in this case are in an all women (men) group. This should have the impact of priming the subjects to this fact, which means this information will be uppermost in the mind of the subjects when they take a decision about contribution. This should not be done with the mixed groups which should be used as control during later analytical exercises.

The same can be done with caste (scheduled caste/upper caste), tribe (scheduled tribe/non-tribal), religion (Muslim/Hindu) or with any other social divide such as rural/urban, agrarian/industrial, literate/illiterate, white/black, rich/poor, etc. Always, priming should be done before the public good game and a few mixed sessions (without priming) should be run as control.

Communication

Interaction and communication between subjects before a public good game is played may have serious impact over the level of contributions. In general, subject pool is divided into anonymous groups and the composition of the groups is changed after every round. This is done to ensure two things. First, if we look at a person (even if we do not speak) we tend to form a subjective impression of the other person. For example we may find a person likeable or dislikeable. This is likely to affect your level of contributions in some way which is random and not necessarily related to the game conditions, creating white noise in the data recovered. Second, communication of any kind often acts as a signal, which too can influence contributions. For example, another subject may tell me that contributing high is a good thing and she is going to contribute high, no matter what others do. Now it is up to me to believe her or not. If I do, then I too may be tempted to contribute high thereby bringing up average contributions. Hence, in general, identity of group members is kept anonymous.

In the present case it is the express purpose of the experimenter to see the impact of communication on contribution. First, of course, several rounds must be played without communication which is to serve as control. Next, an interval must be created during which communication is to take place. Communication may be unstructured or structured. Unstructured communication can take the form of people talking amongst themselves. This has the advantage of giving individual subjects sufficient freedom to communicate and influence each other, but has some disadvantages in the sense that experimental control may be somewhat lost. Some groups may have a subject who is a forceful communicator and this may have an impact on contributions while other groups may not have such a subject, so that replicability is compromised. Alternatively, there could be structured communication amongst subjects. This happens best in a computer laboratory. For example, subjects may play a few rounds without communication and thereafter be given a break. During the break each subject may be allowed to send two email messages (of say not more than 50 words each) which is communicated to all the other players or only players in each player's group. Then a few further rounds are played and contributions before and after communication are compared. Structured communication has the advantage that experimental control is better (hence more replicable) which comes at the cost of individual freedom of expression of the subjects.

Economic theory, however, term contribution commitments (pledge amounts) made during pre-play communication as *cheap talk*. This is to mean that a subject may state her intention to contribute an amount x during pre-play communication, but once the time comes for actual contribution, she may contribute a different (lower) amount. Experience with public goods games, however, show that a large percentage of players do, in fact, honour their pre-play commitments even when these commitment were not binding.

Endowment

An initial endowment is given to each participant before each round of a Public Goods Game. This is done to rule out the difference between rich and poor players. Clearly if players had to bring their own money to play the game, many would not be able to afford it and many would not agree to play the game under these conditions. What is the right amount to be provided as endowment? The endowment that is provided should not be too small so as to become trivial to the subject. It should be a little more than what would be the opportunity cost of time spent by the player in a classroom or a laboratory pro-rated from the local daily wage rate. In the benchmark scenario the endowment is the same for everybody and same in all rounds.

However, two variations can easily be thought of. First, one could create a distributional effect by giving different endowment to players within a group. This is usually done by giving endowments at two levels, high and low, while keeping group endowment the same. Naturally, a few rounds should be played with equal endowment to serve as control. For example, if one has 5 member groups, start with equal endowment of Rs 30 each. Thus group endowment is Rs 150. Now after playing a few rounds try individual endowments within a group in the string Rs 60, Rs 60, Rs 10, Rs 10, Rs 10. This keeps the group endowment the same as in the control creating a distribution between high and low.

Second, the size of the endowment could be itself increased after a few rounds of control. So one may start with endowment of Rs 30 each for five rounds as control, followed by five rounds each with endowments of Rs 50, Rs 100 and Rs 200. It is easy to see that fund requirements can be quite steep if this treatment is tried out but it would bring out the impact of low and high endowment on contribution to the public fund. For comparability, take contribution as percentage of endowment in the analysis.

Reward or profit

As stated earlier, in the basic public goods game the subject's reward or earnings come in two parts. The first part is the amount not contributed to the public fund out of the endowment. The second part is the amount received after the public fund is collected after all contributions are made and is multiplied by some multiplicative factor, usually 2 or 3. Each subject receives an equal share of the public fund after multiplication. So, if each member of a 5-member group gets an endowment of Rs 30 and the amount collected in the public fund is Rs 100, with a multiplicative factor of 2, this will become Rs 200 and each subject will get Rs 40 from the public fund.

In terms of variations, little can be done with the first part. Normally, any amount from the endowment not contributed to the public fund is allowed to be retained by the subject as income. One variation on rewards from the second part is that the public fund after due multiplication can be returned to the members of the group in proportion to the contributions made by each member. This creates additional incentives for subjects to contribute. Another variation can be made if endowments are unequal. Then the amount collected in the public fund, after due multiplication may be returned to the group members in proportion to their original endowments. This creates additional incentives for the high endowment subjects to contribute high.

Provision Point, reward, penalty and risk

Hitherto, we have assumed the public good being provided under the VCM to be continuous in nature. That is to say, the public good could be provided at any level corresponding to the quantity of funds collected through voluntary contributions. A good example may be social forestry. These are schemes where fruit bearing trees are planted by the side of a village road. Now if only a small amount is collected, then only a few trees could be planted; but if a large amount is collected then a large number of trees can be planted. Hence the size of the public good can be adjusted to the contributory fund that is raised.

It is easy to see that there are many public goods for which this does not hold true. A public good such as a bridge or a road will require some minimum level of public fund in order to be at all provided. This is often captured in an experiment by having a threshold for the public fund. Such a threshold is called a *provision point*. Let us turn to our earlier example of a 5-member group with each member having an endowment of Rs 30. So the group endowment is Rs 150. Now we set a provision point at Rs 100. That means the public good will at all be provided if and only if at least Rs 100 is collected.

A provision point is usually associated with a reward-penalty system. This can be designed in one of several ways. One could have a pure reward designed into the game. For example, the subjects are told that if Rs 100 is not reached then the amount collected in the public fund will be simply divided by 5 and returned to the group members (that is the multiplicative factor is 1) but if the threshold of Rs 100 is reached or exceeded then the whole amount will be multiplied by 2 or 3 and then divided by 5 with each member getting one share. Note that subjects continue to retain any amount from the endowment not contributed into the public fund.

One also could have a pure penalty for not reaching the threshold. In its simplest form, the subjects could be told that if the threshold of Rs 100 is reached then they would get an equal share as the return from the public fund after it is multiplied by 2 or 3, but if the threshold is not reached, the entire public fund will vanish (that is come back to the experimenter). In both the above cases, a simple reward or a simple penalty around the concept of a provision point will generally encourage higher contributions in order to reach the threshold. Even so, the rear-end baggage of the tendency to free ride will remain. It is therefore interesting to see how contributions respond to the presence of a reward or a penalty for reaching or not reaching a threshold in the public fund.

Next it is possible to have a reward *and* a penalty around the provision point. This happens when the subjects are told that there is a threshold of Rs 100 for each public fund. If this threshold is not reached by a group, the entire public fund will come back to the experimenter; but if the public fund reaches or exceeds Rs 100 then it will be multiplied by a multiplicative factor of 2 or 3 and returned in equal share to the members of the group. Another variation is when the reward for reaching the provision point is given, not by multiplying the amount collected by some multiplicative factor (say 2 or 3) before returning it to the members of a group, but by making a lump-sum transfer into the public fund when the threshold is reached. This is different from the earlier case of using a multiplicative factor in the sense that the incentive for having reached the provision point is fixed in advance. When a multiplicative factor is used as reward the size of the reward is proportional to the size of total contribution beyond the provision point, while when a lump-sum transfer is used as reward the realisation of the reward is a binary outcome. Either the provision point is reached and the lump-sum transfer is received or the provision point is not reached and the money in the public fund is wiped out.

There are real life situations where the reward for having created a public good or the penalty resulting from having failed to do so is uncertain. For example, if people choose to take defensive action against a cyclone by building a storm shelter, groups of people who succeed in building such a shelter are indeed rewarded only if a cyclone occurs in one's lifetime and groups who fail to build such shelters due to free riding are only likewise penalised if the storm actually occurs. This is often captured in an experimental setting by rolling a die after each round. So one could say that a die will be rolled (or a coin tossed, though people tend to believe the rolling of a die as more unbiased than tossing a coin) and if an even number comes up then the storm will deemed to have been occurred, and the rewards and penalties as announced will operate. Similarly, if an odd number comes up then there is no storm and there will be no reward or penalties. Notice that if you use a standard six-sided die and the alternatives are odd and even numbers, you are effectively assigning 50 per cent probability of a storm happening, which some may consider too high. One could bring this probability down to say 10 per cent by reserving the number 1 for the occurrence of a storm and using a ten-sided die.

Identification

In general, groups formed for a public goods game have members who are anonymous to each other in the sense that each subject knows the group she is in but does not know who the other members in the group are. Identification involves announcing after every round which subject contributed how much. Again, in the simple version of the public goods game, this information is not given out to the participants. Now consider a situation where the names (or participant numbers) and corresponding contributions are announced after each round. What impact is this likely to have?

To answer this we must first understand the role of *peer monitoring* and *social sanction*. Peer monitoring happens when you are in a group situation where others, who are people like you, can observe what you are doing and you are aware of this fact. Social sanction happens when others, who are people like you, can punish you in some way when you do something that others disapprove of. It is generally understood that peer monitoring is a strong social force[6] that can be used as an

[6] Consider a micro credit group such as one proposed by Mohammed Yunus under the Bangaldesh Grameen Bank model, which won him the Nobel Peace Prize in 2006. Under the scheme, members of a small group of micro entrepreneurs are each given a loan by the Bangladesh Grameen Bank (usually with a weekly instalment repayment plan) but each member is jointly liable for all loans in the group. If a single default occurs all members of the group are debarred from

economic force in some group-action situations. The same is true of the threat of a social sanction.

Now, under identification the names (or participant IDs) and the corresponding contributions are announced at the end of every round. This has the clear effect of unleashing peer monitoring on each and every member of the group and the threat of social sanction on low contributors. You may well ask, 'If I am in a group with people I do not know from before and are unlikely to meet in the future, why would I at all care about what others think of me?' As such peer monitoring is not likely to have much effect here. Neither would the threat of social sanction work, as the other members of the group have no recourse to punish me for low contributions. But experimental evidence overwhelmingly shows that identification of subjects with their contributions, publicly, has the unambiguous effect of increasing contributions. The explanation perhaps lies in the fact that the very social nature of human decisions attaches a certain element of social shame with contributing low. Now a player may not hesitate to contribute low if she knows that this will not become public knowledge but will certainly not like to be identified as a low contributor in public even if the other members of the group share no common history and are unlikely to interact with her in the future. The psychological discomfort of being identified as a low contributor—even if for a short duration—most subjects would prefer to avoid.

Partner and stranger matching

All public goods games hitherto described have been played with groups where members are anonymous to each other. So each player

---

future loans. The success of this scheme and its high repayment rate is critically dependent on peer monitoring and social sanction. Since the members of a micro credit group are all from the same village and are neighbours, it is easy for them to ensure that each member of the group are in fact using the loan for the purpose it is given and making every effort to succeed in order to repay. Social sanction is as yet not a well-understood concept in economics. It is the power of a peer group to somehow punish an erring member. It may take the form of social boycott, etc. Both peer monitoring and social sanctions are social forces. The success of Yunus was to be able to make use of these as economic forces.

knows the group she is in but does not know who the other members of her group are. Frequently, these groups are randomly reconstituted or re-matched at the end of every round. There are two issues behind this design. First, it is believed that the particular history of members of a group, as a group, does not matter. So, the members of these randomly formed groups do not begin with any prior presupposition about expected behaviour of other members of the group. The random re-matching at the end of every round ensures that there is no signalling or retaliation within the group. This is called *stranger matching*.

But suppose you are interested to explore the behaviour of a group of persons who know each other from before and have had interactions in the past. You wish to investigate if this would improve contributions. One way could be to recruit subjects with these features and put them in a group. For example you could recruit 20 student subjects with 5 students in each group who are students of the same course in the same semester of your university. If the experiment is held late in the semester, then these 5 students have had some time to know each other and interacted with one another. So, it is now possible to put the students from the same class in a group and play say 5 rounds without changing the groups. This is called *partner matching*. This could be followed up with 5 more rounds of randomly re-matched groups that will act as control.

Two things could be investigated here. First, do the partner matchings demonstrate higher average contributions compared with the control. Second, are decay rates lower in partner matchings than in stranger matchings.

Rounds and termination

A first critical decision for the experimenter is to decide whether to play the public goods game for a single round (period) or to play multiple rounds. In general one is interested to have a data set as large as possible within the allotted budget for the research project. In that sense it is perhaps simpler to have multiple rounds in a single session rather than to have many single-round sessions. Also, with multiple rounds, the collected data may be more amenable to analysis using panel data methods. Further, multiple rounds allow investigation of decay rates in contributions.

A word of caution pertaining to the attention span of the subjects. In order to maintain experimental control it is required that subjects do not talk, leave the room or use mobile phones or play computer games during the course of the experiments. Also they play each round with full attention to the game at hand. It is generally true that it is not possible to hold subjects in these conditions for more than 90 minutes. Beyond this, some talking will happen or someone will want to make a phone call (citing an emergency) or visit the toilet, thus loosening experimental control. This puts a physical limit on the number of rounds you can have in a single session. If you allow for a total of about 30 minutes for allotting subject IDs, explaining the instructions, giving examples and taking a quiz before the game begins and making payments after the experiment is over, you are left with about 60 minutes to play the actual game. In a computer laboratory it will take about 3 minutes per round, so you can never have more than 20 rounds per session. If the game is hand-run, the number of rounds planned for must be less.

Once the number of rounds is decided, the next critical decision to take is whether to announce the number of rounds that will be played at the beginning or not. If the experimenter announces the number of rounds to be played at the beginning, there remains the possibility that subjects will make use of backward induction. This happens when a subject decides it is not worth contributing in the last round as the signal of high contribution to other players will not be carried forward. Given this, it is not worth contributing in the last-but-one round as no contribution will take place in the last round. In this way no contributions happen from the first round itself. This sort of an outcome may be prevented if the number of rounds to be played is not announced at the beginning. Then the subjects have no way of knowing which the last round is.

On the other hand the number of rounds to be played in a session must be strictly decided in advance and should be the same across sessions when there are multiple sessions. Otherwise, one can face a possible accusation from a reviewer that the experimenter has decided the number of rounds on the spot by considering how the result of each round is going.

SOME NOTABLE PUBLIC GOODS GAMES

Marwell and Ames had concluded from experimental evidence that subjects did, in fact, contribute under a VCM and the degree of free riding, where it exists, is nowhere near the levels predicted by economic theory. As a direct response to the Marwell and Ames study, two studies were taken up that hoped to challenge this conclusion. These were Kim and Walker (1984) and Isaac, McCue and Plott (1985).

The main innovation of these two studies over the earlier study by Marwell and Ames was repetition. Isaac, et al. had ten students who were undergraduates in sociology and economics as subjects in a public goods game with nine treatments, thereby yielding 90 observations per treatment. Each treatment had multiple rounds. Another innovation in the experiment was a show up fee of \$5.00. This was endowed to them at the start of the game and earnings from all rounds of the game were in addition to this. Individual earnings were artificially related to the size of the public good provided through contributions. This was different from calculating earnings based on contributions itself and was calculated as follows. The experimenters set a price of \$1.30 as the cost of providing one unit of the public good, and so the contributions to the public fund in each round was divided by this figure to determine the size or level at which the public good was provided.

Each subject was assigned to two payoff conditions, high or low. The earnings of a subject in a round was the subjects payoff as determined by the size of the public good provided in that round plus the value from the subject's payoff chart minus the amount contributed by that subject for the public good in that round.

Each subject received a subject payoff chart at the beginning of the game showing marginal and total payoffs for public goods level zero to 40. The functions which generated these marginal payoffs for each level of public good was $\$0.44 - 0.011q$ for high payoffs and $\$0.276 - 0.008q$ for low payoff where q was the size of the public good. Notice that the use of these functions ensured that marginal payoffs declined as the level of public good increased. In this case, the optimal group allocation that maximised total payoff was for $q = 23$ or 24. Individuals were not allowed to communicate during the experiment and were not allowed information about payoffs received by others.

As to the results of the study, contributions in the initial rounds of the study were very similar to those obtained by Marwell and Ames, but very soon, with multiple rounds, there was considerable decay in the contributions. On average, first period contributions yielded public goods levels of 8.8 but decayed quickly to 2.1 by the fifth round. Corresponding contributions were 53 per cent of endowment in the first period but declined to only 16 per cent of endowment in the fifth round. This decay, high initial contribution rate which then decays or declines over rounds, has been found by many subsequent studies (Isaac, McCue and Plott 1985; Isaac, Walker and Thomas 1984; Isaac and Walker 1988; Kim and Walker 1984). The possible reasons for the decay have been discussed in general terms earlier in this chapter.

Kim and Walker (1984) with a very similar design and multiple rounds found contributions of 41 per cent of the maximum group payoff in the first round which declines to only 11 per cent by the third round. Mention should also be made of a slightly earlier study by Isaac, Walker and Thomas (1984) who also got similar results from 8 VCM sessions under various treatment conditions. This experiment was run in a computer laboratory to estimate different factors that may affect free-riding. Such factors included group size, repetition, the value of the multiplicative factor that is used to determine payoff to subjects from the public fund and experience of subjects. They used two group sizes of 4 and 10. Each treatment had 10 rounds. Multiplicative factors used were 1, 2, 3 and 7.5. The average contribution over all treatments was 42 per cent and an average contribution over first rounds of all treatments was 51 per cent. Contributions increased with group size for low multiplicative factor but no perceptible effect of group size was observed for the high multiplicative factor of 7.5. Similarly, repetition with a lower multiplicative factor decreased contributions. On the other hand the effect of increasing the multiplicative factor from 3 to 7.5 increases contribution in all cases. Inexperienced subjects contributed more than experienced subjects suggesting that some learning does happen with more rounds of play.

What drives contributions in public goods games? Various explanations have been suggested to explain positive (often high) contributions to a public fund even when not contributing is the dominant strategy. These include (but are not limited to) group size, multiplicative factor, repetition, communication between subjects and the opportunity of punishing free riders. Yamagishi (1986, 1988), Ostrom, Walker and Gardner (1992) and Fehr and Gaechter (2000, 2002) show that subjects tend to exhibit higher levels of cooperation when they have the option of punishing free riders, even when there is a cost associated with punishing others. In Ostrom, et al. subjects were allowed the opportunity to punish free riders by paying a fee. Clearly the cost of punishment, thus, would be borne by the individual but the consequent benefit of higher contribution would go to the group as a whole. A pure self-interested subject would not choose to punish when a fee is required. Thus the Nash equilibrium would be no punishment but the results of the experiment showed considerable punishment taking place.

In Fehr and Gaechter (2000) subjects were placed in two types of groups, strangers and partners. In stranger groups, subjects were randomly assigned to a group after each round. There were 4 subjects in each group who played 10 rounds with punishment and 10 rounds without punishment. In the rounds with punishment, in addition to the normal VCM, there was an additional stage where subjects could punish low contributors by paying a fee and the final payoffs were adjusted accordingly. Punishment meant that the subject punished would receive only 10 per cent of the amount the subject earned in that round. This resulted in improved contributions compared to no-punishment rounds.

Pre-play communication is another important factor influencing contributions. Though theory holds that non-binding and non-enforceable commitments made by people can be cheap talk, Isaac and Walker (1988) showed that pre-play communication had significant positive impact on contributions. The rate of decay was also slower with pre-play communication.

Bochet, Page and Putterman (2006) conducted an experiment with free-form communication, removal of anonymity and communication with number commitments only (i.e., no verbal or visual inputs). The different treatments designed were: a) a baseline public goods game, b) with monetary punishment, c) face-to-face communication, d) face-to-face communication with punishment, e) chat room, f) chat room with punishment, g) numerical communication, and h) numerical communication with punishment. An important finding of the study was that face-to-face communication was most effective in improving contributions. Without punishments, numerical communication was not at all effective. Punishments improved contributions but not as much as face-to-face communication.

Chakravarty, Sebi, et al. (2013) uses a standard VCM game with a group of 10 subjects and face-to-face communication. The subjects who were villagers of Gori-Ganga Basin of the Central Himalayas in India were not re-matched every period. They find that even with a relatively low MPCR (= 0.2) and a large group, subjects contribute around 55 per cent of their endowment which diminishes slightly towards the end of the session to around 50 per cent. This is quite different from laboratory experiments using a similar design such as Isaac and Walker (1988).

It is easily seen from all the above cases that there is serious departure in actual results obtained in public goods games (in all its treatments) from corresponding predictions in economic theory. While theory predicts that the *n*-person Nash equilibrium will yield complete free riding by subjects, this is virtually never seen in experimental results. The actual behaviour can only be explained by altruism, sentiments prone to making charitable contributions and ties of kinship in families and communities. For example, Ghate, Ghate and Ostrom (2013) bring out the role of peer monitoring and social sanctions in communities when subjects participate in a VCM. Communities in real life are prone to punish free riders even when such punishment is costly to the community. This may also have serious consequences when communities may have to vote on the size of a local public good when the cost of the public good may have to come from voluntary contributions from the members of the community, by mutual agreement. This is discussed in the next section.

VOTING FOR A PUBLIC GOOD

In the real world, public goods are rarely provided through voluntary contributions. Most public goods are provided by the government or parastatals (government-like institutions such as municipalities) by raising taxes. In fact, this is by far the most usual way of providing public goods. Often taxes are raised without telling the tax-paying public which specific public good is to be provided and at what level.

Once the tax has been imposed and the tax-imposing body has collected the tax or has a good estimate of how much tax will be collected, the specific bouquet of public goods and their levels are decided. This is most often done through voting[7] in committees or bodies that control these governments or parastatals.

Davis and Holt (1993: 360–64) constructs a nice example of an experiment to capture the decision-making process to provide a public good through voting in a small committee where the consequent conflicts can be studied. In this example, there is a city council with 9 members. They are debating the level of public funding of schools in the city. We are told that apart from schools that run on public funding (therefore charging very little from the students) there are private schools in the city which run entirely by charging high fees from the parents of students. While private schools are naturally more expensive than publicly-funded schools, they are usually associated with better quality of education. Now the council has 9 members, 3 members each representing high-income (*h*), middle-income (*m*) and low-income (*l*) groups. For simplicity, let there be three levels of funding possible, high (*H*), medium (*M*) and low (*L*) . The preferences of each of the 3-member factions in the committee are as follows. High-income (*h*) members would in any case send their children to private schools, so they are unlikely to support high levels of public funding of schools, which would result in high taxes. Hence their preference ordering is low funding followed by medium funding followed by high funding. Middle-income (*m*) members would prefer to send their children to public schools provided such schools receive high levels of funding (representing superior quality of education), otherwise they prefer to send their children to private schools and give low levels of funding to public schools, so that taxes would be lower. So, their preference ordering is high funding followed by low funding followed by medium funding. Finally, low-income (*l*)

[7] Voting behaviour has been a popular subject of investigation in experimental political economy. There is a large body of literature that use experiments to explore voting behaviour of human subjects under various experimental conditions, voting rules and rules of winning. Starting with the work of Fiorina and Plott (1978), economists and political scientists have used laboratory experiments to study a range of issues in voting behaviour. For a more comprehensive coverage of voting issues, see Palfrey (1991).

members are compelled to send their children to public schools as they simply cannot afford the fees in a private school. However, they find the tax burden that is associated with high funding also quite heavy. So their preference ordering is medium funding followed by high funding followed by low funding.

Indicating funding levels high, medium and low in upper case initials and voter type, according to income class high, middle and low by lower case initials, the preference ordering of the 9 voters are shown in Table 3.3 below.

Table 3.3 Preference Ordering of Voters in the City Council (> indicates preferred to)

Voter Type	Preference Ordering	Number of Voters
h	$L > M > H$	3
m	$H > L > M$	3
l	$M > H > L$	3

Source: Drawn by the author for this publication.

It is clear that there can be no consensus on the level of funding the city council will provide to the public school system. A simple vote with three options will result in a three-way tie with no method of breaking the stalemate. Moreover, pair-wise voting between *H* and *L*, between *H* and *M* and between *M* and *L* will also not yield an outcome as 6 members prefer *L* over *M*, 6 prefer *M* over *H* and 6 prefer *H* over *L*. This makes the preference ordering of the committee as a whole cyclic where in a pair-wise vote, *L* would lose to *H*, *H* would lose to *M* and *M* would lose to *L*.

One way to break this stalemate is to resort to pair-wise voting, where the vote is taken in two stages. In this case, first, any two of the alternatives are taken up and members asked to vote for any one of the two alternatives. The winner of this contest is then matched against the remaining alternative in the second stage. Now members vote for either the winner of the first stage or the alternative not considered in the first stage. The winner of the second stage voting is the overall winner. To keep matters simple we assume that members resort to sincere voting—that is, vote according to the preference ordering given in Table 3.3.

Thus, before the voting can begin, an *agenda* has to be drawn up. The agenda simply tells the members the order of business, that is, which two alternatives will be considered in the first stage and which two in the second stage. The agenda for such a meeting is shown in Table 3.4 below.

Table 3.4 Agenda for the Meeting of the City Council

Item Number	Agenda
1	To decide between levels of public funding *H* or *L*
2	To decide between the levels of public funding chosen in Item 1 or *M*

Source: Drawn by the author for this publication.

The rationale behind drawing up the agenda in the above manner may be some pre-existing convention. For example, let *M* be the level chosen last year, hence *M* is the status quo. Supposing the convention is that the first stage vote will be between alternatives other than the status quo, the winner of which will be matched against the status quo in the second stage of voting. It can be shown that the agenda or the order in which the alternatives are considered will be crucial in deciding the final outcome. In fact with equal sized factions, cyclic preference ordering and the agenda convention mentioned above the status quo will always be the overall winner.

Take the present case, following the preference ordering given in Table 3.3 and agenda as set in Table 3.4. In item number 1, in a contest between *H* and *L*, all *h* type voters vote for *L*. Hence *L* has 3 votes. All *m* and *l* type voters vote for *H*, so *H* has 6 votes. Hence *H* wins in the first stage. Now we go to agenda item number 2. This is a contest between *H* and *M*. In this item all *h* and *l* voters vote for *M*, so *M* has 6 votes and all *m* voters vote for *H*, so *H* has 3 votes. Hence *M* is the winner of the second stage and the overall winner. The reader can easily verify that, in the same way, if we start with *H* as the status quo (the first stage contest is between *M* and *L*) then *H* will be the overall winner and if we start with L as the status quo (the first stage voting is a contest between H and M) then L will be the overall winner. Notice that sincere voting implies that if the most preferred alternative is not available to a member at any stage of voting, members will vote for the second-most preferred alternative.

How can we actually conduct experiments of this kind and what can we learn from them? First, the subjects are recruited from among students (say) of the university. They may be told that they are members of a committee that will take a decision regarding provision of a public good. The alternatives are given to the subjects. To begin with students may not have clear preference ordering among the alternatives and these will have to be induced in them by promising each group differential rewards for different outcomes of the entire voting game. For example, we can begin by selecting 9 subjects and divide them into 3 equal factions by using a lottery. Now, the 3-member faction who needs to behave as h voters may be told that they will get Rs 50 if L is chosen, Rs 25 if M is chosen and nothing if H is chosen. Similarly the 3-member faction who is required to behave as l type voters may be told that they will get Rs 50 if M is chosen, Rs 25 if H is chosen and nothing if L is chosen.

It is now possible to make three variations. First, one can try out different faction sizes. For example, instead of having 3 factions of 3 voters each, one could have factions of unequal size. Still keeping 3 factions they could be of 2, 3 and 4 members, so that we can study the effect of faction sizes on the final outcome. Second, the preference that is induced in the subjects of the 3 factions with differing incentives could be made non-cyclic. One possible alternative is to reverse any one preference for any one faction (any one row) in Table 3.3. For example, in the third row of Table 3.3 instead of the preference being $M > H > L$ it could be made $H > M > L$. This allows us the opportunity of testing the impact of preference over formation of temporary coalitions. Finally, one could change the number of factions. For example, instead of 3 factions, one could have 4 or 5 factions. But in that case it is preferable to have more number of subjects in each session. All these variations can then be conducted along with the base case described earlier as control and the outcomes compared. This will allow for situations where the final outcome is not entirely agenda-controlled.

Before finally taking leave of this subject, it is important to mention that members in small committees tend to follow long term strategies. Because, a small number of people who serve on a committee tend to meet repeatedly over a long period of time and voting on agenda items are often done openly and not by secret ballot, most voters know what to expect of another member on the committee. So strategic relationships tend to form between voters which may reach beyond the positions one voter may take with respect to a particular item on the agenda. This often leads to a departure from sincere voting to other strategies such as logrolling[8], where voter A always (or mostly) votes in favour of motions moved by voter B and this favour is always (or mostly) reciprocated by voter B.

Voting behaviour in small committees lends itself to many such experiments which can be carried out to gain insights into the actual strategies people adopt when taking decision through a vote. Especially, repetition and lack of anonymity may have major impacts on how people vote as well as the final outcomes.

[8] Lumberjacks of Canada move the trunks of felled trees by floating them in large numbers on river water and allowing the tide to carry these downstream. The lumberjacks then follow the timber on floating rafts. However, logjams do often happen when a few pieces of timber get stuck somewhere and other pieces end up in a heap creating a jam. In such situations the jam has to be cleared physically. This is done by lumberjacks carrying poles, jumping from one floating timber to another till they reach the source of the jam and release the pieces causing the jam. In this situation, lumberjacks work in pairs. While one of the pair is jumping from log to log, which makes the logs roll in the water, the other member uses his pole to steady the log. This is important or else the first lumberjack will fall off a rolling log. This is known as logrolling, and is the origin of the term in political science.

four

Individual Decisions under Uncertainty

A crucial assumption in much of economic theory is that economic agents behave in a rational manner, where such rationality implies self-interested behaviour. This self-interested behaviour is based on two fundamentals: a) the situation in which an individual finds herself, and b) the knowledge or information set that she possesses at that point in time. Self-interested behaviour implies that she takes such decisions that she believes is best for herself. This is how conventionally, rationality has been described.

It is in this context that information plays a vital role. In the preceding paragraph, the particular self-interested decision that a person takes will critically depend on the information available to the decision maker at that point of time. Now, in a simple situation, this does not tax the imagination. In everyday situations like buying bread or going to a cinema, most information is available in the public domain. So people take similar decisions when faced with similar situations. But in more complex situations, say when there is a time gap between decision and outcome, the information set available to the individual as well as individual attitudes begin to matter. So when you choose a subject for a major in the university, buy a house or contemplate migrating to another country, information plays a crucial role.

This centrality of information has evolved economics in the 1970s and 1980s, and changed economics from a subject with a mechanistic approach to one which is more nuanced and capable of addressing interpersonal differences in decisions even when two persons are situated in similar conditions. This central role of information is important due to the presence of uncertainty. Uncertainty is an intervention between an individual's decision and its outcome. Rawls

(1971) had called it 'a veil of ignorance'. You take a decision today which will deliver an outcome sometime in the future. That future you can see, but only imperfectly, as if through a veil. For example when accepting a job offer, proposing marriage to someone or deciding on a school for your child, you are really choosing behind a veil of ignorance. All these decisions have outcomes that you realise only in the distant future. Moreover, if you do not like those outcomes, these outcomes are sometimes irreversible or reversible at great cost.

What decision makers normally do is try to gather more information about the outcomes possible. What this information does is help us make the veil more transparent by allowing us to assign probabilities to every outcome consequent upon each decision. For example, you try to find out if the company offering you a job is a good employer, what kind of a person is he whom you are planning to marry and how happy are kids in the school you plan to send your child to. So if there are at least 2 possible outcomes to every decision you are about to take, one good outcome and one bad outcome, you need to have an estimate of the probabilities associated with each such outcome, before taking a decision.

Finally, when you have multiple choices attached to every decision, then each option for a decision is like choosing between multiple lotteries, each with 2 outcomes, one good (high) and one bad (low). And now, the risks involved with each such option are there before you. The economic rationale for taking a particular decision is modelled by the Expected Utility (EU) theory which is due to von Neumann and Morgenstern (1947). This is the theoretical basis for making choices under uncertainty when there are multiple options ex ante but only one outcome ex poste. Even though some readers may be familiar with EU theory, in the next section we provide a short review of the relevant theoretical premises. This will be followed by experiments designed to test the validity of EU theory, mainly in the nature of lottery choice experiments.

REVIEW OF EXPECTED UTILITY THEORY

The principal theory of choice underlying decision-making under risk is EU theory. This theory is based on the existence of an ordinal utility function by which alternatives can be ranked. The foundations of this theory were developed by von Neumann and Morgenstern (1947) and later by Luce and Raifa (1957). The theory rests on a set of axioms the most important of which include: ordering, transitivity, continuity and independence. Ordering requires that for any two choices A_1 and A_2, the decision maker either prefers A_1 over A_2, or A_2 over A_1 or is indifferent between the two. Transitivity requires that if A_1 is preferred to A_2, and A_2 is preferred to A_3, then A_1 must be preferred to A_3. Continuity requires that if A_1 is preferred to A_2 and A_2 is preferred to A_3, then there must be a combination of A_1 and A_3 that is preferred to A_2 and A_2 is preferred over some other combination of A_1 and A_3. The independence axiom requires that if A_1 is preferred to A_2 and A_3 is some other option, then the decision maker will prefer a combination of A_1 and A_3 to the same combination of A_2 and A_3.

Given the existence of an ordinal utility function, the expected utility maxim can be illustrated by a simple situation. Let us consider a decision maker faced with the problem of choosing among alternative courses of actions, the outcomes from which are determined by the state of an uncertain environment where:

A_j = the *j*th act or alternative course of action,
S_i = the *i*th possible risky outcome,
$p_i = p(s_i)$ = the probability that s_i occurs, and
Y_{ij} = the outcome of A_j given that s_i occurs.

Then, for the utility function $U(y)$, we know

i. If any risky action A_1 is preferred to another risky action A_2 then $U(A_1) > U(A_2)$, and
ii. $U(A_j) = EU(y_{ij}) = \Sigma_i p_i \, U(y_{ij})$

Following EU theory, the optimal act A_j^* is the one which maximises expected utility.

$$EU(A_j^*) = Max\ U(A_j) = Max\ \Sigma_i p_i \, U(y_{ij}) \qquad (4.1)$$

This theory, therefore ranks alternatives according to the probability of states of nature occurring, and relative preference regarding outcomes as represented in the utility function. The utility function $U(y)$ is assumed to be single-valued function of some measure of wealth y. There are several assumptions regarding $U(y)$.

First, it is assumed that the economic agent prefers more wealth to less. This implies a monotonically increasing utility function where marginal utility of wealth is strictly positive, $U'(y) > 0$. Second, it is assumed that the utility function demonstrates decreasing marginal utility of wealth implying a concave function with $U''(y) < 0$; this is the same as assuming that the decision maker is risk averse.

Because of the shape of the utility function, a risk averse person prefers a sure amount to taking a risk, that is $U[E(y)] > E[U(y)]$. This is demonstrated in Figure 4.1 for a simple lottery. Suppose an individual is given the choice of playing a lottery which pays y_1 units of y with probability p_1 and y_2 units of y with probability p_2 (where $p_2 = 1 - p_1$). Note that expected outcome is calculated as $E(y) = \Sigma_i p_i y_i$. As is shown in Figure 4.1, for a risk averse individual the utility function is concave and hence the utility of the expected outcome, $U[E(\bar{y})]$ will always be higher than the expected utility of the lottery, $E[U(\bar{y})]$.

Notice that $E[U(y)] = E_i p_i U(y_i) < U[E(\bar{y})] = U[\Sigma_i p_i y_i]$

Figure 4.1 The Expected Utility Hypothesis

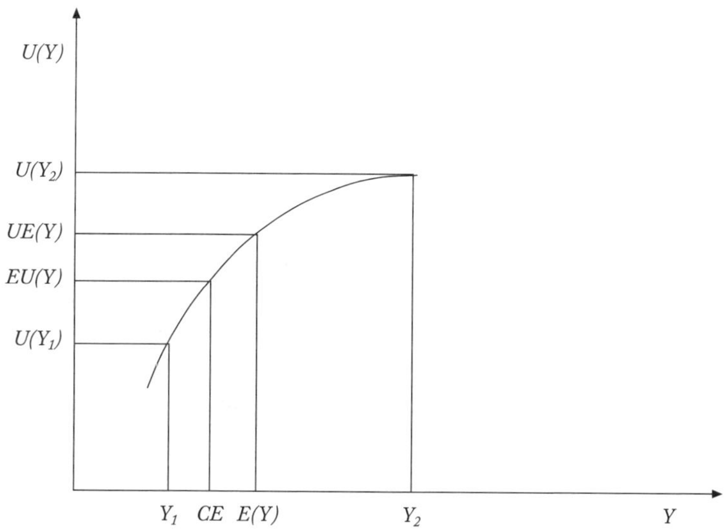

Source: Drawn by the author for this publication.

The certainty equivalent, *CE*, is the amount (in units of y) that will give the same utility as the lottery. That is, $U(CE) = E[U(y)]$. It is the certain amount that risk averse individuals are willing to accept in exchange for the chance of giving up playing the lottery. Further, risk averse individuals are willing to pay an insurance premium to avoid the uncertainty involved in playing a lottery. The risk premium, $\pi(y)$ is the difference between the certainty equivalent and the expected outcome of the lottery, or, $\pi(y) = E(y) - CE$, such that

$$U(CE) = U[E(y) - \pi(y)] = E[U(y)]$$

The risk premium is the amount of y that will make an individual indifferent between receiving the certain amount, *CE*, or playing the lottery. Naturally, for risk averse individuals, the risk premium will be positive. The degree of risk aversion can be uniquely measured in absolute terms by the Arrow-Pratt absolute risk aversion parameter: $r(y) = -U''(y)/U'(y)$. Notice that this measure is independent of the level of wealth y at which the individual exists. Alternatively, one can also measure the degree of risk aversion with a measure that is sensitive to the level of wealth of the individual. This is the relative risk aversion parameter:

$$R(y) = -yU''(y)/U' = yr(y)$$

INDIVIDUAL CHOICE UNDER UNCERTAINTY: THE ALLAIS PARADOX

Following the popularity of EU theory, there were a surge of lottery choice experiments, that is experimental sessions where individual decision makers were faced with two lotteries in which the outcomes and their associated probabilities are known to the players and then the subject is required to choose one lottery which she wants to play. By having the individual face a number of pair-wise choices, it was possible to comment upon the risk-attitude of individual subjects. Perhaps the most well known of these experiments is the one that contains the Allais paradox (Allais 1953). Allais asked subjects to make two hypothetical choices. First they were asked to choose between lotteries A and B, and then between lotteries C and D.

The outcomes and their associated probabilities are given in Table 4.1 below.

Table 4.1 The Allais Lotteries

Lottery	Outcome	Probability
A	100	1
B	500	0.1
	100	0.89
	0	0.01
C	100	0.11
	0	0.89
D	500	0.1
	0	0.9

Source: Adapted from Allais (1953), by permission of The Econometric Society.

It is not difficult to show that a risk averse expected utility maximiser, who prefers lottery A (not really a lottery) over B in the first pair-wise choice must also prefer lottery C over D[1].

Allais showed that a common pattern of choices that emerged in the experiments was that subjects preferred A over B but D over C. It is intuitively easy to see why this is the case. In the first pair-wise choice lottery A is a certainty of 100 but lottery B offers 500 with a small probability of 0.1. The decision maker thinks she is unlikely to realise 500 due to the small probability and if she opts for B she may even end up with 0 that carries a probability of 0.01. Under the circumstances she prefers 100 with certainty. Now compare C and D. C has a high

[1] There are three outcomes: 500, 100, 0. The probabilities of each outcome in each lottery are shown in Table 4.1. Utility of outcome at level x is written here as U_x. Since the decision maker in the first pick chooses A over B, it must be true that:

$U_{100} > (0.1)U_{500} + (0.89)U_{100} + (0.01)U_0$

Now adding $-(0.89)U_{100} + (0.89)U_0$ to both sides, we get

$-(0.89)U_{100} + U_{100} + (0.89)U_0 > (0.1)U_{500} + (0.89)U_{100} - (0.89)U_{100} + (0.01)U_0 + (0.89)U_0$

or, $(0.11)U_{100} + (0.89)U_0 > (0.1)U_{500} + (0.9)U_0$

Hence, $C > D$.

reward of 100 and a low of 0. D has a high reward of 500 and again a low of 0. The associated probabilities differ by only 0.01 which the decision maker interprets as being an almost negligible difference in probabilities. So she feels it is better to go for D which has a high reward of 500 rather than C which has a high reward of only 100.

Allais had performed these experiments with hypothetical choices, without providing real monetary rewards. But these experiments have subsequently been reproduced with real monetary incentives and the results turn out to be the same.

COMMON RATIO LOTTERIES

In order to conduct a simple lottery choice experiment, we first require to construct what are called common ratio lotteries. To keep matters simple we restrict the number of outcomes of each lottery to two outcomes. The representation of each lottery will be made as follows: First, each lottery will have a name, viz. S1, S2 or R1, R2, etc. This will be followed by some numbers in parentheses. The first number is the high outcome followed by the probability of this outcome, separated by a comma and followed by a semicolon. Again the third number is the low outcome of this lottery followed by the probability of this outcome, separated by a comma. The lottery choice experiment thus constructed can be played with real monetary rewards indicated in the lotteries.

Now consider a pair of lotteries S1 (a safe lottery) and R1 (a risky lottery), such that S1 (300, 1; 0, 0) and R1 (400, 0.8; 0, 0.2). Ask an experimental subject to make a choice as to which lottery she wants to play. The predominant response pattern is that participants tend to choose the safe lottery S1 (not really a lottery since getting 300 rupees is a certainty). Now consider another pair of lotteries, S2 and R2, such that S2 (300, 0.25; 0, 0.75) and R2 (400, 0.2; 0, 0.8). Again ask the same participant which lottery in this pair she wants to play. The likely predominant response is that she will choose R2 over S2.

Although the choice of S1 over R1 followed by a choice of R2 over S2 is typical, it poses the same paradoxical situation as the Allais paradox described in the previous section. This is because the pair of lotteries S2, R2 is derived from the pair of lotteries S1, R1 using a common ratio. In this case, the common ratio is ¼. That is, S2 is derived from S1 and R2 is derived from R1 by taking the high outcome in S1 and R1 and multiplying the corresponding probabilities by ¼ and assigning the residual probabilities to the 0 outcome to get S2 and R2 respectively. Hence it would be the theoretical prediction of EU theory, that if a participant is risk averse she would prefer S1 over R1 as the outcome in S1 is a certainty but the outcome in R2 is risky and the same participant will prefer S2 over R2 as S2 and R2 are derived from S1 and R1 respectively by using a common ratio. Intuitively though, it is not difficult to see why a participant may choose R2 over S2 in a situation of practical choice. She looks at the high outcomes in each, namely 300 (0.25) and 400 (0.2) and compares both. She perceives the probability difference, 0.25 and 0.2, to be negligible but the value difference 300 and 400 to be substantial, thus favouring R2 over S2.

PROBABILITY TRIANGLE REPRESENTATIONS

Most lottery choice experiments that yield results which violate predictions based on EU theory involve pairs of lotteries which are related via a common ratio. When all lotteries involved in an experiment have no more than a total of 3 outcomes, such lotteries can be represented in a probability triangle. Such triangles were first devised by Marschak (1950) and popularised by Machina (1982). These triangles make it easy to study the relationship between lotteries and compare them.

Here we illustrate such a probability triangle using the specific example of the lotteries described in the previous section, namely lotteries S1, S2, R1 and R2. These 4 lotteries involve 3 prizes or outcomes—Rs 0, Rs 300 and Rs 400. As shown in Figure 4.2, first, a 3-dimensional axes is drawn and the probabilities corresponding to the 3 outcomes are represented along the 3 axes. The probability of the most preferred prize Rs 400 is denoted along the vertical axis and the least preferred prize Rs 0 along the horizontal axis and the probability of the intermediate prize of Rs 300 is denoted along the third axis. We denote these as p_1, p_2 and p_3. Since these probabilities can take a maximum value of unity, points denoting $p_1 = 1, p_2 = 1$ and $p_3 = 1$ must first be marked on the 3 axes. These points need to be joined by 3 straight lines denoting the boundary on which each of the

Figure 4.2 Probability Triangle Representation in Three Dimensions

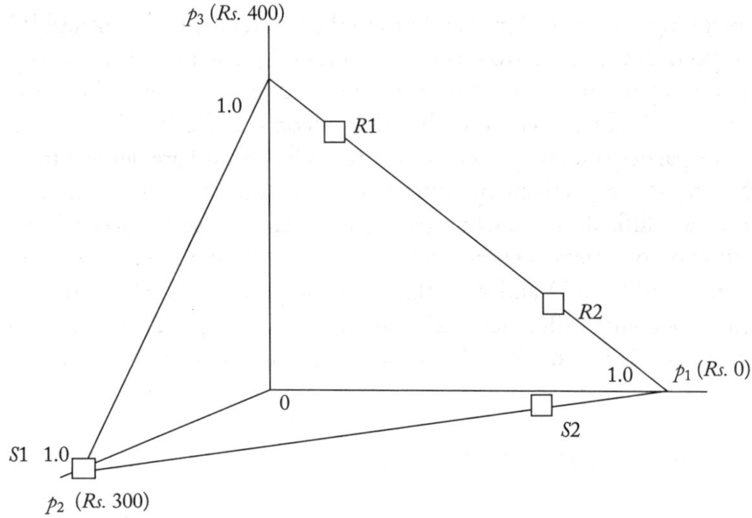

Source: Republished with permission of Princeton University Press, from Davis and Holt (1993); permission conveyed through Copyright Clearance Center, Inc.

four lotteries can be represented. Thus, S1 is Rs 300 with probability 1 will be represented at $p_2 = 1$ and the other two probabilities at 0. Similarly R1 will be depicted on the straight line joining p_3 and p_1 axes at coordinates 0.2 (for Rs 0) and 0.8 (for Rs 400). Likewise, S2 will be represented on the straight line joining p_2 and p_1 at coordinates 0.75 for Rs 0 and 0.25 for Rs 300. Finally R2 will be located on the straight line joining p_3 and p_1 axes, further down from R1.

Notice, however, that since there is a total of 3 outcomes in the exercise, the sum of the probabilities must add up to 1.[2] Hence, $p_1 + p_2 + p_3 = 1$. It follows that $p_2 = 1 - p_1 - p_3$. Using this last relationship the 3-dimensional triangle in Figure 4.2 can be converted to a 2-dimensional probability triangle by eliminating p_2. This leads to Figure 4.3.

[2] Although each lottery here has two outcomes, one can think of the outcome left out to be included in the lottery with probability zero. Thus S2 has outcome Rs 400 (0), Rs 300 (0.25) and Rs 0 (0.75).

Figure 4.3 Probability Triangle Representation in Two Dimensions

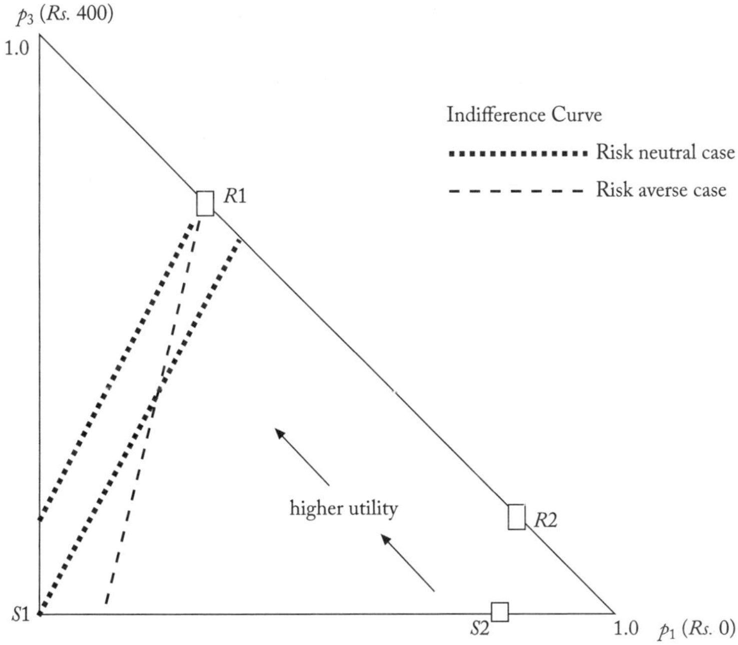

Source: Republished with permission of Princeton University Press, from Davis and Holt (1993); permission conveyed through Copyright Clearance Center, Inc.

In Figure 4.3, as before, we represent p_1 along the horizontal axis and p_3 along the vertical axis. In this figure p_2 is left out and is present by implication only. Note that the triangle in Figure 4.3 formed by joining points $p_1 = 1$ and $p_3 = 1$ is the collapsed version of the simplex in Figure 4.2 which had been formed by joining points $p_1 = 1, p_2 = 1$ and $p_3 = 1$. Now, to locate the lotteries on the triangle in Figure 4.3: first, consider S1. This lottery is Rs 300 with probability 1, therefore for this lottery both p_1 and p_3 take value 0. Hence this lottery is represented at the origin. Next let us look at R1. This lottery is (400, 0.8; 0, 0.2). Hence, as shown, R1 is represented on the line $p_1 + p_3 = 1$, as here $p_2 = 0$. In the same way, S2 and R2 can be represented as shown in Figure 4.3. Recall that the pair of lotteries S2, R2 is derived from the pair of lotteries S1, R1 using a common ratio which is ¼. That is,

S2 is derived from S1 and R2 is derived from R1 by taking the high outcome in S1 and R1 and multiplying the corresponding probabilities by ¼ and assigning the residual probabilities to the zero outcome to get S2 and R2 respectively. Consequently they will be located on the horizontal axis and the hypotenuse respectively. Also a straight line joining S1 and R1 will be parallel to a straight line joining S2 and R2. Such a set of parallel lines are known as *lottery indifference curves* as an individual with a certain risk preference, risk neutral or risk averse, will be indifferent between lotteries represented on any one straight line.[3]

ATTITUDE TOWARDS RISK

First consider a risk neutral individual. Such a person is, by definition, indifferent between lotteries that have the same expected value. The indifference curve passing through the origin has all lotteries whose expected value is Rs 300.

This locus is constructed by using the following equation:

$$300 = p_3(400) + p_2(300) + p_1(0)$$

As the three probabilities add up to unity, p_2 can be eliminated to yield

$$300 = p_3(400) + [1 - p_3 - p_1](300) + p_1(0)$$

which simplifies to $p_3 = 3p_1$

This is represented, in Figure 4.3, by a straight line through the origin with slope of 3. All indifference curves that are parallel to this straight line shall also have a slope of 3. Such a straight line is one that has a slope of 3 and passes through R1. The most preferred outcome is Rs 400 with certainty represented by the point $p_3 = 1$. Hence, higher utility is obtained by moving to the left. Therefore, if we consider the two indifference curves passing through S1 and R1, the one passing through the latter will be above and to the left of the indifference curve passing through S1. This implies that to a risk neutral individual R1 will be preferred to S1. This is borne out by the fact that R1 has higher expected value.

[3] The description in this section closely follows chapter 8 in Davis and Holt (1993: 435–504).

Now we try to develop a more general expression for the slope of an indifference curve in the lottery triangle facing a risk neutral individual. Let there be a family of lotteries with 3 prizes ranked $x_1 < x_2 < x_3$ and three associated probabilities p_1, p_2 and p_3. Then a risk neutral individual's preference can be written as $p_1x_1 + p_2x_2 + p_3x_3$ in the sense that more preferred lotteries take higher values in this expression. Since the above expression is linear, it follows that the indifference curves will be linear in the (p_1, p_3) space, and using $p_2 = 1 - p_1 - p_3$, the slope of the indifference cure of a risk neutral individual is $(x_2 - x_1) / (x_3 - x_2)$.

Next we consider a risk averse individual. By definition, such a person will prefer the safe lottery S1 over the risky lottery R1, even though the expected value of the lottery is higher in R1. It follows that the indifference curve (straight line) passing through S1 must lie entirely to the left of the indifference curve passing through R1. Recall that indifference curves more to the left represent higher utility. This is the dashed pair of straight lines in Figure 4.3 clearly showing that a move from being risk neutral to risk averse makes the set of indifference curves steeper.

A risk averse individual who is a utility maximiser will choose one lottery over another so as to maximise her expected utility rather than expected value. If a risky outcome is x_i with the corresponding utility being $U(x_i)$, then a risk averse person will select a lottery that maximises: $p_1U(x_1) + p_2U(x_2) + p_3U(x_3)$.

Indifference curves for utility functions are obtained by equating this expression to a constant, since the utility along an indifference curve remains the same. Again, by analogy with the risk neutral case, using $1 - p_1 - p_3$, to eliminate p_2 and solving for p_3 as a linear function of p_1 the slope of the indifference curve for a risk averse individual will be given by $U(x_2) - U(x_1)/U(x_3) - U(x_2)$.

This is analogous to the case of the risk neutral individual.

SOME IMPORTANT LOTTERY CHOICE EXPERIMENTS

We have now discussed how to construct a series of lotteries where subjects are asked to make pair-wise choices. In this section we discuss the results from some important lottery choice experiments.

The bulk of experiments conducted in the lottery choice format ask participants to make a series of choices about the lottery a participant would prefer to play when faced with pair-wise alternatives between 2 lotteries in each pair. The objective is to verify if the Allais paradox actually exists in practice. That is, if the choice to be made by a risk averse subject, as predicted by EU theory will actually be made by the subject in an experimental situation. It will be seen that the predictions made by EU theory will not hold in experimental situations. Similar experiments are also conducted to elicit a participant's attitude towards risk. This is usually done after these participants have participated in some other experiments, where they were required to take some risky decisions. Then a lottery choice experiment is given to the participants where the choice is confined to a single pair, one relatively safe and another risky lottery. The result enables the investigator to separate the subject pool into two groups, one more risk averse and the other less risk averse. Now a dummy variable can be used as an explanatory variable in a regression where the subjects' decision in the earlier experiment is sought to be explained.

Kahneman and Tversky (1979) conducted a series of experiments where lottery choices of the type S1 versus R1 and S2 versus R2, as described in this chapter, were offered to the subjects. As was common in those days, real financial rewards were not given, hence the results somewhat lacked credibility. However, these experiments have since been repeated by many others with financial rewards and the results were largely confirmed. Kahneman and Tversky offered hypothetical financial rewards, denoted in Israeli dollars, and observed that 80 per cent of subjects preferred S1 over R1, indicating high degree of risk aversion. Of this 80 per cent subjects, a majority of 65 per cent also preferred R2 over S2. This is interpreted as a violation if the independence axiom of EU theory, since the choice between S1 and R1 should be independent of the irrelevant prospect of a 75 per cent chance of getting zero.

Conlisk (1989) gave 236 subjects the pair-wise choice of S3 versus R3 and S4 versus R4. Here, S3 (5 million, 0; 1 million, 1; 0, 0) and R3 (5 million, 0.1; 1 million, 0.89; 0, 0.01). Again S4 (5 million, 0; 1 million 0.11; 0, 0.89) and R4 (5 million, 0.1, 1 million,0; 0, 0.90). Hypothetical payments were used. In this case, 60 per cent of subjects switched between the S lottery and the R lottery in the 2 pair-wise choices. Note that the latter pair S4, R4 is constructed by an additive transformation of the pair S3, R3, by adding a 0.89 probability of earning zero and keeping the probability of earning 5 million constant. Such lotteries are known as common-consequence lotteries.

Results described above involved hypothetical payoffs. If financial incentives did not matter in lottery choice experiments, then payments in money terms would be unnecessary and the cost of running the experiments would be quite low. Experimental evidence however seems to suggest otherwise. Battalio, Kagel and Jiranyakul (1990) finds that comparing across experiments with hypothetical and real payoffs, subjects tend to be more risk averse when payoffs are in real money. Similarly, Starmer and Sugden (1991) report that monetary incentives alter the quantitative nature of lottery choice inconsistencies, though not the qualitative ones.

The use of real monetary payoffs brings into focus some special methodological concerns in the context of lottery choice experiments. For instance, one may ask how the subjects' attitude towards risk may be altered by wealth. It would seem that the participants' attitude towards risk changes as she continues to accumulate money over several rounds of lottery choice experiments. The experimental evidence on this question is a mixed bag. Cox and Epstein (1989) report that wealth changes do not affect lottery choice decisions. They offered participants a series of pair-wise lottery choices and each lottery selected was played immediately and the earnings were added to the subjects' cumulative total. But in the context of a lottery-like asset market with randomly determined dividends Ang and Schwarz (1985) show that observed risk premiums are affected by wealth changes.

Ideally, when testing for the Allais paradox, one would like to eliminate the effect of wealth on observed choices. This is most conveniently done by the so-called random selection method. In this method, subjects are gives a series of pair-wise choice of lotteries. The subjects are required to choose one in each pair, the one they would like to play. The lotteries are not played out immediately. At the end, after all the choices have been made, one lottery pair is selected randomly, ex poste, and the chosen lottery played. This is used to determine the subject's earnings. It is easy to see that when the subject is making the choices she has no money. Hence she is not influenced by wealth effects. Yet she knows, that one of these lotteries will be randomly chosen and played and that will determine her earnings from this session. Hence she will take all the decisions seriously. Even though only one lottery is selected to determine the subjects payoff, the investigator needs to ensure that monetary payoff for each of the pairs that may be selected are high enough, so that all decisions are salient.

Starmer and Sugden (1991) set out to test the effectiveness of the random selection method. They had 160 subjects play some lotteries with hypothetical payoffs. Then they were divided into three groups of 40, 40, and 80 each. Group A participants made a single real payoff choice followed by a choice between another pair with hypothetical payoffs. Group B participants were offered the same two pairs of lotteries and the payoffs were hypothetical in the first case and real in the second case. Finally, Group C participants faced the same two pairs of lotteries but they were told that their earnings would be determined by one pair of lotteries being randomly selected and played, ex poste. The results do not clearly indicate that random selection works well to eliminate wealth effects and conclude with only guarded support for the success of the random selection method in being able to eliminate wealth effects.

Camerer and Ho (1990) has commented that the random selection method works well and this is because subjects may derive psychological benefits from considering each lottery separately, instead of viewing the random selection process as a choice between compound lotteries, composed of the component choices in each lottery. According to Kahneman and Tversky (1979) this is called the isolation effect.

Chew and Waller (1986) conducted a pair-wise lottery choice experiment that had a total of three prizes. X_H = \$20, X_M = \$10 and X_L = \$0. There were four pairs of lotteries, coded by letters. There were 56 participants. The lottery pairs are shown in Table 4.2 along with the number of participants who chose a particular lottery.

The pairs were constructed to efficiently pick up 2 important effects with only 4 choices per subject. Pairs O-L and O-H were used to detect common ratio effect and pairs I-L and I-H were used to detect common consequence effect. Subjects were not allowed to be indifferent between 2 lotteries or refuse to play any lottery. The common ratio effect occurred because 35 subjects chose in a risk averse manner in the O pair but only 17 did so in the L pair. A weak common consequence effect was detected as 23 subjects chose risk aversely in the I pair but 17 did so in the L pair.

Table 4.2 Chew and Waller's Structure of Lottery Pairs

Lottery Pair Name	Lottery Number in Pair	Outcomes with Probabilities	Number of Subjects Choosing
H	1	\$20, 0.95; \$0, 0.05	31
	2	\$20, 0.75; \$10, 0.25	25
I	1	\$20, 0.25; \$10, 0.75	33
	2	\$10, 1.0; \$0, 0	23
L	1	\$20, 0.20; \$0, 0.80	39
	2	\$10, 0.25; \$0, 0.75	17
O	1	\$20, 0.8; \$0, 0.2	21
	2	\$10, 1.0; \$0, 0	35

Source: Drawn by the author for this publication.

Lottery choice experiments generally offer the choice of a pair of lotteries to a subject where one lottery is more risky than the other. These types of experiments are mainly used for two purposes. First, to test for individual rational behaviour as predicted by EU theory versus the occurrence of the Allais paradox. Second, to elicit a subject's attitude towards risk so that this can be used in analysing results from some other previously conducted experiment in which the same subject had participated and made a decision under conditions of risk. This rather elegant tool is useful for both purposes as has been discussed in this chapter.

five

Various Types of Experimental Designs

Field Experiments, Experiments with Gender and Religion & Multicultural Experiments, Natural Experiments, Non-Monetised Experiments

In the early days of experimental economics, methodology and protocols were not well developed or standardised. More or less, by default, two fundamental beliefs dominated. The first was the belief that the composition of the subject pool did not matter. Human beings, whatever their demographic, social, cultural and economic characteristics, would react similarly to the external stimuli administered during an experiment. Consequently, university students became the most frequently used set of subjects, simply because they were the one group of people most readily available to the experimenters, who were mostly university professors. It is still the case that the bulk of studies in experimental economics reported world-wide are conducted with student subjects who are Western Educated, Industrialised, Rich and Democratic (WEIRD)[1].

The second belief was that the subjects need not be monetarily rewarded for participating in an experiment. Consequently, most experimenters did not use monetary incentives. There is anecdotal evidence that in some cases student subjects were rewarded with extra points in an examination if they participated in their professor's experiment. Both these beliefs have undergone much change in more recent times. As to the continuous use of students as subjects, this is still the case. However, there is increasing awareness about the fact that

[1] The term was coined by Henrich, Hein and Norenzayan (2009) for their paper 'The Weirdest People in the World'.

the social, economic and cultural markers as well as lived historical experiences do often determine how a subject will respond to an external stimuli delivered during an experiment. It is not unusual now for identical experiments recording remarkably different responses when the subject pool differs in history, culture, demographics and the lived experience.

The first major multi-cultural study was undertaken by Roth, Prasnikar, et al. (1991) during 1989–90. This study will be discussed in some detail below. The study was conducted in 4 locations in 4 countries. They were able to pick up important differences due to differing social norms. They still used university students as subjects in all the locations. This was soon to change though. Boyd and Gintis put together a team of 12 experimenters working in 12 countries in 5 continents who conducted experiments with subjects drawn from non-student common people in 15 small scale societies with wide differences in economic and cultural conditions. The results of this study can be seen in Henrich, Boyd, et al (2004) . The day of the multi-country field experiment had arrived. Nowadays, it is quite common for researchers from several countries to collaborate and agree on a common research problem. Next, a mutually agreeable experimental design must be generated. Then each researcher can conduct experimental sessions in her own country and in her own language. The subjects can be either students or drawn from the common people. The data can then be used to pick up important differences that can be attributed to cultural and social factors. More recently, multi-country and multi-cultural experiments are also being conducted over the internet. Here, several designated computer laboratories are used in as many countries. Subjects are brought into these laboratories and administered the experiment over the internet, with some local agency proctoring to ensure experimental control. Subject payments are made through any of the international money transfer organisations.

As to the second question of using monetary payoffs as incentives, it has now become almost compulsory to pay the subjects according to some previously announced rule. This is done to ensure that in the face of non-trivial payoffs, subjects take their task seriously. However, non-monetised experiments continue to be conducted whenever the researchers are able to defend how the absence of monetary incentives do not act as a barrier for subjects engaging seriously with their given tasks and the credibility of the experiment has not been compromised simply because monetary rewards were not promised or given. This will be discussed in some detail below.

The rest of the chapter is divided as follows. The first section will describe field experiments and offer certain taxonomy of such experiments. The second section describes a few multi-country (and multi-cultural) studies both with student and non-student subjects. The third section will discuss experiments involving the use of gender, religious and class differences among the subject pool. The fourth section will discuss one multi-country experiment where subjects share a common lived experience. This study involved a very large subject pool across two countries. The fifth section will talk about experiments conducted in the field, i.e., outside the university laboratory where the subjects are in their natural habitat. The sixth and last section will describe two related non-monetised experiments conducted in recent years.

THE FIELD EXPERIMENT

Broadly speaking, field experiments are experiments conducted outside the university classroom or laboratory environment with non-student subjects. A more detailed typology of various types of field experiments is discussed below. Before we start, however, it would be convenient to begin by looking at the rationale of conducting field experiments. Take the experimental economist, recruiting student subjects, putting them in a computer laboratory, having them face an artefactual situation, making them play a game or otherwise take decisions with monetary incentives, then collecting the generated data and econometrically analysing the same to come up with results. A standard objection to this method of collecting data (often put forward by economists who are more used to collecting data through questionnaire-based field surveys) is that the responses of student subjects in a computer laboratory facing an artefactual situation can hardly be representative of real life responses of people facing a real life situation. Take next, the case of the empirical economist out to test a theoretical prediction. She designs and pilots a structured questionnaire, selects a region and draws a sample of units (say, households), trained enumerators conduct interviews based on the questionnaire and the collected data is again econometrically analysed to show results that may or may not bear out the relevant theory. Objections to this manner of gathering data are well known. First, many theoretical precepts do not lend themselves readily to such empirical testing. Theories about strategic decisions or decisions involving risky choices fall in this category. Further, any field-survey depends to some extent upon the power to recall the past by the Respondent, and here the Respondent may be well intentioned but provide erroneous responses. Finally, the Respondent has no incentive to provide truthful answers. She may be unable or unwilling to provide an accurate response but would often provide any response rather than admit the inability or decline to respond outright.

Field experiments provide a very good meeting ground for the two approaches, and may offer valuable lessons both for the experimental economist conducting lab-based experiments as well as the empirical economist gathering data through field surveys. Following Harrison and List (2004) we outline 6 important factors that may be used to determine the field context of an experiment:

i. The nature of the subject pool
ii. The nature of the information that the subjects bring to the task or the decision-making process
iii. The nature of the commodity or good, if any, that are involved in the task
iv. The nature of the task, decision-making process or trading rules
v. The nature of the stakes or rewards promised, and
vi. The nature of the environment that the subject operates in

Each of the above can play a vital role in influencing the design of an experiment. Based on the above factors 4 kinds of experiments can be identified. These are:

i. A conventional classroom or laboratory experiment that is hand-run or run using a computer network respectively, using student subjects, abstract framing and an imposed set of rules and monetary incentives.
ii. An artefactual field experiment is the same as a conventional classroom or lab experiment but employs a non-student subject pool. The subjects may be chosen at random from the population (one member of every tenth house on a road) or chosen with a particular focus (from among persons visiting a mosque or a shopping mall).

iii. A framed field experiment is the same as an artefactual field experiment but with a field context in either the commodity under question, task or decision-making process or the information set that the subjects can use to complete the task. The public goods games in the Sundarbans in India and Bangladesh described below are examples of this type of experiment.
iv. A natural field experiment (often simply called a natural experiment) is the same as a framed field experiment where the environment is such where the subjects naturally undertake these tasks, where the subjects are not aware of the fact that they are in an experiment. A natural field experiment involving charitable fund-raising in the University of Central Florida is described in detail later in this chapter.

EXPERIMENTS ACROSS REGIONS AND CULTURES

The first major multi-country (and multi-cultural) experiment was conducted by a team of 4 researchers under the leadership of Alvin Roth during 1989–90. Other members of the team were Shmuel Zamir, Vesna Prasniker and M. Okuno Fujiwara (Roth, Prasnikar, et al. 1991). We already know that much of the behavioural response of the Respondents in a UG is motivated due to fairness. The Respondents respond positively only when they feel that they have received a *fair* offer. But it remains a moot question as to what constitutes such a fair offer. Up to this point of time the UGs had largely been played with university students in the US and, of course, in Germany where the first such study by Guth, et al. was conducted. Therefore, all clues about the division of the original pie considered fair came from the Western industrialised developed countries. It could be the case that the notion of fairness is also culturally contextualised and may vary across cultures. Roth and his team were interested to find out if that is the case. They took the UG to 4 locations in 4 countries. These were Pittsburgh (USA), Ljubljana (in Slovenia, which was part of Yugoslavia), Tokyo (Japan) and Jerusalem (Israel). They however continued with the use of university students as subjects. There were 20 student subjects in each session who were divided into 10 pairs of Proposers and Respondents. Each Proposer played with all 10

Respondents sequentially over 10 rounds. So at the end of the session every Proposer had played with every Respondent in any one round. As usual Proposers and Respondents were anonymous to one another.

In the Pittsburgh sessions the initial endowment to the Proposer was $10. Comparable purchasing power amounts were offered in the other 3 countries. These were 400,000 dinars in Slovenia, 20,000 yens in Japan and 20 shekels in Israel. In practice, Proposers in all sessions across countries were asked to propose a division of 1000 experimental tokens and the tokens earned by each subject were converted to real money at the end of the session. The authors point out 2 major problems of multi-country multi-cultural studies. The first is the effect of translating the instructions from one language (usually English) to another (usually the local language). Often exact synonyms are not found and another closely associated word is used which may lead to a different meaning being conveyed. This problem was solved by translating the English instructions to the other language and having a different person re-translate it back to English. This is then compared to the original instructions to iron out differences in meaning in the two language versions. Second, as the experiments in different countries were being run by different persons, a slight shift in manner and demeanour may alter subject response. This problem was solved by having all the authors run some sessions in Pittsburgh, and then have 1 or 2 other author(s) present as observers in the 3 other countries. In the US and Slovenia, most Proposers chose the 50:50 split, while in Japan and Israel the split mostly offered was 60:40 in favour of the Proposer. While these numbers were statistically significant, there were no significant differences in the rejection rate by the Respondents. Hence, it is perceived that Proposers in Japan and Israel were more aggressive and the authors conclude that the main cultural difference across countries is in what is believed to be an offer fair enough not to be rejected.

One issue that remains with the above study is that the study itself is quite multi-cultural in the sense that the cultures of the 4 countries studied are quite diverse. However, the subjects in each case were undergraduate students. One could argue that students are quite similar in their attitudes across cultures. Also, students are often not a good representative of the cultures they belong to. This is especially true of college students who get exposed to similar ideas in their course of study. To address this concern, in a more ambitious multi-cultural study Henrich, Boyd, et al. (2004) put together a team of 12 researchers in 11 countries. They played the simple Ultimatum game, Dictator Game and Trust Game with members (not students) of 15 small scale societies[2] spread over 12 countries in 5 continents. Of the 15 societies studied, 3 were foraging societies, 6 were involved in slash and burn agriculture, 3 were nomadic groups and 3 were small scale agrarian societies. Because the task was quite complex, it is possible that some experimental replicability and control was compromised due to problems of translation and the fact that different researchers were conducting the sessions in each country.

The results were quite striking and unlike other UGs played in the West with student subjects. While no society demonstrated the predicted very low offer, there was substantial variation across cultures in the offer the Proposers made to the Respondents. Three societies had offers of around 25 per cent of endowment, 2 societies offered around 40 per cent and 2 others between 51 and 58 per cent. These were the extreme values with others in between. Turning now to the rejection rates we find extremely low rejection rates, typically less than 20 per cent with only 2 societies at 28 and 40 per cent. This would imply a broad consensus between Proposer and Respondent in each society as to what constitutes a fair offer.

Hoffman, McCabe and Smith (1996) was the first to explore how Proposer and Respondent behaviour changed as stakes increased. They chose 2 levels of endowment for the Proposers, \$10 and \$100. A hundred dollars is a serious amount of money for student subjects. They assigned 24 Proposers to the \$10 treatment and 27 Proposers to the \$100 treatment. One would expect that Proposers in the \$100 treatment would offer amounts that are higher in absolute value but lower in percentage terms to the Respondent and the Respondents would tend to accept such offers. What they found is quite striking.

[2] Small scale societies are well defined, small and tightly knit communities that have little contact with the outside world. In this case they were Orma in Kenya, Hadza and Sangu in Tanzania, Torguuds and Kazakhs in Mongolia, Lamalera in Indonesia, Au and Gnau in Papua New Guinea, Achuar and Quichua in Ecuador, Machiguenga in Peru, Tsimane in Bolivia, Mapuche in Chile, Ache in Paraguay and Shona in Zimbabwe.

Proposers in both treatments behaved similarly and offered close to 50 per cent of the endowment to the Respondent and these offers were accepted.

Boarini, Laslier and Robin (2009) presents a 'Transcontinental Ultimatum Game' implemented between India and France. They find that when French subjects made offers to Indian subjects, bargaining mostly ended up with unequal splits of money in favour of French, while nearly equal splits were the most frequent outcome when Indian subjects made offers to French subjects.

These are but just a few examples of some very important multi-country and multi-cultural studies. The literature is now bursting with such studies with many throwing up very interesting results which are often in the nature of a commentary on the cultures themselves. We shall have occasion to review some of these below.

EXPERIMENTS INVOLVING GENDER, RELIGION AND CLASS

Identity is an important reason why economists study social categories such as gender, religious belonging or caste. By identity is meant a person's sense of self or how a person sees herself as belonging to a socio-demographic category. In a ground-breaking paper, Akerlof and Kranton (2000) show that identity can affect economic outcomes. They developed a utility function that included identity, and used it to explain many phenomena that current economic theory cannot fully explain. For example, ethnic and racial conflicts, discrimination, intractable labour disputes and separatist politics all invite identity-based analysis and all of which affect economic outcomes. Hence the need to conduct experiments with subject pools chosen from specific categories. Akerlof and Kranton applied their model, more specifically to look at gender discrimination in the labour market, household division of labour and the economics of social exclusion and poverty.

Continuing on the more recent realisation that the demographic, social, economic and cultural characteristics of the subject pool does matter, investigators repeated well known experimental games with well defined experimental protocols but with subject pools drawn so as to bring out the difference in responses to experimental stimuli that can then be related to specific socio-demographic factors. In all such experiments, it is necessary to run some sessions where the subject pool is mixed or the socio-demographic feature in question is unknown to the players. It could also be the case that the identities of the subjects were kept anonymous to each other. The purpose is to have some sessions to be treated as control. The crucial factor in all such experiments is to choose the subject pool according to some required criterion and adapting an experimental design for the purpose at hand.

Experiments Involving Gender Differences

With the coming of age of multi-country and multi-cultural (across countries or within the same country) studies, any one social, economic, demographic or cultural attribute could be varied within the subject pool to produce a new result. Any well known experimental design could be used as a template and the possibilities are endless. An area now well investigated is the role of gender. As to studying the role of gender, only two kinds—male and female—have been studied. Transgender subjects, to the best of my knowledge, are yet to be used as subjects. Solnick (2001) conducted an experiment with 178 subjects, half of them male the other half female. She chose to play the simple 2-person UG described in Chapter 2. She had 2 treatments. In the first, the Proposers were not told the gender of the Respondent and vice versa; and in the second treatment the gender of the Proposer and the Respondent were common knowledge to each other.

She did come up with some really interesting results. Average offers did not differ between male and female Proposers. But average offers were affected by the gender of the Respondent, with male Respondents attracting higher offers, particularly from female Proposers. This could mean the male Respondents are perceived as no-nonsense hard bargainers with high retaliatory instincts who would quickly reject low offers whereas female Respondents are perceived as being more flexible and forgiving. Turning now to Respondent behaviour, both male and female Respondents had higher levels in mind that were acceptable as offers when such offers were being made by a female Proposer than a male one. This could mean that both male and female Respondents expected female Proposers to make higher offers than their male counterparts.[3] All this, of course, made substantial difference in earnings between male and female players.

Differences in responses by gender have been studied quite extensively by experimental researchers using the DG. You may recall this game from Chapter 2 where, in its basic version, we still have the Proposer-Respondent set-up, as in the UG, except now the Respondent has to accept whatever she is given by the Proposer. Hence, any amount given out by the Proposer from her endowment is nothing short of a charitable donation and can be interpreted as a mark of altruistic behaviour (there now being no fear of rejection). Eckel and Grossman (1998) experimented with a double-blind DG. Thus neither the Proposer nor the Respondent knew the gender of his/her matched partner. This was done to permit the emergence of basic gender differences in economic behaviour. They found that women, on average, gave away twice as much as men to their anonymously matched partners. This, after all other factors that may have confounded cooperation had been eliminated. The authors comment that this finding is consistent with research results in the social sciences, other than economics, which find substantial differences in behavioural responses between men and women.

In a more nuanced experimental design Andreoni and Vesterlund (2001) use a DG where the Proposer is endowed with some tokens, which are to be divided by the Proposer between the Proposer and the Respondent, but the rate at which each token is to be converted into money at the end of the game keeps on increasing. It is found that men tend to be quite generous initially but tend to keep more for themselves as the value of the tokens rise, whereas women tend to divide the tokens more evenly even when the value of a token has risen quite a bit. Thus this design not only picks up the amounts donated by a subject by gender but is also able to record the effect of changes in prices on such donations. Their results, as may be expected, are not straightforward. First, they find that when altruism is cheap (incomes are high and/or prices are low) men donate more than women but as

[3] This is at some variance with another study by Eckel and Grossman (2001) who found that in a UG male Respondents displayed 'chivalry' by accepting lower offers from women than men, and women Respondents displayed 'solidarity' by accepting lower offers from women than men.

incomes fall and prices rise, making altruism more expensive, women outdo men in donations. Following the concept of 'warm glow', earlier developed by Andreoni (1990) in the context of altruism, they attempt to construct demand curves for altruism by gender. They find that as prices rise, the demand curves for 'warm glow' for men and women tend to cross. This leads them to conclude '... men are more likely to be perfectly selfish or perfectly selfless whereas women tend to be *equalitarians* who tend to share evenly' (Andreoni and Vesterland 2001: 293).

There are very many uses of the DG in experiments that attempt to pick up several aspects of the gender differences. A meta-study of these research papers can be found in Eckel and Grossman (2008).

A game that has been much in use in recent years to investigate difference in response by men and women in economic situations is the TG. The reader will recall this game described in Chapter 2, is quite like the UG. Here the Sender (Proposer) offers a certain part of her endowment, which is multiplied by some factor and given over to the Receiver (Respondent), and then the Receiver has the option of sending some of this money back to the Sender. This game was originally designed as an extension and refinement of the UG to pick up the degree of cooperation or reciprocity with an anonymously matched partner but has now found a plethora of uses.

In the context of the study of gender differences the all-women team of Buchan, Croson and Solnick (2008) investigated if gender could influence trust. Their study compares choices made by men and women in an Investment Game (a variation of the TG where the Sender is a bank and the Receiver is a borrower). Next, they administer a questionnaire to the male and female subjects to try and find out the motivations behind the choices they have already made. In order to understand the results of this study one needs to recall that the percentage of endowment sent by the Sender to the Receiver (which is tripled by the experimenter) is seen as a measure of trust and the amount sent back by the Receiver as a percentage of what she receives is considered to be a measure of trustworthiness. In this study, it was found that men trust more than women but women are more trustworthy than men. Also, the relationship between expected return and trusting behaviour is stronger among men than women, implying thereby that men view these interactions more strategically than women. Women, on the other hand, feel more obligated by any trust reposed on them and therefore reciprocate.

Surely, culture must also play a role in all this. As it turns out, it does not, in the sense that women, at least in this context, tend to behave similarly across cultures. In an ambitious multi-cultural study Buchan and Croson (1999) recruit a total of 186 student subjects across 4 countries (cultures). These are China (48 students from Nakai University), South Korea (50 students from Seoul National University), Japan (44 students from Tokyo University) and USA (44 students from University of Pennsylvania). They play a standard Sender-Receiver TG where the amount sent by the Sender is tripled by the experimenter and handed over to the Receiver. The protocol is double-blind as the Senders and Receivers are seated in two different rooms. So the players have no information about the identities (and therefore gender) of their matched partners. The experimenter effect is eliminated by having the experimenter sit in another room, with monitors running between rooms bearing the money in numbered envelopes. There is therefore no relevance of *face-saving* behaviour, considered important in East Asian cultures.[4] Hence the experimenter too has no idea of the identities of the players and the subjects know this.

There are 2 very important results obtained from this study. First, there are no significant gender-based differences in the amount sent by the Senders. Second, women Receivers return significantly more than male Receivers. In summary, therefore, it seems likely that women are, in general, more prone to cooperation while men are more competitive. Trust and trustworthiness form part of this overall attitudinal difference. However, such trust, and therefore cooperation, especially with anonymous persons are contextualised. The jury is still out on what a man or a woman will do in a specific context.

Chattopadhyay and Duflo (2004) found differences in the investment policy of female and male policymakers in village councils of West

[4] Face-saving behaviour is closely connected to the experimenter effect. The subject may actually wish to take decision A but changes it to decision B to save face before the experimenter. This may be important when subjects are university students and the investigator their professor. Face saving behaviour is considered more important in East Asian cultures. As held by Greif (1989), Asian cultures are more collectivistic than western cultures.

Bengal and Rajasthan, India. They found that, in a public goods game, women invest more in public goods linked to women's concerns (drinking water, etc.) and invest less in public goods linked to men's concerns (education, etc.), i.e., women leaders increase the provision of public goods that benefit women.

Any discussion on gender inevitably turns to the issue of persistent differences in rewards between men and women, especially in the workplace. For some time now, there have been conscious efforts made by governments of many countries to erase such differences through affirmative action and other public policies designated to give women a handicap. In spite of all this, such differences in rewards and achievements in the public sphere have persisted. The reasons for this are not difficult to find. The standard answer is that most societies are patriarchal and male-dominated and have been so for a very long time. As a result, biases against women are hardwired into most systems and women are prevented from reaching positions of wealth and power. While most countries have laws that prevent active discrimination against women, the ground reality is very different in practice. So, in most situations, women are allowed to proceed thus far and no farther and this gives rise to the idea of a 'glass ceiling'. There is much truth in the argument. A casual look at the economics department of any leading university in India will demonstrate the story. While the bulk of the student population is female, the faculty is predominantly male. True, there are women to be found in positions of power and wealth. There are women prime ministers and CEOs of large multinational corporations, but these are largely seen as cases of patriarchal face-saving tokenisms.

This mode of analysis continued to hold sway until Elizabeth C. Arch (1993) came up with an alternative theory that was bound to generate much controversy, which it did. While accepting the dominant explanation about inherent anti-female bias, she extends her explanation of persistent differences in achievement between the genders to the fact that women and men have widely differing attitudes towards risk. According to Arch, hardly anything can be achieved in life without engaging in situations that are potentially risky. Here, though, men and women differ in their attitudes. Men perceive a risky situation as a challenge and are mostly inclined to accept such a challenge while women perceive the same risky situation as a threat and are therefore inclined to avoid it. Her study was actually a survey of 50 studies and therefore could be termed as a meta-study.

Naturally, this paper by a psychologist generated much debate not only in the field of psychology but also in economics. As risk-taking is inherent in many economic decisions, this difference in attitude towards risk had implications in economic decision making. Do men and women really have differing attitudes when it comes to taking risky decisions? Masters and Meier (1988) had shown that male and female entrepreneurs had the same ability to take risks. Another empirical study by Atkinson, Baird and Frye (2003) investigated the investment behaviour of male and female mutual fund managers to show that gender differences in investment performance disappeared when other factors are controlled for. These studies, however, did not attempt to directly measure the degree of risk aversion.

The ball now rolls into the court of the experimental economist, and the lottery choice experiments described in Chapter 4 provides a handy template. Holt and Laury (2002) construct a series of 10 pair-wise lottery choices where the subjects are required to choose one lottery in every pair. Subjects were 212 college students. As discussed in Chapter 4, in every pair of lottery offered for choice one is a high risk and the other a low risk lottery. The pair-wise choices are so structured that the crossover from the low risk to the high risk lottery in a subsequent choice can be used to infer the degree of risk aversion. With normal payoffs of a few dollars most subjects are risk averse and a few risk taking. Scaling up the payoffs by a factor of 20, 50 and 90 make little difference as long as the payments are hypothetical. Subjects become sharply risk averse when these high payoffs are actually paid out. In particular, it was found that both men and women are risk averse when the size of the gamble is big but women are significantly more risk averse than men when the size of the gamble is small.

In another typical study, Eckel and Grossman (2002) asked 148 student subjects to choose between 5 lotteries. Each decision has 2 equally probable outcomes. Each gamble has 1 outcome which is certain and the remaining 4 with linearly increasing expected payoff and risk. They ran 2 treatments, one with a no loss environment and another where a loss was possible. In the no-loss environment all payments were scaled up by $6 so that the lowest payment was zero (the subjects did not have to pay anything out of their own pocket, in case they lost the gamble). In the environment with losses, subjects were paid $6 to complete a questionnaire and this $6 could be lost in the gamble. Eckel and Grossman (ibid.) report that in both environments there is a significant gender difference in risk aversion. The mean choice by male subjects exceeds the mean choice by female subjects: 3.76 for men versus 3.14 for women in the environment with losses and 3.63 and 2.95 without losses. A means test confirms these differences are statistically significant.

There are many more similar studies but they all bear in the same direction. Further, marital status seems to exacerbate the situation. Sundén and Surette (1998) studied allocation of assets in retirement plans to find that marriage make both men and women more risk averse. This study was not based on experiments.

In general, all studies using experiments point to the fact that women, in comparable circumstances, are more risk averse and prefer more certain outcomes to less certain ones, even in the face of higher payoffs. Whether this explains the relative failure by women to attain positions of wealth, status and power, as originally claimed by Arch will, of course, remain a subject matter of some debate.

Before leaving the topic of gender differences it is worthwhile to make some concluding remarks. Sex refers to the physical differences between men and women, the differences in the construction of their bodies and bodily functions. Gender captures a more nuanced concept involving social and cultural constructs that have much to do with upbringing, assignment of social and familial roles and moral precepts held by a particular society and social environment. Without doubt, one can see difference in responses by individual decision makers, which are clearly coloured by gender differences. It is interesting to investigate if these differences in responses impact economic decision making and performance. If you have a contract with a woman and you know the contract is not enforceable are you less likely to be cheated? If you invest in a mutual fund scheme and the fund manager is a woman are you less likely to take a loss even though the growth of your portfolio is likely to be smaller. Hopefully, these and similar questions will be answered and a general truth emerge with more studies of the kind discussed above.

Experiments Involving Religious Differences

In the summer of 1993 *Foreign Affairs* published an article 'The Clash of Civilisations' by Samuel P. Huntington. In this article that remains controversial till date Huntington claimed: 'The great divisions among humankind and the dominating source of conflict will be cultural. ... but the principal conflict of global politics will occur between nations and groups of civilisations. The clash of civilisations will dominate global politics' (1993: 22). In particular, the two groups of civilisations that were bound to come into conflict were religious groupings—Christianity and Islam.[5]

While Huntington's theory would seem too simplistic and far-fetched to most thinkers, it does generate interest in researching the relationship between religious groups in everyday situations. Do such interactions between members of different religious groups give rise to cooperation or conflict? Is there trust between members of different religious communities who live in close contact to one another, or does religious identities have nothing to do with trust?

Most modern-day religions teach of universal brotherhood and tolerance. The message is one of amity and tranquillity and the search for the inner self. Most religious teachings also prefer to send a message of peace. It is unfortunately true that the reality on the ground is otherwise. Much hatred has been spread and much blood spilt across the world in the name of religion. Religious bigotry very often overshadows tolerance and the acceptance of the right of every person to practice according to one's own spiritual belief. There are two major ways in which religion can influence economic and social behaviour. First, religion acts as an identifier of a social group. Thus a person can think of herself as being (among other things) a Christian or a Muslim or a Jew. This may become important when

[5] Huntington expanded his article into a book *The Clash of Civilisations and the Remaking of the World Order* (1996) in which he tried to address all the criticism he faced for his earlier article by claiming that in the post–Cold War era, cultural groups, rather that the state, will act as the locus of war. He shifted his emphasis on possible Christian-Islamic conflict by identifying 8 cultural groups who are likely to be in conflict with one another alternatively. In Huntington's taxonomy, these 8 groups were Western, Latin American, Islamic, Chinese, Hindu, Orthodox, Japanese and African.

some decisions are being taken or some activities carried out where the individual believes this particular identity marker is important. Subjects' choice, behaviour or strategic decision may depend on how she perceives persons of her own group identity versus persons not belonging to such group identity. Second, religion may, consciously or otherwise promote a certain set of values. Often this set of values may not be formally codified in any religious text of that particular religion but may exist as a social belief associated with communities belonging to a particular religion.

Here an important distinction should be made between religion and religiosity. The former simply refers to a person's religious affiliation, which is mostly inherited and only sometimes consciously opted for. It is often the case that a person inherits a religious affiliation but does little in terms of practice. In that case, the person will answer in the affirmative if asked if she belongs to that particular religion but little indoctrination or absorption of the religious values of that religion will have happened. Religiosity is, of course, a more serious business. This involves imbibing the rituals and practices of that religion as well as the diktats and doctrines. This comes from direct participation and practices. In this section we shall look at some research which has tried to explore the relationship between religion, religiosity and generic individual decision making. There are 3 areas where religion may have played a role in shaping human beliefs and directed decision making: these are altruism, trust and cooperation. We will take up each in turn.

Altruism has been discussed at length in Chapter 2 and it is generally agreed that the experimental economics format which most closely captures pure altruism (about as pure as it gets) is the DG. Eckel and Grossman (2004) had 167 US college students play the DG, where subjects were asked to divide a cash endowment between themselves (Proposer) and a non-religious charity they could choose from a list (Respondent). There were 12 treatments which varied the initial endowment, rebates and matching funds provided by the experimenters. Subjects were classified as religious or non-religious according as they had self-reported that they attend religious services regularly. It was found that the religious group donated a little more than the non-religious group, the difference was not statistically significant in 10 of the 12 treatments.

Ahmed (2009) recruited 103 student subjects in rural India, some of whom were studying in Madrassas[6] and others for non-religious degrees. He got his subjects to play the DG with fictitious recipients and with endowments which the subjects had earned from an earlier public goods game they had played. It was found that the Madrassa students (presumed to be more religious than others) donated 22 per cent of their endowment while the other group donated only 13 per cent. It would appear then that religious training prompted people to be more charitable. However, it should be noted that the endowments were not uniform and the donations in the DG may have been influenced by the size of earnings in the public goods game and the experience gained there. Also, the study did not control for other potentially differing aspects between the religious and non-religious groups.

Malhotra (2010) in a game somewhat similar to the DG constructed a bidding game for online auctions where the proceeds go to charity. When a particular subject loses a bid she receives an on-screen message to continue bidding. The on-screen message makes an appeal to the subject's religious sentiments as well as to her competitiveness. Subjects who, by their own declaration, attend religious functions never, rarely or occasionally are classified as non-religious, and by the same token those attending regularly are classified religious. Using a logistic regression, the probability of re-bidding by the religious group was found to be 40 per cent against the same probability for the non-religious group which was only 12 per cent. Curiously, this happened only on auctions held on Sundays. On other days the probability of re-bidding was not significantly different between the 2 groups and was around 26 per cent. The explanation provided was that Sunday served as a prime for the subjects and aroused religious sentiments among the members of the religious group.[7]

We now turn to a few studies that use the TG. Trust, as has been mentioned earlier, has been found to be an important factor in macro-economic studies as it generally facilitates economic interactions and

[6] Islamic religious schools from where many students would go on to be priests in mosques.

[7] Prime is a term in psychology which refers to an unimportant or irrelevant factor that influences a certain decision simply because the decision maker's attention has been drawn to it immediately before the decision was taken.

reduces transaction costs. The structure of the TG which is being used here to examine differences in response between religious groups, if any, has been discussed in detail in Chapter 2. It may be recalled that the amount sent by the Sender is usually tripled (but also sometimes doubled) by the experimenter before being given over to the Receiver. On average, Senders send half the amount of their endowment and Receivers tend to return the absolute amount sent (that is, before doubling or tripling). We shall see what effect, if any, religious belonging has on such responses in a TG.

Fehr and Gaechter (2002) got 429 German non-student subjects to play the TG. Using a regression model with religiously unaffiliated subjects as control, they found that Catholic affiliation among Christians raised Sender amounts significantly. No effect was found for Protestant affiliation on Sender behaviour and for affiliation to any denomination on Receiver behaviour. Another important variable they considered was church attendance of more than once a month, but this too had no effect on either Senders or Receivers. Other variables such as age and education were significant in the regression.

Bangladesh presents a unique religious mix in its population. The country (formerly East Pakistan till 1971) was carved out of the undivided Bengal province of colonial India on religious grounds in 1947. Presently, Muslims constitute 90 per cent of the population, 9.6 per cent are Hindus and 0.4 per cent are others. Ethnically and linguistically the population is homogenous between Muslims and Hindus. Johansson-Stenman, Mahmud and Martinsson (2009) had Muslim and Hindu subjects in Bangladesh play the TG. They had Muslim-Muslim, Muslim-Hindu, Hindu-Muslim and Hindu-Hindu pairings of Senders and Receivers with religious identities disclosed immediately before each session began (the pairings were otherwise anonymous). One can presume that this would serve as a prime. The responses were compared against some control sessions where religious identity was not disclosed. Surprisingly, religious identity or its disclosure played no role on the behaviour of Senders or Receivers.

The province of Bengal was divided on religious grounds at the time India gained Independence from British rule in 1947. The eastern part became East Pakistan, and eventually Bangladesh (in 1971). The western part (about one-third of the erstwhile Bengal province) became the state of West Bengal within independent India. In that sense, the ethnic and linguistic composition of the population in West Bengal and Bangladesh are similar. The only major difference in the population is the religious composition, the state of West Bengal being Hindu majority and Bangladesh being Muslim majority. Hindus are a majority in West Bengal (73 per cent) and Muslims (23 per cent) are in the minority. As mentioned above, the opposite is the case in Bangladesh with Muslims comprising 90 per cent of the population and Hindus 9.6 per cent.

Gupta, Mahmud, et al. (2013) felt that this religious composition provided an ideal ground to investigate if religious identity considerably influenced individual decision making. This was done by conducting framed field experimental sessions in both countries in the format of a TG. The research questions of this study were: a) Do individuals discriminate based on religious identity; b) Do individuals discriminate based on majority/minority status within society; c) Does discrimination take the form of in-group bias or systematic discrimination against members of all other groups; d) Is there a significant difference between individuals who are religious and those who are not so.

A TG was conducted in both countries to investigate the research questions above. Subjects were individuals living in villages approximately 80 kilometers (about 2 hours driving distance) south of the relevant capital—Kolkata in West Bengal and Dhaka in Bangladesh. In a typical village in either West Bengal or Bangladesh, with mixed populations, the Hindus and Muslims tend to live in separate clusters within the same village, usually separated by some natural demarcation. Sixteen villages were chosen in each country and 3 sessions were conducted for each village in a nearby location (typically a school building). Each session was conducted in 2 adjacent rooms, one room (Room 1) being randomly assigned for the role of Senders and the other room (Room 2) being assigned for the role of Receivers. Each session had 8 subjects in each room, all 16 having been recruited from adjacent villages, 8 each from the Hindu cluster and the Muslim cluster. Thus between the role of Sender and Receiver, there were 4 treatments, namely Hindu-Hindu, Hindu-Muslim, Muslim-Hindu and Muslim-Muslim, with a few sessions in each country where the religious identity of the matched partner was not disclosed to serve as control. In each session, one subject from Room 1 was randomly paired with one subject from Room 2, but identities were kept anonymous.

Subjects were told that there were 8 persons in the other room, and they came from a nearby village.

Each subject in Room 1 (Sender) was given an endowment of Tk 160 in Bangladesh and Rs 120 in West Bengal.[8] Given the cognitive ability of subjects in rural Bengal and to keep things manageable, Senders were allowed to offer integer amounts in fixed equidistant percentages of the endowment. This translated to the option set in West Bengal {0, 15, 30, … 120} Indian Rupees and in Bangladesh {0, 20, 40, … 160} Takas. The amount sent was tripled by the experimenters. In a slightly different protocol than the standard TG, the Receivers' responses were obtained in a strategy format, where they had to say how much they would send back for each of the (tripled) values received.

The Senders' contributions in the TG may be influenced by her preference towards altruism, efficiency or risk. Likewise, the Receivers response may be influenced by altruism. To account for these possibilities each subject in this experiments, Sender and Receiver, played a Triple Dictator[9] Game and a Risk Game. Each subject also responded to a short questionnaire which, among other things, collected information about the subject's religiosity and belief about who to trust.

This framed field experiment delivered some very interesting results. These are summarised below. The commonality found in behaviour of subjects in the 2 countries was interesting; it was status (as a religious minority) that drove decisions in the TG rather than religious identity (Hindu or Muslim). In both countries, the minorities, that is Muslims in West Bengal and Hindus in Bangladesh demonstrate positive in-group bias in trust. Strikingly, the majority community in both countries—that is, Hindus in West Bengal and Muslims in Bangladesh—show positive out-group bias in trustworthiness. There is, therefore, systematic benefit for minorities in both locations; from positive in-group bias in trust from fellow minorities and positive out-group bias in trustworthiness from members of the majority

[8] Taka (Tk) is the currency of Bangladesh. At the time these field experiments were conducted the exchange rate was Indian Rs 1.00 = Bangladeshi Tk 1.5; $1 = Rs 60 = Tk 90.

[9] A Triple Dictator game is a DG where the amount donated by the Proposer is tripled by the experimenter before being given over to the Respondent. This was being done here to make the move at par with the TG, where the Sender's amount was being tripled.

community. Religious identity itself (being a Hindu or a Muslim) does not drive behaviour in the game and this result is consistent with those obtained by Johansson-Stenman, Mahmud and Martinsson (2009). Religious individuals show systematic in-group bias in trust compared to non-religious subjects though non-religious subjects exhibit positive out-group bias in trustworthiness. This result holds in both countries.

A related area of investigation is whether religious identity and religiosity promote cooperation among groups of individuals. This becomes more important when an individual does not know who the other members of such a group are. The role of cooperative behaviour in promoting economic efficiency and growth cannot be overstressed. The public goods game with VCM provides a ready format for this investigation. The basic format of this game has been discussed in Chapter 3. Recall that the number of players in a group is denoted by n, the amounts deposited by the subjects in the public fund is multiplied by an integral factor denoted m and the number of rounds or repetitions is denoted r.

Anderson and Mellor (2009) is one of the earlier studies in this genre where they have subjects in the 50+ age group in the US play the public goods game with VCM. In this experiment, subjects were categorised as Catholic, Protestant and Other. In this study using a public goods game, number of participants (n) = 8, multiplicative factor (m) = 2 and rounds (r) = 10. They found that average contributions to the public fund as a percentage of endowment was Protestant (52 per cent), Catholic (40 per cent), Other (30 per cent) and No religious affiliation (51 per cent), and these percentages were not statistically significantly different from one another. Turning now to religiosity of the subjects, information was collected about attendance in religious service in the last one month. The amounts contributed to the public fund as a percentage of the endowment was as follows: those who did not attend religious service even once (52 per cent), once (45 per cent), 2–3 times (50 per cent), 4 times (43 per cent) and more (57 per cent). These percentages are averages over all 10 rounds and there is no clear pattern here. Only the percentage contribution of subjects attending more than 4 times is significantly different from those who did not attend at all with all other differences turning out to be not significant. Also, only Protestant subjects seem to sustain cooperation over rounds in the sense there is less decay in contributions. A subsequent study by the same investigators Anderson, Mellor and Milyo (2010) with US college students as subjects find no effect of religion on public good contributions, but subjects with high attendance in religious services contribute more than those whose attendance is low.

As mentioned above, Ahmed (2009) had 103 school students in rural India play a public good game with $n = 3$, $m = 1.5$ and $r = 1$. They found that the average contributions of Madrassa students was 66 per cent of endowment while the corresponding percentage of students studying in secular institutions was 51 per cent, and this difference was statistically significant. In a similar study across three countries, Ahmed and Salas (2009) asked college students in India, Mexico and Sweden if they would classify themselves as religious or not. Based on this self-declared classification, a public good game was conducted in each country with a mix of religious and non-religious students participating in each session. They found that average contribution of religious students as a percentage of endowments were Indian (47 per cent), Mexican (63 per cent) and Swedish (66 per cent). This is to be compared with the corresponding contribution percentages of non-religious students, which were Indian (55 per cent), Mexican (61 per cent) and Swedish (57 per cent). The differences between the contributions of religious and non-religious students were statistically not significant. In both studies factors other than religion seem to account for most of the differences.

Benjamin, Choi and Fisher (2010) recruited college student subjects in 4 categories: Catholic, Protestant, Jewish and No religious affiliation. The students were given some sentences with words jumbled and their task was to unscramble the sentences to make sense. The natures of the sentences were such that this exercise served to prime religion. They were then made to play a public goods game. The researchers then estimate separate regressions for each of the 4 groups to estimate if the religious priming influenced cooperation. It was found on average that the Catholics contributed the most and the non-religious group least in the public good game.

Before leaving the subject of exploring religious differences and religiosity in experimental economics it should be mentioned that research in this area is of relatively recent vintage and many religious identities and their effects have not yet been explored. While experiments in the North countries largely compare Catholics,

Protestants or Jews; in the South countries comparisons have been done between Hindus, Muslims and Buddhists. No work yet can be seen which compares the behaviour of Christians and Muslims. Hence there is much work to be done in this regard.

Experiments based on Class Differences

This section will explore the effect of income class on behaviour of subjects in experimental situations. A few experiments have been conducted in this regard. Basu, Mitra and Gupta (2013) chose to have 18 college student subjects play a 6-stage Centipede game. The Centipede game, as described in Chapter 2, has 2 players, marked Red and Blue. Red is always the first mover. This game was played with a pot of Rs 25 offered to Red and Rs 10 offered to Blue in the first stage with the stakes doubling after every stage. The stakes were alternated between the two players who could either Take or Pass alternately. In order to investigate income class differences the experiment was set up in the following way. First, 18 student subjects were recruited from the same department of Jadavpur University, Kolkata, India. They were first brought into a classroom and a questionnaire was administered to them. There were some general socio-economic questions in the questionnaire but the 2 questions of interest were the student's family income and her own personal income.[10] These 2 figures were added to obtain the total income. Based on this students were ranked in descending order. The first 6 were classified as High Income Group (H), the next 6 as Middle Income Group (M) and the last 6 were marked as Low Income Group (L). It should be noted that the income status H, M or L is merely relative and does not indicate affluence or deprivation in any absolute sense.

After the students had filled out the questionnaire, they were let go and asked to come back at a later time and date. By this time the ranking, classification and groupings had been done. As there

[10] In addition to family income, student's own personal income becomes important in the urban Indian context as students do tend to earn money through various kinds of part-time work, including tutoring junior students. Often this income is not need-based but is earned to obtain a sense of affluence by the student.

were 18 players, they were divided into 9 pairs. In each pair in each round one player was designated Red and the other player Blue. Once the players returned, they were given the instructions and then the game commenced. To capture the effect of income class, there were 3 treatments. Each treatment was played over 5 rounds. In the first treatment Red and Blue players were matched across income classes randomly. In the second treatment players played within the same income class, that is H-H, M-M and L-L. In the last treatment they played with a player of a different income class, that is H-M, M-L and L-H. This information was given to the players before each treatment.

Now let us look at the results. As expected, there was very little use of backward induction, with very few first stage takes. Most takes happened in the second or third stage. Thus we see partial cooperation, even though there were a few players in every treatment who did not 'take' in any stage of the game and allowed the game to continue till their partner terminated it or the game ended after the sixth stage. The results of the effect of income classes on 'take' decisions were also interesting. Using paired *t*-tests on the number of takes in each treatment significant differences between treatments 1 and 2, between 2 and 3 and between 1 and 3 were found. Thus pairing subjects within own income group as well as pairing subjects with subject from another income group induced behaviour significantly different from pairing subject where income group is randomly determined. Evidence of significant positive in-group bias in cooperation was found. As to interaction with a subject from another income group, the results were significantly different from random income matching. but the direction of the bias could not be conclusively determined.

Conducting experiments to explore differences in human behaviour due to differences in socio-demographic or cultural attributes is a relatively new area in experimental economics. Many dimensions of this class of problems remain unexplored. Further research in the area will require continuous use of non-student subject pool and often the conduct of the experiments in the field. Appropriate protocols for the conduct of artefactual or framed field experiments need to be developed in each case so that the experiment can be carried out quickly and efficiently. There is also much scope for multi-country experiments.

FIELD EXPERIMENTS WITH SUBJECTS HAVING A COMMON LIVED EXPERIENCE

This section describes in some detail an experiment with subjects spread over a wide geographical area who share a common lived experience. The motivation springs from a concern that there may be real life situations where it is important to measure the response of the participants to a situation on the ground and therefore responses from student subjects are not appropriate.

We have earlier described the partition of the Bengal province in colonial India, On both sides of the international border at the very south, lie the sprawling and majestic Sundarbans forest, which is considered to be a World Heritage Site. This area which is partly forested and partly inhabited has some unique features that affect the life and livelihood of the people who live there. This is where several rivers including the mighty Ganges (in West Bengal) and the Padma and Meghna (in Bangladesh) flow from the north into the Bay of Bengal. This creates innumerable distributaries that divide the basin into an intricate delta with more than 200 islands. About half of the islands are uninhabited and form the Sundarbans forest, home to the Royal Bengal Tiger and the mighty Gangetic estuarine crocodile. Other wildlife and numerous flora, particularly mangroves, are found here making it a biodiversity hotspot. The inhabited islands are home to the people of the Sundarbans. These islands are separated from each other and the mainland by large rivers or narrow creeks. The area is entirely rural where the unique feature is that the heights of the islands are mostly below the high tide level of the adjoining river. Normally, this would mean that the island would be inundated with brackish water twice a day. As the water is a backwash from the Bay of Bengal it is brackish and saline and inundation would make agriculture impossible. In order to make habitation and agriculture possible on the islands the people of the area build dykes around the island such that the dyke keeps the saline water out as well as serves as a road around the island. These embankments are crucial to life in the Sundarbans and there is approximately 3500 kilometers of such dykes and embankments in the total area.

This feature is common to both the West Bengal and Bangladesh part of the Sundarbans whereas about two-thirds of the land mass is on the Bangladesh side and the rest on the side of West Bengal. The entire area suffers from acute shortage of potable water and mostly the ground water too is saline. Agriculture is therefore dependent mainly on the monsoon making only one crop possible every year. The entire area is extremely disaster prone, especially prone to cyclones and hurricanes as well as erosion of the coastline of the islands. Both factors contribute to embankment failure leading to quick inundation with saline water. The remedy to this is creating mangrove plantation on the outer edges of the dyke or embankment. These mangrove varieties have roots that run deep into the soil and help to bind the earth such that the embankment that stands over the water level can withstand a certain amount of outside force generated by a storm or tide.

Thus, embankment protection and repair and mangrove plantations in the islands are vital to the habitation and agriculture on the islands, in fact to the very existence of the people and their livelihood in the Sundarbans. These embankments and the peripheral mangrove plantations act like local public goods. The upkeep and repair of embankments and the mangrove plantations are technically under various government departments such as irrigation or forest, but as with many local public goods that are spread over large areas, there is very little government investment or intervention with the upkeep of the local public good being largely the concern of the local community.

This poses 2 problems. First, in the matter of embankments and dykes, especially in case of a breach due to storm or tide, intervention in the form of repair work must be quick and immediate. This precludes formal government intervention which is at best tardy. The local people must intervene immediately and ensure repair work by contributing voluntary labour. This naturally requires the effective circumvention of the well known free rider problem. Successful intervention does have its own rewards with gains from effective dyke repair being either equally distributed or pro rated by land ownership or crop cultivated. So, whenever there is a need for community action (donation of labour time, which is costly) to protect a public good, the cooperation level that the local community can achieve in a very short time becomes crucial to the life and livelihood of the village concerned.

Second, there could be problems of unrestricted extraction. This is particularly true of the peripheral mangrove plantations created to protect the embankments from external shocks due to storm and tide. The problem of extraction becomes particularly challenging in the light of an acute shortage of fuel, especially cooking fuel. Local rural household have very little access to more modern fuels such as electricity or gas and have to make do for most of the year with crop residue, dung and wood chopped from the neighbourhood plantations and forests. In this case, given that a mangrove plantation has been effectively created there is a high likelihood that members of a nearby community, who have had no stake in the creation of the plantation, but who have de facto extraction rights on fuel-wood decide to chop down a part of the mangrove plantation for fuel, thereby making the embankment vulnerable.

To investigate the above two tendencies—namely, a) the propensity of the village community to contribute towards a common fund in order to be able to create a local public good (building dykes, embankment repair or mangrove plantation) by overcoming the free rider problem, and b) to refrain from extraction (of wood from the mangrove plantations)—Joseph, Sopher, et al. (2013) designed two closely related public goods games to be played, one each in the Sundarbans in West Bengal and Bangladesh. The idea was to ensure the participation of common rural people from agrarian communities in West Bengal and Bangladesh Sundarbans who share the common lived experience of residing in villages on islands protected by embankments, close to the forest and the river, conducting agricultural activities or fishing, where storm and tide often cause embankment failure and gives rise to occasions when voluntary collective action is necessary. The subjects also share the daily lived experience of creating peripheral mangrove plantations where extraction by members of neighbouring communities poses a hazard.

The Public Goods Game in the West Bengal Sundarbans

The experiments conducted in the West Bengal (India) Sundarbans was a public goods game with VCM conducted in 20 randomly selected villages in the 19 administrative blocks of the districts of 24 Parganas (North) and 24 Parganas (South). Each session had 20 randomly selected villagers who were assembled in a large room, typically a classroom in a school or a hall belonging to the panchayat.

As the participants are seated (in a manner that they cannot easily communicate with each other or see the decision sheets of each other) they are randomly assigned identification numbers 1 to 20, which are prominently displayed on the table in front of the subjects so that both subject and experimenter/monitors can identify any subject by that number. These numbers remain the same throughout the duration of one session. Next, a short questionnaire containing some questions on the socio-economic characteristics of the subject was administered. Subjects are asked to record their IDs and fill out the questionnaire with monitors at hand to help out subjects who may be illiterate, semi-literate or physically challenged.

Once the filled-in questionnaires are collected back the main experiment begins. The room is cleared of all people except the subjects, experimenters, monitors and assistants. Experience suggests that in rural situations there are always the possibility of idle onlookers and self-appointed busybodies. Such people should be dealt with tactfully and it must be ensured that there is no intervention from such sources during the execution of the public goods game.[11]

Now, the 20 subjects are seated around the room and their IDs are prominently displayed. To begin the public goods game instructions are delivered at this point. While requirement of replicability require that instructions delivered in each session be as close to each other as possible, it is also important that the instructions not be merely read out and that subjects comprehend the task at hand. It is also important in field experiment sessions, especially in rural settings,

[11] This may sound trivial to the reader but in terms of running a field experiment what follows may turn out to be important. The room where the experiment is being conducted must be made secure in every way during the runtime of the experiment including the time to distribute the monetary payoffs. The subjects must be instructed to visit the toilet, drink water and make emergency phone calls before they settle down. They should be told that the duration of the experiment will be approximately 2 hours (say) during which time they will not be allowed to talk, make phone calls or leave the room. All mobile phones are to be switched off for the entire period. The experimenter need to ensure that the runtime does not overlap with the *namaaz* (prayer) hour when Muslim subjects are present. Also, women subjects often tend to turn up with small children and a temporary day-care facility may need to be established with a woman care-giver so that such subjects are not distracted during the session.

for the experimenter to develop a certain rapport with the subjects. This ensures that subjects remain obedient to the experimenter and experimental control is not lost during the session.

In each session in this experiment there were 20 rounds with 20 subjects present in the session. The subjects were randomly divided into 4 groups of 5 subjects each (Groups A, B, C and D). The groups were only valid for that round and re-matched at the end of every round. The groups must be formed before the commencement of the experiment with subject IDs and stored in a spreadsheet format in a laptop in the main table that is being manned by an assistant. Response record sheets are therefore created in advance for each round and put in round-wise packets. Each response record sheet (numbered 1–20) for the 20 subjects in each round contains 3 pieces of information: the subject ID, the subject's group (A, B, C or D) and her endowment in that round. This is followed by a blank space where she has to record her contribution to the public fund.

All subjects, at the beginning of each round are handed out the response record sheet so that each subject knows the group she is in and the endowment she has. She does not know who the other members of her group are. They have to record what they wish to contribute to the public fund. They have already been told that any money they do not contribute to the public fund remains in their private account and is theirs to take home. Any money they contribute to the public fund will be added up for each group and announced. This was a public good game with a threshold (also called provision point). In this experiment the threshold was always Rs 100. If Rs 100 is reached, the amount is totalled for each group and returned to the members of that group according to a sharing rule already explained to the subjects at the beginning when the instructions were given. There were several sharing rules according to the treatment being played. Each session had one treatment and the sharing rule was explained to the subjects at the beginning using a chart. If the threshold was not reached, then the money in the public account was returned to the private accounts so each subject had just her endowment. This is equivalent to the embankment not being repaired.

Next, the subjects face a possibility of a breach in the embankment due to storm or tide. This may happen with some probability. For this, this game had two levels of risk, 10 per cent and 50 per cent. Always, of the 20 rounds, 10 were played with risk level at 10 per cent and the other 10 at 50 per cent. This was explained with the help of visual aids. To take care of order effects these were alternated between sessions so that of the 20 sessions played, 10 were played with risk at 10 per cent followed by 50 per cent and the other 10 with 50 per cent followed by 10 per cent.[12] If the roll of die indicated that a storm or tide had struck, all money in the private account was wiped out, or else the subjects retained the money in the private account as earnings.[13]

There were 5 treatments (called versions here) in the West Bengal experiment. They differed in the endowment and the sharing rule from the public account in case the threshold was reached. These are summarised in the Table 5.1 below.

Table 5.1 Treatments in the Public Goods Experiment in West Bengal Sundarbans

Version	Risk	Number of Sessions	Sharing Rule	Endowments
A	High/Low	2	Equal	Equal
B1	High/Low	6	Equal	Unequal
B2	High/Low	6	Proportionate	Unequal
C1	None	3	Equal	Unequal
C2	None	3	Proportionate	Unequal

[12] A 10-faced die was used. First, for each group, the total in the public fund was announced. Whenever this did not cross the threshold of Rs 100, one member of the group was called to roll the die. In rounds where the risk level was 50 percent, it was announced that an odd outcome means subjects retain their private account and an even outcome means they lose all the money in that round. In rounds where the risk level was 10 per cent it was declared that if the outcome is '1' subjects lose all the money, in the other 9 cases they get to keep the total in their private account.

[13] Recall that once the subjects in each group have declared their contributions to the public fund, the information is collected, totalled and announced. If this amount falls short of the threshold value of Rs 100 then all money in the public account is returned to the private account of the subjects. Thus when the die is rolled each subject has her original endowment in her private account and that is at stake at the roll of the die.

Versions or treatments are explained as follows:

Version A: This is the base case or the control version. In this version, the endowment to each subject was Rs 30. When the threshold of Rs 100 was reached, the amount collected in the public fund was shared equally among the group members (that is $m = 1$, $MPCR = 1/5$). There were 2 sessions of this version.

Version B1: In this version, endowments were randomised within each group, so that 2 members of each group in any one round got Rs 60 and the three others got Rs 10 each.[14] This kept the group endowment at Rs 150 (same as Version A) but put a higher obligation on those who had an endowment of Rs 60 towards reaching the threshold. If the threshold was reached, the group members shared equally in the outcome.

Version B2: This was same as the earlier Version B1, except that if the threshold of Rs 100 was reached, the amount in the public fund (up to Rs 100) was shared among the members of each group in the proportion of their endowments. So the subjects who started out in this round with an endowment of Rs 60 got a return from the public fund of Rs 40 and the subjects who started this round with an endowment of Rs 10 got a return of Rs 6.70 (actually Rs 6.66 rounded off). Any amount collected above Rs 100 was shared equally.

Versions C1 and C2: Version C1 is exactly like Version B1 and Version C2 is exactly like Version B2 except that in Versions C1 and C2 there is no risk of losing any money when the threshold is not reached. The 10-faced die no longer rolls. This version was conducted to pick up any differences in responses when there is a threat perception against one where there is none.

Finally, the investigators realised that subjects have inherent responses built into them about how each person faces a risky situation. To control for this individual attitude towards risk, the main public goods game was followed by a risk game (in the form of a lottery choice game). In the risk game each subject was presented with a series of pair-wise lottery choices

[14] The randomisation of endowments was done in such a way that in the 20 rounds each of the 5 members in a group got an endowment of 60 rupees 8 times (40 per cent) and 10 rupees 12 times (60 per cent). This tallied exactly with the proportion of 'rich' subjects in a round (2 out of 5, that is 40 per cent), and the 'poor' subjects in each round (3 out of 5, that is 60 per cent).

(this is the same structure discussed in Chapter 4). The first lottery was a no-risk lottery in the sense that the payoff for a win and the payoff for a loss was the same. From then on the spread begins to widen. In all the pair-wise lotteries the probability of a win was 50 per cent. Each subject had to decide which lottery she wanted to play. The lottery was actually played at the end of the session and the realised winnings were added to the subjects' total payoff. This allowed the investigators to divide the subject pool by the relative degree of risk aversion into high, moderate and low levels of risk aversion (captured by dummy variables in a regression).

In another study Kulkarni (2014) selected 4 villages in Maharashtra for a finitely-repeated public good game. Two of them (Ralegan Siddhi and Hiware Bazar) are well known for having a history of community action by villagers and the other 2 do not have any history of collective action. She found that the established history of the norm of cooperation makes individuals behave with more cooperation even under anonymity.

The Public Goods Game in the Sundarbans in Bangladesh

The Sundarbans in Bangladesh spreads over 5 districts, which is where these experiments were conducted. To maintain parity with the West Bengal experiments, here, too, 20 sessions were conducted distributed over 4 villages in each district[15] which are adjacent to the river and forest. The terrain is very similar to the West Bengal Sundarbans as are the socio-demographic profile of the subjects. The only difference is that there is a much larger proportion of Muslims in the subject pool. The experimental set up was exactly similar to the experiments in West Bengal, including the survey, the main experiment followed by the lottery choice game. There is one crucial difference in the main experiment, which is discussed below, the logic of which should become clear as you read the details of the design.

The main difference between the public goods game played in the West Bengal Sundarbans and the present case of the public goods game in Bangladesh (hereafter called the Common Pool Resource

[15] A district in Bangladesh is quite small compared to one in West Bengal. Just to give the reader an idea of the scale, Bangladesh is about twice the size of West Bengal. While West Bengal is divided into 19 districts for administrative purposes, Bangladesh is similarly divided into 50.

[CPR] extraction game) is that the CPR game was played in the form of an extraction game with rewards for retaining a threshold level of the CPR. Recall that in the public goods game subjects are provided an endowment from which they are asked to contribute to a common fund. The rest follows. In the CPR game, the endowment is provided to the common fund (and not to the subjects) from where the subjects have extraction rights which they can exercise or choose to leave more (or all) in the common fund. The Bangladesh experiments were played in this format with the endowment being put in the common fund and the subjects having withdrawal rights which they could exercise or otherwise. Again there were 3 versions (treatments) with 2 sub-treatments each. This is now explained in some detail below. You should be able to see the similarities with the West Bengal experiment. The treatments (called version here) and their design description of the experiment is shown in Tables 5.2 and 5.3 below.

Table 5.2 Treatments in the CPR Extraction Game in Bangladesh Sundarbans

Version	Treatment Description	Sessions
A	Equal withdrawal rights with equal sharing	3
B	Unequal withdrawal rights with equal sharing	9
C	Unequal withdrawal rights with proportionate sharing	8

Version A, B and C have two treatments each: a) one with a risk to the lump sum transfer and b) with a fixed lump sum transfer without risk.

Table 5.3 Experimental Design in the CPR Extraction Game

Version	Risk	Number of Sessions	Sharing Rule Rights	Withdrawal
A1	50%	2	Equal	Equal
A2	None	1	Equal	Equal
B1	50%	6	Equal	Unequal
B2	None	3	Equal	Unequal
C1	50%	6	Proportionate	Unequal
C2	None	2	Proportionate	Unequal

Versions A1, B1 and C1: In each round, the 20 participants are grouped into 4 groups (A, B, C and D) with 5 members each. Each participant is given a cash withdrawal rights from a public fund. The total value of the public fund was Tk 150 and the sum of the cash withdrawal rights of all participants in the group added up to Tk 150. A participant could withdraw any amount from zero to the maximum of her cash withdrawal rights that was allocated to her. If the total cash withdrawal by the group exceeded Tk 50 (or if the group as a whole failed to maintain a threshold balance of at least Tk 100 in the public fund), then whatever was left was distributed to the participants either equally or based on their initial withdrawal rights (equal or proportionate sharing). If the total cash withdrawal was below Tk 50 (or if the group as a whole was able to maintain a threshold balance of at least Tk 100 in the public fund), then the public fund received a lump sum transfer of either Tk 70 or Tk 210 with equal probability (50 per cent chance). Then the total amount (whatever was leftover in the public fund) and the lump sum transfer was distributed to the participants either equally or based on their initial withdrawal rights (equal or proportionate sharing). Then the next round would begin. There were 20 rounds in each session.

Versions A2, B2 and C2: In these versions, if the total cash withdrawal was below Tk 50 (or if the group as a whole was able to maintain at least Tk 100 in the public fund), then the public fund received a lump sum transfer of either 70 or 210 which was announced beforehand at the beginning of the round. There was no uncertainty about this amount. For the first 10 rounds, the lump sum transfer was Tk 70 and the next ten rounds, lump sum transfer was Tk 210. This order was reversed in half the sessions to eliminate order effects.

All participants were seated in a classroom with enough space between them so they were not too close. Participants were assigned ID numbers at the beginning, which were taped to the desks or chairs they were seated in so that the monitors could easily identify them. Instructions were read out by the experimenter, and then the experiment began. Twenty decision periods (rounds) were conducted in every session in each of which participants were randomly assigned to be a member of a group (A, B, C, and D) of 5 people each. The randomisation was done in advance.

In each period, each participant was handed a sheet of information by an assistant for that period, which included the participant number, the group she belonged to in that period, the cash withdrawal right for the participant for that period, the cash withdrawal rights received by members of her group, the minimum amount in the public fund that must be maintained for the group to be eligible for the lump sum transfer for that period (this is fixed at Tk 100 in all periods), and the payment from the public fund that the participant would receive if the threshold balance was maintained. There was also a space to enter the final payment received, which is the sum of the initial cash withdrawal made and the share from the public fund and share from the lump sum transfer at the end of the period. Any money not withdrawn remained in the public fund. Any money remaining in the public fund was distributed according to the prevailing sharing rule if the threshold was not maintained. If the threshold was maintained, then the total in the public funds including the lump sum transfer was distributed. There could be situations where even after all the participants have made their withdrawals, the total amount left in the public fund was more than the threshold of Tk 100. In that case, the money which is above the threshold was divided based on the prevailing sharing rule within the group.

In each period, the participants made their withdrawal decisions. The assistants collected the sheets and brought them to the monitor. The monitor, with the help of the assistants, sorted the sheets into the 4 groups for that period. The withdrawals of the participants in each group were entered on the monitor's record sheet to check whether the threshold was maintained or not. If the threshold was maintained, a die was rolled to determine the lump sum transfer. Then the result was entered on each participant's sheet (the amount going to participant which included her initial cash withdrawal and her share from the public fund and the total amount, depending on whether or not the threshold was reached and the sharing rule). The sheets were then returned to the participants.

NATURAL FIELD EXPERIMENTS

A natural field experiment[16] is a rather recent innovation in the area of experimental economics. This method of conducting experiments seeks to investigate a class of problems where running experiments in a classroom or a laboratory is neither possible nor appropriate. Natural field experiments are conducted in a natural setting of the real world and in that sense 2 essential criteria of experimental economics—replicability and experimental control—are compromised. Essentially, the experimenter has advance knowledge that some event is about to take place in the future. The experimenter is able to build-in one crucial economic stimulus into the already about-to-happen event and thereafter record the response of economic agents to the stimulus delivered. Thus subjects are not brought into an experiment room or a laboratory but remain in their natural environments. Typically, they do not know that they are in an experiment. The economic stimulus is typically delivered by a letter or a phone call (lately often over the internet) and the subjects are given a longish period of time to respond. Hence, the subjects are free to review the situation at length, consult with family or friends and gather information from sources outside the control of the experimenter. In this sense, there is some loss of experimental control in that each subject may go through a process of one's own choice not open to the experimenter's scrutiny. Further, there is, for this reason, some loss in replicability as a repetition of the same experiment will not follow an identical protocol. The main advantage of the natural experiment is that it can observe economic variables that normally remain buried in a person's mind even when it is not possible to bring such persons over to an experiment room to play artefactual games. In the following subsection we discuss one of the first such innovative experiments contrived by List and Lucking-Reiley (2002).

[16] Natural field experiments were earlier called field experiments. This is because when natural experiments begun in 2002 field experiments of the type described in the first section of this chapter had not become popular. Hence earlier papers on natural field experiments refer to these as field experiments.

A Natural Experiment in the University of Central Florida

List and Lucking-Reiley[17] was possibly the first to conduct a natural experiment at the University of Central Florida, USA. They had come to know that the university was planning to raise charitable donations from the public in the Central Florida area to purchase computers for the Centre for Environmental Policy Analysis (CEPA) located in the university. The investigators sought and obtained permission from the university authorities to design and run the charitable fund raising campaign.

They were attempting to empirically verify two theoretical predictions about charitable donations that had already existed in the relevant literature. If one sets out to create a public good by way of raising charitable contributions or voluntary contributions, and there is a threshold level of money below which the public good cannot be provided, literature predicts the following:

i. If the prospective donors are told that a certain amount of money (seed money) has already been raised for the stated purpose, this tends to improve donation levels.
ii. If the prospective donors are told that in case the threshold is not reached after the campaign is over and the public good concerned cannot be created, the donor shall be refunded her contribution (refund policy), this tends to improve contributions.

They began by purchasing a mailing list with the names and addresses of 3000 persons in the Central Florida area who met two criteria: first that the person belonged to a household that had an annual income in excess of $70,000 and second, the household has been known to have contributed to charity in the past.

They calculated the price of a computer to be $3000. They chose 3 levels of seed money, namely 10 per cent, 33 per cent and 67 per cent of the price of a computer which translated into a collection requirement

[17] John A. List has worked extensively on the economics of charitable donation using natural field experiments. The paper being discussed here is one of the earliest works and sets out very cogently the methodology and protocol of natural experiments. John A. List has a website where all his publications are available (http://home.uchicago.edu/jlist/ accessed 9 September 2015).

of \$2700, \$2000 and \$1000 respectively for the 3 levels of seed money \$300, \$1000 and \$2000 chosen. Further, for each level of seed money they had one treatment where refund was promised when the collection requirement was not met and another where refund was not promised. Instead, the prospective donor was told that the money collected would be used for other purposes at CEPA.

Thus they had 6 treatments named 10, 10R, 33, 33R, 67 and 67R where the numbers refer to the level of seed money shown and R refers to the presence of a refund policy. The total sample of 3000 individuals was randomly divided into 6 sub-groups of 500 each and each sub-group received a solicitation letter containing the treatment administered. All donors were told that they were in a cohort of 500 persons and the university expected to buy one computer worth \$3000 from the donations received from each block of 500 persons. Any money raised above \$3000 will be used to fund CEPA's other needs.

Now a brochure was designed that contained the solicitation letter. The first part of the brochure was common to all treatments and talked about the need to establish a Centre like the CEPA, its aims and objectives and possible scope of work. The last part of the solicitation contained the treatments. After explaining that the potential donor is in a cohort of 500 persons and the university expects to buy one computer worth \$3000 out of the donations from this group, there would be one or two lines that differed from version to version which were the treatment lines. For example, the 10 treatment had a line 'we have already obtained funds to cover 10 per cent of the costs for this computer so we solicit a donation from you to cover the remaining \$2700.' Again the 10R treatment would have the additional line, 'if we fail to raise the \$2700 from this group of 500 individuals, we will not be able to purchase the computer, so we will refund your donation to you.'[18]

[18] Please note an important difference between a laboratory version of a public goods game under VCM with a threshold and a natural field experiment for providing a public good with a threshold. In the former the subjects receive an endowment from which they contribute and can get a return, but in the latter individuals contribute out of their own income and get no return. Therefore, to some extent, the subjects' behaviour in the laboratory may be strategic but in the natural experiment it must be completely altruistic.

Turning now to the results of the natural experiment, it was found that a total of 183 donation cheques were received from as many individuals and a total of $5509 was collected which the authors consider to be quite high. The detailed analysis of each 500-strong cohort shows the following:[19] In the 10 treatment 17 persons contributed a total of $202 which changes to 20 persons contributing $379 in the 10R treatment. Likewise, in the 33 treatment 33 persons contributed a total of $805 which changes in the 33R treatment to 31 persons and $863. Similarly, in the 67 treatment 42 persons contributed $1485 but in the 67R treatment 40 persons contributed $1775. The investigators found strong evidence that increase in seed money perceptively increases donation rates and per capita donations. The existence of a refund policy, if threshold was not reached, also positively influences donations but to a lesser extent.

In a somewhat similar natural field experiment Mitra and Gupta (2009) came across a Community Based Organisation (CBO) whose members had a history of engaging in collective action based on voluntary labour targeted to benefit the local community, such as planting trees alongside a state road (social forestry), regeneration of a local degraded water-body or designing mechanisms for recycling solid waste. This organisation, located in a rural area of the district of 24 Parganas (South) in West Bengal, had obtained as donation a sizeable plot of land, where they were planning to set up a community medicinal garden.[20] The investigators offered to run a fund raising campaign in collaboration with the CBO, on the basis of a solicitation letter to every household in the neighbouring villages. The letter was first distributed to each household by hand. The letter explained the need for such a project and the benefits it would bring to the community. It provided a budget for the project and promised that the investigators would contribute an amount equal to the shortfall of the amount collected from the required amount. The investigators would also bring

[19] For detailed results, see Table 1 in List and Lucking-Reiley (2002: 221).

[20] In various parts of India there continues to exist a strong tradition of non-Western alternative medicine where local varieties of plants are grown and traditional knowledge is used to administer the leaves, roots or extracts of these plants for common illnesses such as cough and cold, headaches, minor injuries or stomach-related ailments.

in an expert phyto-chemist who would provide technical expertise on setting up the medicinal garden. Donations were actually collected at a later date by providing receipts from the CBO. The total amount was recorded and the shortfall (there was a shortfall) was provided by the researchers out of a university research grant. An expert was brought in from the government forest department and the medicinal garden gradually took shape. The upkeep and protection depended on community labour voluntarily provided by members of the CBO. A short survey was administered to the households (both contributing and non-contributing). It was found that land ownership and membership of the CBO had the most positive impact on donations.

NON-MONETISED EXPERIMENTS

It is now a strict requirement in experimental economics that experiments be monetarily incentivised. The monetary incentives are to be linked to the decisions taken by the subjects during the experiment. This so that the decision-making process is not trivialised by the subjects and all decisions are taken seriously and diligently after careful thought and consideration. A show up fee is also now a requirement. Yet, experiments without monetary incentives continue to be conducted. This is possible when the researchers can show that the absence of monetary incentives do not lead to the subjects taking the experimental tasks lightly. In this section we describe two such experiments to provide a brief introduction to the reader to this area.

Carlsson, Gupta and Johansson-Stenman (2003) were interested to measure social inequality aversion. The reader will recall the discussion around risk aversion in the context of the lottery choice experiments described in Chapter 4. It has been argued that when a person takes a decision behind a veil of ignorance,[21] relative risk aversion is actually a

[21] The term *veil-of-ignorance* was used by John Rawls (1971) to describe a situation where there is a finite time gap between a decision and its outcome so that it becomes necessary for the decision-maker to hazard a guess about what may happen in the future, yet the decision-maker is able to see the future imperfectly, as if through a veil. Inequality aversion in this situation implies that the decision maker will choose a more equal distribution of income so that even if she ends up in the down-end of the distribution she will not lose much.

measure for social inequality aversion. This is the framework chosen by the investigators. The experiment was conducted with undergraduate students in 4 Indian universities. Participation was voluntary and no monetary reward was paid. Of the 364 students who participated, 338 passed the consistency check in the responses; that is, they did not contradict themselves given the assumed utility function. This is the data used for further analysis.

In order to create a veil-of-ignorance situation, the students were asked to 'imagine that in the future you have a grandchild, and you have the power to place him or her in a society of your choice.' The students were told that all societies in the experiment were identical in terms of language, culture, availability of goods and services and their prices as well as government policies and affirmative action. The subjects were also told that they could not know the position of the future grandchild in the income distribution of the given societies. The logic of asking the students to imagine a grandchild is as follows. It was believed that most people have a good estimate of their own abilities and would therefore not hesitate to choose an unequal society if they felt they had the ability to climb socially. One could extend this line of thought to a son or a daughter. However to a student subject a grandchild is too distant in the future to form any impression about the child's future abilities or potential.

The subjects were handed out a printed response sheet. They faced 8 pair-wise choices between a Society A and a Society B. Each society was represented by the highest, lowest and average income of that society. For econometric convenience, Society A was always the same (a very unequal society) and was pitted pair-wise against 8 Society Bs numbered B_1–B_8 which ranged from very unequal to less unequal.

The median relative risk aversion was found to be around 3, but about 20 per cent of the subjects exhibited extreme risk aversion. It is likely that the less developed nature of the Indian economy makes a significant proportion of young people extremely risk averse.

The above investigation spawned a new series of discussions between Carlsson and his two colleagues. The main theme of these discussions was about the constituents of happiness or satisfaction with life. There have been many studies on the subject. The most frequently used method is to take a survey where people are asked to rate their own subjective happiness (e.g., Easterline 1995; Clark and

Oswald 1996; Blanchflower and Oswald 2004; Luttmer 2005). These studies clearly show that it is not only the absolute level of income that determines happiness or satisfaction with life but also the position one has relative to other people. Thus, it was thought proper to design an experiment where subjects would have to compare one's own income with the average in society. However, a further question arises. Do people compare their own income with the average in society or some other average of income in her peer group? Certainly happiness or satisfaction with life must be influenced by all 3—namely, one's own absolute income, own income relative to the average in society and own income relative to some average income of the person's peer group. For experimental purposes it is extremely difficult to define a peer group. However, the caste system in India presented a unique opportunity with respect to income comparison: first, because caste is hereditary and cannot be changed, and second, in spite of much political effort to build awareness against caste-based discrimination, caste identity remains extremely important in Indian society. Thus, caste could be used as a good proxy for the peer group. Moreover, Muslims and Christians, being minority communities in India, also could serve as a proxy for a similar peer group.

It may be mentioned that caste identity itself has been the subject of experiments. Brooks, Hoff and Pandey (2015) conducted a field experiment in India with subjects drawn from men of high and low castes. They were made to play a simple coordination game with efficient and inefficient equilibria. They found that high caste men coordinated less efficiently than their low caste counterparts. This difference can be explained by the response of an individual to a low payoff that results when an individual is trying for efficient coordination but his partner is not. In an earlier paper, Hoff, Kshetramade and Fehr (2010) conduct field experiments in Uttar Pradesh, India. Each session consisted of 3 players in various caste combinations of high and low. They played a variation of the TG with third-party punishments when the other 2 players cooperate. They were investigating the presence of spiteful behaviour and found that between 61 and 73 per cent of decisions were the results of spiteful behaviour when 2 other players cooperated. Again Hoff and Pandey (2006) conducted another experiment in the field with high and low caste subjects from Uttar Pradesh. In the control the caste of the participants was not revealed and in the treatment it was. The participants were then asked to solve a series of mazes where the payoff increased as the subject solved more mazes. It was found that high caste participants solved 7 per cent more mazes than the low caste participants when caste was not revealed and 34 per cent more when caste was revealed.

Carlsson, Gupta and Johansson-Stenman (2009) designed a choice experiment to study the relative income effect. The subjects were undergraduate students of 4 Indian universities. The survey-type response sheet was in three parts: a) a general introduction, b) the relative income experiment, and c) questions regarding the Respondent's socio-economic status. The relative income experiment consisted of 3 sets of choices between Society A and Society B. In each set there were 3 pair-wise choices. Each society, A or B, was represented by individual income, average income of the individual's caste and the average income in that society. Again, following Carlsson, Gupta and Johansson-Stenman (2003), the choice was being made on behalf of an imaginary grandchild in the future. The structure of the experiment was similar to Carlsson, Gupta and Johansson-Stenman (2003). No monetary compensation was paid to the participants. A typical page in the present relative income experiment is shown in Figure 5.1.

A total of 498 undergraduate students participated in the relative income experiment. After eliminating inconsistent responses 429 responses were available for analysis. The Indian Hindu society was broken up into 4 distinct peer groups. These were General (that is, upper) caste, Scheduled Caste (SC), Scheduled Tribe (ST) and Other Backward Classes (OBC). This classification follows the Government of India policy on affirmative action (called *reservation* in India) whereby the last 3 categories are eligible for reservations in education and employment. Likewise, Muslims and Christians being minorities also formed 2 more sub groups. Traditionally, there has been a chasm between the general (upper) castes and SCs, with little or no marriages happening between the two groups. Thus, one's relatives and friends tend to be from such a peer group only. Further, due to affirmative action for SCs, STs and OBCs these have become well defined peer groups. Likewise, religious minorities too form well defined peer groups.

The main result of the study was that between half and two-thirds of the Respondent's marginal utility of income came from relative income effects. This is comparable with results from earlier studies in Western

Figure 5.1 The Relative Income Experiment in Carlsson, Gupta and Johansson-Stenman (2009)

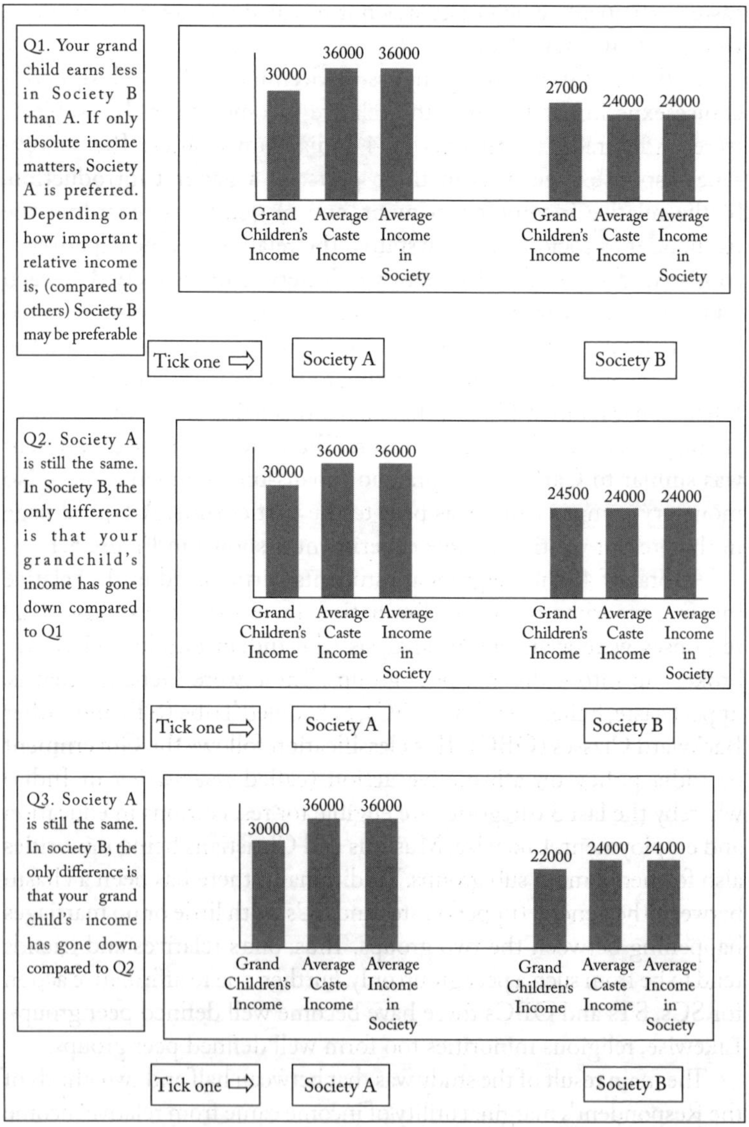

Source: Drawn by the author for this publication.

countries. Another important query in this study was whether an increase in the average income of the subgroup to which an individual belonged increases or decreases the individual's utility (holding the individuals own income fixed). The answer is not straightforward since there are 2 effects that work in opposite directions. First, people derive utility from having a high relative income compared to others in the peer group. Second, people derive utility through improved social identity from belonging to a caste with higher average income and status. This study finds that the former effect dominates the latter; that is, on the whole, people's utility tends to decrease with increased average income of the peer group to which they belong.

This chapter has tried to showcase various types of experimental designs that are in many senses not typical. This is to mean a generation of experimental problems and designs that arose out of the first generation experiments on strategic choice, public goods games, uncertainty experiments or auction and market structure experiments. Here, innovation is the key word. Innovations continue to happen and newer and newer areas are being constantly brought in under the scope of experimentation in economics.

six

The Methodology and Protocol of Experimental Economics

When economics began with Adam Smith, it was not perceived to be a subject amenable to the conduct of experiments, in the same sense that physics or chemistry were seen as experimental subjects. It was widely held that the nature and content of the class of problems addressed in economics was such as not to lend itself to observation under controlled or laboratory conditions. Rather, it was held that like astronomers or meteorologists, economists must largely be content to observe and study naturally-happening phenomena. It took almost 150 years to change this perception even slightly and over 200 years and considerable effort on the part of many economists for a major change of this position. But experimental economists could take heart from the fact that in Aristotle's time some 2000 years ago, physics was not considered to be a subject amenable to experiments. It is only some 400 years ago that scientists such as Galileo and Bacon established a tradition of conducting controlled laboratory experiments in physics.

Edward Chamberlain (1948) was perhaps the first reported proper experiment in economics. He induced a natural market with students as buyers and sellers. Even though no monetary rewards were paid, he tried to see, with hypothetical profits and gains, whether a group of buyers and sellers could discover a market clearing price (see Box 6.1). This generated a strand of literature in market experiments. This was followed by another set of experiments testing behavioural properties of agents participating in experiments using non-cooperative game theory. Third, a further set of experiments followed where individual decision making was investigated, mainly in situations where some uncertainty was involved.

EXPERIMENTAL METHODS

First, it is important to understand what classes of problems are amenable to solutions involving experiments. As discussed in Chapter 1, the answer to this question must begin from economic theory. We begin with a theory that is attempting to explain some economic phenomena. Next, we try to enquire if the solution or prediction of the problem, as suggested by relevant economic theory is empirically validated with real life data. Here, we will prefer secondary data over primary data. Secondary data is happenstance data where the passivity of observation is almost always guaranteed, that is to say that the fact that the action of an economic agent is being observed does not affect or alter the observation itself. In case secondary data is not available, primary data must be collected, usually through a field survey. Here, the subject is aware that she is being observed, and to that extent her behaviour (or its reporting to the investigator) may be altered due to the act of observation itself. Data collected by way of secondary data or field–survey based primary data is then put to use with the help of statistical or econometric techniques to seek validation or otherwise of the relevant economic theory. If the theory and its predictions are not (even partially) validated, this causes occasion for the development of a new theory and theoretical extensions.

Box 6.1 Chamberlin and his Experiments on Markets

Chamberlin wrote *The Theory of Monopolistic Competition* in 1933. This book reflected his concern about the fact that markets did not perform adequately during the Depression. He felt that some of his theoretical predictions could be tested in an experimental format by creating a simple market environment using students as economic agents. He reported his first market experiment in 1948. He divided the students into 2 groups of equal size and designated them as buyers and sellers. Each seller got a card with a per unit cost printed on it. Likewise each buyer got a card with a per unit value printed on it. These represented the per unit cost of producing a hypothetical good for the seller and the per unit value that the buyer gets from consuming the same hypothetical good.

(Box 6.1 contd...)

(...Box 6.1 contd)

During trading, the buyers and sellers were required to negotiate the price of one unit of the good. The trading process was unstructured and the students were free to communicate with other sellers and buyers and negotiate with others in a decentralised manner. Buyers and sellers were each given different costs and values. A buyer could earn the difference between the value he has and the price he negotiates. Likewise the seller earned the difference between the price she negotiates and the cost given to him. Monetary rewards were not given to the subjects. From the experimental results Chamberlin concluded that in this competitive situation actual outcomes deviated from theoretical predictions and that trading volume was higher than that indicated by the intersection of underlying supply and demand curves.

According to one view, only in situations where the collection of data through secondary or primary observations is not possible or data gathered though such methods are considered to be wholly unreliable, should conduct of experiments be even considered. However one need not be so very restrictive about the use of experiments. Experiments may offer precision in identifying the impact of different economic variables, which could be meaningful even when observational data is available. It is also possible to gather data through primary or secondary observations as well as through an experiment and then to compare them to yield useful results.

The main advantage of conduct of experiments are: a) replicability and b) control. First, the experiment must be conducted in such a way so that it may be repeated in another location with another set of subjects in exactly the same way. For this reason, the experiment must be so designed that it is completely structured. It must not have any component which is decentralised or unstructured. Suppose you are playing a UG. The simple anonymous UG can be played in a structured manner quite easily. This has been discussed in Chapter 2. Suppose now you wish to run a treatment where you wish to see the effect of pre-play communication on the amount the Proposer offers to the Respondent and the consequent response of the Respondent. If you explain the game to both players and then simply allow a few minutes to the players to talk to each other, you will lose replicability. This is because when the same treatment is run in another location with another set of subjects the discussion between Proposer and Respondent may take a completely different turn from the one that took place in the earlier session, thereby affecting the outcome. Thus communication poses a challenge in terms of keeping it structured and centralised.

One option could be to tell the subjects that pre-play communication will not take the form of an actual discussion about what offer is to be made and whether it will be accepted or not, but this communication will be in the nature of a promise to be made by the Proposer about what to offer to the Respondent and a counter promise by the Respondent about whether she will accept or not. In a sense, you are testing to what extent these pre-play promises are genuine or cheap talk. This can be achieved in the following way. Suppose the Proposer's endowment is Rs 50. Next several alternative figures such as Rs 0, Rs10, Rs 20, Rs 25, Rs 30, Rs 40, Rs 45, Rs 50 appear on the computer screen of the Proposer under the statement 'When the Ultimatum Game will actually be played, I will offer the Respondent the amount Rs __.' When the Proposer clicks on any one figure this will be placed at the end of the sentence and this sentence will be transmitted to the screen of the Respondent. This will be followed by an option for the Respondent such as 'I will Accept/Reject this offer.' Now, the Respondent will record her decision and this will be communicated to the Proposer on her computer screen thus 'Your offer of Rs __ will be accepted/rejected by the Respondent.' Again, in case of a rejection the Proposer may be allowed to send a revised offer. The number of times the offer may be revised will need to be decided in advance and informed to the players. Thus, open, face-to-face unstructured communication has been replaced with communication through computer terminals which is structured and option based. Therefore, if the communication method is kept the same it can be easily replicated in another location with another set of subjects.

Next we turn to control. Control is the ability to manipulate laboratory conditions so that observed behaviour can be used to study theory and policies. The experimenter should be able to exercise absolute control over the subjects in an experiment, without which the situation that is sought to be induced in a laboratory will not be effectively transmitted to the subjects and consequently the response of the subjects will also be random and meaningless. Experimenters should especially look out for the following problems that result in loss of control.

i. Communications between subjects in the form of talking or other non-verbal signals, when communication is not required
ii. Unplanned interruptions after the experimental process has started
iii. Experimental process continuing for too long resulting in loss of concentration among the subjects
iv. Subjects looking at the screen of another subject and being influenced by the decisions taken by the latter
v. Subjects leaving at the end of an experimental session talking about the experiment to another subject waiting to enter for the next session

Take the case of the simple anonymous UG. It is easy to see that if subjects talk amongst each other, if the proposer in one pair looks at the screen of the proposer from another pair sitting next to her, or if the experiment goes on beyond, say, 90 minutes, experimental control may be compromised and then the data collected through the experiment will be quite useless.

THE PROTOCOL OF EXPERIMENTS IN ECONOMICS

To begin with, you must have the design of an experiment. It bears repetition that the design must be checked and re-checked, again and again. This is usually done by discussing the design with friends and colleagues, even a spouse or partner. As famously claimed by Alvin Roth,[1] it is even better to run the design of your experiment by your enemies. Roth further states, that this is what he mostly did and in the process he lost many enemies (because they became friends), but the point is that you must be prepared to face, without rancour, the harshest criticism about the design of your experiment, from friends or foe alike, *before* the experiment is actually conducted. It is good to remember at these times that an experiment costs time, effort and money—especially money. If an experiment is run with a design flaw, and the flaw is discovered *after* the experiment is over, there is nothing to be done except shed some tears and begin all over again.

[1] See Roth (1994) for a more detailed account of the do's and don'ts of running experiments.

And all this with one objective in mind. You began by creating an artefactual experimental environment. In this environment you have delivered a stimulus to your subjects. The subjects, in return, have delivered a response, which you have recorded. It is vitally important to ensure that the response is only, *and only*, due to the stimulus[2] and not something else. There is always something else. Be sure to filter that something else out before you begin to process the data from the subjects' response. This alone ensures the effectiveness of experiments. Let no reviewer be able to say later that the response data was contaminated because the experimenter did not take some factors into consideration that influenced the subjects.

It is always best to test the design of the experiment with a dry run. This means that the experiment is conducted in a laboratory or classroom with student subjects but who are not actually paid any money. Even though this somewhat diminishes the seriousness with which the student subjects take the decisions, such dry runs help to bring out any problems with the design and programming of the experiment.

We discuss here the process and protocol to follow, when running experiments. In this there will be a difference when you run an experiment in a computer laboratory or in a room (irrespective of whether this room is in your university or institute or in the field). In what follows, both processes will be discussed.

Choosing the Venue

It is absolutely vital to choose the venue of your experiment right. This is important from the point of view of exercising experimental control. If the experiment is being run in a computer laboratory, it is important to ensure that all the terminals are running and functional. The one thing you do not want is one terminal malfunctioning while the experiment is on. It is therefore important to do several dry runs with subjects who are not being paid but (perhaps) being given a bar of chocolate. The computer laboratory must be made completely secure, in the sense that there should be no interruptions from outside once the

[2] See section 'Advantages of Experiments' in Chapter 1.

experiment is on. The seating arrangement must be thought through. There must be partitions between computer terminals to prevent subjects from peeking at adjacent terminals (which they inevitably have a tendency to do). They should be able to see their own screen and the experimenter at all times.

A hand-run version will usually be run in a room. Again, the room must be made secure from outside intrusions. This is especially important when the experiment is being run in the field. One has to encounter the curiosity phenomenon. Bystanders will simply gather to find out what is going on, and they must be dispersed before the experiment can actually begin.

In the field or in a classroom, subjects should be seated in chairs in a manner that the experimenter has access to every one of them at all times, they can hear the experimenter clearly and can see any visual aids being used for instructions. They must be sufficiently spaced out to discourage communication among subjects. In order to ensure anonymity between say, Proposer and Respondent in a UG, if you are using 10 pairs, it is better to put all the Proposers in one room and all the Respondents in an adjacent room, with a couple of assistants running between the rooms. One should also ensure that the two groups do not meet before the session while entering the rooms.

Recruiting Subjects

When experiments first began in the 1950s and 1960s, no particular importance was attached to any specific pool of subjects. It was felt at that time that the results of an experiment would be invariant to the subject pool as long as subjects were human beings. As a result, most experiments were conducted with university students, both undergraduate and graduate. This was simply because the experiments were conducted by professors of universities and the one pool of subjects readily available to them was university students.

This resulted in a chronic situation, where the bulk of results in experimental economics were obtained by conducting experiments with student subjects who came from WEIRD society backgrounds. This term was coined by Henrich, Heine and Norenzayan (2009) who analysed top journals to find that 68 per cent of subjects came from the US and a whopping 96 per cent from the developed North. This is easily explained by looking at the first authors of these journal articles where 73 per cent were from the US and again a whopping 99 per cent from the developed North. Yet, these studies claimed their results were universally valid.

However, with time it was observed with the help of multi-country studies that there could be substantial variation in the results when a) non-student subjects are used and b) non-WEIRD subjects, whether student or non-student, are used. A number of large projects have sought to map the world on several dimensions. These are values (Hofstede 2001; Inglehart, Basanez and Moreno 1998; Schwartz and Bilsky 1990) personality traits (McCrae and Terracciano 2005; Schmitt, Allik, et al. 2007) and levels of happiness (Diener, Suh, et al. 1995).[3] These studies find that there are serious differences in results when the same game is played with non-student subjects more closely associated with the problem being investigated as well as student subjects in the South countries.

So, it is important to consider the subject pool carefully. If the problem at hand or its real life parallel is of such nature that not much difference is expected between student and non-student subjects, then it is usually logistically simpler to use student subjects. Here again some difference in motivation has been reported between student subjects who study economics and those who study other subjects,[4] and this should be borne in mind when selecting the subject pool.

Often it is desirable to work with not-students subjects altogether. This is especially true when the real life parallel involves a decision that a certain group of people normally take. Suppose you have re-tooled the public goods game to reflect decisions taken by members of a local community involved in forest conservation,[5] it may be preferable to take the experiment to the field where the subjects shall actually be members of such a community.

In any case, it is best to talk to each subject briefly well before the session and tell them a little bit about what the session is about, explain

[3] For a comprehensive discussion, see Henrich, Heine and Norenzayan (2009).

[4] See Marwell and Ames (1981) for some interesting results in this regard.

[5] See Ghate, Ghate and Ostrom (2013) for an example of this type of experiment.

to them that they will earn some money and ask them to come to the venue at a particular date and time. If you require a specific number of persons it is always best to ask for one or two extra people. In the field it is always preferable if the experimenter arranges for to and fro transport and the subjects are accompanied by assistants. This ensures participation and punctuality.

Delivering the Instructions

This is the most vital part of running experiments. Remember, your subjects, whether student or non-student, have no idea about experiments and most likely never participated in one. They will not know what to expect. In creating the instruction sheet the two important factors to be considered with due importance are *replication* and *cognition*. The experiment being conducted should be replicable in the sense that another researcher should be able to take the design and instructions elsewhere and repeat the experiment in some other location with a different pool of subjects and (hopefully) get similar results. Else, if the results are different then the difference is explainable in terms of known factors. Hence, all instructions should be written out. Any tendency to extemporise should be avoided. The language should be simple and easy to follow. Long sentences should be avoided. Examples should be given, wherever appropriate, but care should be taken to ensure that specific examples do not influence the decision of the subjects. For example, you are playing a public goods game with a 5-member group with Rs 30 as the initial endowment. Now you want to explain how subject profits are to be calculated. Suppose you say that each person contributes Rs 30 to the group fund, it may indicate to the participants that the rules of the game *require* the subjects to contribute the *entire* initial endowment. The best way to offset this is to give a second example where the subjects contribute nothing or very little.

The language can be English if subjects are comfortable with English. Often, especially when conducting experiments in the field, English instructions will not be comprehensible to the subjects. It is best to still write out the instruction in English (rather than in the local language) and then have it translated. The English instruction sheet will be required during the publication process. Though most journals will not publish the instruction sheet to save space, they are still required to be produced during the review process. Care should be taken to ensure that the translation is faithful. Ambiguities should be avoided. Some terms may not have one-word translations, in which case the original term may be retained but explained at length. The instructions should be tested out by reading it out to friends and colleagues quite a few times. Care should be taken to ensure that every time subjects understand the same thing. This can be ensured by administering a short quiz where questions are asked on situations that arise in course of the session. A high percentage of wrong answers indicate ambiguity or excessive complexity in the instructions.

Visual aids by way of posters and banners giving a tabular or graphic description of the experiment should be used to emphasise points. The instruction should be read out as well as put up on the computer screen of the subjects (when possible). If this is not possible then the instructions should be projected on a screen from a laptop via an LCD projector and the subjects should be required to read along. This ensures that the subjects read along while the instructions are read out. This further ensures that some subjects will not finish earlier than others and then have to wait and get bored. All this is to ensure complete comprehension of the instructions by the subjects. It is safe to assume that subjects have limited cognitive ability. You need to ensure that subjects understand the entire exercise and what options they have and the consequence of exercising those options. Also, that all subjects understand the same thing.

Running the Experiment

It is always good to begin by welcoming the subjects to the experiment and expressing your gratitude at the fact that they have taken time out to participate. This should be done even though the subjects may be your students and you will be paying them good money at the end. This is followed by assigning them seats and numbering the locations and assigning the subjects a unique identification number. If there are multiple sessions of your experiment, the unique identification number must capture the session in which a particular subject participated. For example, if you are going to have 10 sessions with 20 subjects per session, a identification number such as 0313 tells you that this is subject number 13 in session number 3.

Once the subjects are seated, the instructions should be handed out (non-computerised experiment) or put up on the screen (computerised). The instructions are then read out and subjects encouraged to read along. You should read out the instructions, rather than make an extempore speech. This ensures replicability. Visual aids and examples should be used when appropriate with the usual caution. You may safely assume that there will be some subjects who will want to ask clarificatory questions. You need to decide in advance whether you want the subjects to ask their questions out loud so that everyone can hear the question and the answer or you want the ones wanting to ask questions to raise their hand and you can go close to them and hear and answer their question so that only the person asking the question can hear the answer. But whatever you do, it should be uniform throughout the experiment.

This is followed by administering a quiz designed to test the subjects' understanding of the experimental exercise, the options before the subjects and the consequences of these options. Questions must be so designed to have a unique answer. They can also be multiple choice questions with (usually) 4 answers provided of which only one is correct. The subjects should write their identification number on the quiz sheet. The quiz should have a time limit which is clearly spelt out. Once the quiz is over, the sheets should be gathered and corrected. In a computer laboratory this could be so programmed that the computer will correct the quiz and inform the subject and the experimenter with the corrected quiz and the scores. The occurrence of wrong answers will tell you areas which need further explaining. This should be done at this stage. You may repeat part of the instructions and give examples. No remonstration or blame should be apportioned on a subject for performing poorly in the quiz.

Now the actual experiment is started. This could be hand run or computerised. In case of hand run experiment the paper-instrument used for providing subject-specific information (group number, endowment, rewards in a lottery she is facing) and recording of subjects' decision must be printed in advance and used. These sheets will be gathered at the end of each round and used to compute the monetary reward of the subjects for each round. It is best to give each subject a sheet where she may record the money she is earning in each round so that she can tally the total over all rounds with the amount actually being given to her at the end of the experiment. Tabulation of the decisions taken by the subjects may be done while the experiment is going on (enter the data pertaining to one round when the next round is going on) or after the session is over. This part can be easily programmed in a computerised experiment. In hand-run or field experiments, there are advantages in carrying a laptop where a spreadsheet format is already created. Then the decisions of the subjects can be entered right away and this not only completes the tabulation for each session as the session is completed, but also helps in computing the monetary rewards of the subjects automatically.

Nowadays it has become customary to conduct 1 or 2 trial rounds. This is particularly important when the design of the experiment is quite complex and/or the experiment itself is in multiple rounds. It has been found that even though the instructions are amply clear, subjects may have difficulty in comprehending these or may be confused about some aspects of the game, especially how the reward is calculated. So it is best to have 2 trial rounds, where the full game is played out and the rewards calculated. Compensation is not actually paid in the trial round, and this should be informed to the subjects before beginning the trial round. Since it is inevitable that some learning takes place in multiple-round experiments, the presence of 2 trial rounds helps the subjects to get a better grasp on the game and what to expect during the course of the game. This way she starts at a higher point on the learning curve.

Monetary Incentives for the Experiment

As earlier mentioned, monetary incentives were not part of experiments in economics initially. Professors wielded sufficient power over the students and participation was ensured without incentives. When experimental economics began gaining respect, providing monetary incentives became important; particularly to ensure that the choices made by subjects were consistent with what they thought was best for herself and not make random or spurious choices in a casual manner.

It is important to recall a critique of Thurstone's experiment. L. L. Thurstone (1931) had considered the problem of empirically determining an individual's indifference curves. He reported the results of an experiment in which each subject was asked to make a large number of hypothetical choices between commodity bundles consisting of hats and coats, hats and shoes and shoes and coats. He reported the data for one individual in detail to conclude that the fitted indifference curves that followed from the observed data were indeed convex to the origin. W. Allen Wallis and Milton Friedman came out with a detailed critique of this experiment. Their main argument was that since the environment in an experimental situation is entirely artificial, subjects do not know what decisions they would take in a similar real life situation. Therefore, such subjects, in entire good faith are likely to produce systematic but spurious results. They wrote:

> For a satisfactory experiment it is essential that subject give actual reactions to actual stimuli. ... Questionnaires or other devices based on conjectural responses to hypothetical stimuli do not satisfy this requirement. The responses are valueless because the subject cannot know how he would react. (Wallis and Friedman 1942: 179–80)

This raises the serious question whether the subjects are taking the same decisions in an experimental set-up that they would otherwise have taken in the real world. One way in which you can make the subjects take the experiments seriously and compel them to take decisions that are consistent with their real life preferences is to provide non-trivial monetary rewards that are linked to the decisions the subjects take and the outcome of the game. Thus, it has now come to be mandatory to provide monetary incentives to subjects in an experiment.[6] The monetary incentive is nowadays provided in 2 parts. In the first part, a show up fee is given. This is usually a small fixed amount that is given to every participant who comes to participate in the experiment. The amount is the same for everyone regardless of the performance of the subject in the experiment or the decisions she takes. The second part is variable and contingent on the decisions taken by the subject in the experiment and its outcome. So, for example, in a

[6] It should be noted here that experiments are still conducted by some researchers, without monetary incentives. In these experiments an instrument is normally used that looks like a survey questionnaire where a hypothetical situation is described to the subject and she is then asked to take some decisions.

public goods game all subjects are provided with an endowment. The endowment is hers to take away. However the subject has the option of contributing a part or whole of her endowment to a group fund. When all subjects have contributed the amounts they choose to contribute, the amount is tallied and is multiplied by some multiplicative factor and distributed equally among all subjects. The sum of what she did not contribute out of her endowment and the amount she receives from the group fund after multiplication by the multiplicative factor constitute her earnings from this round of the game. This, of course, is in addition to the show up fee.

The point is that monetary incentives must be linked to the decisions taken by the subjects and the outcomes of the experiment. This makes the stimulus delivered very actual rather than hypothetical and hence the responses recorded in the nature of decisions are consequently real and not hypothetical. Further, monetary incentives tied to decisions and the outcomes ensure that subjects take the decision-making process seriously. Non-trivial amounts must be used and should, at the least, be equal to the opportunity cost of the subjects' time.

There are several ways to design the payment structure:

i. One can begin by awarding points for each round of the game. These points can be added up, for each subject and converted to money at some rate that has been previously announced. For example, in an experiment where the subjects are shown inflation rates in the past 10 periods and are asked to predict the inflation rate in the next period, rewards were linked to prediction errors. If E is the prediction error in percentage, points were calculated using the formula:

$$\textit{Points earned} = \frac{375}{1+E} - 75$$

And Re 1 was given for every 100 points earned. As the formula is a convex function, zero points are earned for error rate of 4 per cent and any error rate above 4 per cent are awarded negative earnings. However, conventionally, any negative earning is considered to be equal to zero earning so that no money is actually deducted from the personal fund of a subject.

ii. The simplest way to compute earnings from a game is to provide the subject with some endowment and then ask the subject to take a decision. The decision then leads to an outcome which is measured in monetary terms. The reward exactly equals the monetary outcome. For example, in a UG the Proposer is provided with an endowment of Rs 50. She is asked to propose a division of this amount between herself (x) and an anonymously matched Respondent ($50 - x$). If the Respondent accepts the proposal the Proposer gets Rs x and the Respondent gets Rs ($50 - x$) and if the Respondent rejects the proposed division both get Rs 0.

iii. One way to reduce the total amount required to be paid out to subjects without offering trivial amounts in each round of a multi-round experiment is to offer a substantial amount as endowment, say Rs 200, in a public goods game. Next, have the game played for say 10 rounds, and then randomly choose any one round of the experiment by draw of lots in a transparent manner and pay all subjects the actual earning of that round only.

CONSENT AND OTHER ETHICAL ISSUES

It is extremely important that the subject pool consist of only volunteers. That is, each subject has been told that there is going to be an experiment and each has voluntarily agreed to participate in it. A written record of their willingness to participate must be kept by the experimenter by getting the subjects to sign a consent form. The experimenter's institute or university may already have the template of such a consent form, in which case it should be followed. If no such template exists, the experimenter should create one for herself.

Many institutes or universities nowadays have committees (often called ethics committees) that are charged with the responsibility of vetting experiments where human subjects are involved. Clearance or permission must be obtained from such a committee before the experiment is conducted. Failure to do so may attract penal action on the investigator at a later stage. Apart from this, instructions are to be worded in such manner as not to contain rude words or any gender or other kind of bias. Care should be taken to ensure that nothing in the design of the experiment or the instructions may give offence to any subject. No deception should be used and no untruth told. Certain religions prohibit gambling. When subjects from such groups are present, care should be taken to explain the difference between the money earned by a subject from the experiment, which is based on performance and money earned from a gamble or a pure game of chance. Finally, a subject has the right to walk out of an experimental session, even after giving consent, and this right should be fully respected at all times, even when it is costly to the experimenter.

FOLLOW UP

There are two kinds of follow ups that you could consider. These are meant to give more substance to the data generated through the experiment.

i. *Exit interview*: This is usually done to find out more about the motivation of the subject regarding the decision she has taken in the experiment. However, for purposes of analysis it is best if the interview is conducted through a structured questionnaire. In this questionnaire, each question should have several alternative answers provided by the experimenter and the subject may be asked to pick one answer for each question that comes closest to the reason that particular subject had in mind when taking the decision in the experiment.

   For example a follow up exit interview after a UG for a Proposer could have a question as follows:

   You chose the amount you proposed that should be given to the Respondent because:
   a) You wanted to be generous to the Respondent
   b) You were afraid that a lesser amount would be rejected by the Respondent
   c) You wanted to keep as high an amount as possible for yourself
   d) You believe a 50:50 split is fair to both players

ii. *Survey*: A second type of follow up is to conduct a socio-economic survey on the subjects who have participated in an experiment. This survey would gather information about age, educational qualifications, gender, religion, caste, income and socio-demographic characteristics. The questionnaire could also have questions that elicit information about the belief structure of the subject. For example, information about the subjects' attitude towards risk taking, trust, trustworthiness, generosity, etc. could be included.

USE OF DECEPTION

Experimenters in other disciplines such as psychology habitually resort to deception to conduct their experiments. In experiments in economics, however, deliberate deception of subjects by the experimenter is now a taboo. First, most experimenters are concerned about developing and maintaining a reputation among the student population for honesty. Even if it is the case that you have not used that particular group of students, but have used another group of students in the past where you had used deception, the present group is likely to be affected for word gets around. This jeopardises future experiments by any other researcher. This is particularly important in universities where several researchers are engaged in conducting experiments, the very idea of participating in experiments might become suspect with the student subjects. Second, deception must be avoided to ensure that the decisions being taken by the subject are motivated by the induced monetary rewards rather than as a psychological reaction to suspected manipulation.

BUILDING A COMPUTER LABORATORY

If you are planning to conduct many more experiments or thinking of creating a centre where many other researchers will eventually come and conduct experiments, you are better off creating a computer laboratory for the purpose. Ideally, it should be a laboratory dedicated to the conduct of experiments, but even if it is a shared facility, it will suffice. Basically you need a room of about 30 feet by 20 feet and equipped with about 21 desktop computers (See Figure 6.1).

Box 6.2 Computer Configuration for a Lab

Computer Configuration:
Processor: Pentium (R) Dual Core 3.2GHz
RAM/Memory: 2GB
HDD: 250GB
Display: G41Express
CDDVD

The computers are best located along the 3 walls of the room with one wall left free for showing projections for instructions and the like. One will need an LCD projector hooked up to a suitable computer for the purpose. All the computers must be connected by a Local Area Network (LAN). Nowadays many experiments are conducted over the internet so it is better for the laboratory to have internet connection. The room should be protected by a router and a firewall.

One of the desktops is to be treated as a server leaving the rest of the 20 computers as terminals where subjects will sit. Chairs should be swivel type so that they can turn around when receiving instructions and turn back when participating in experiments. There should be partitions between terminals so that subjects cannot see the screen next to them, even by accident. Figure 6.1 will make the design clear.

You may need some special devices in your laboratory. These include devices that reflect different probabilities in an unbiased way. Dies are good for this. You need a set of 3-faced, 4-faced, 6-faced, 8-faced, 10-faced and 20-faced dies. In addition, bingo cage[7] with a hundred numbered balls is sometimes helpful.

[7] Bingo or housie is a popular parlour game in which a round cage that rotates is used. The cage contains a hundred numbered balls and a trap such that on every rotation one numbered ball is trapped and brought up. It is useful to create a probability of one per cent.

Figure 6.1 The Layout of an Experimental Computer Laboratory

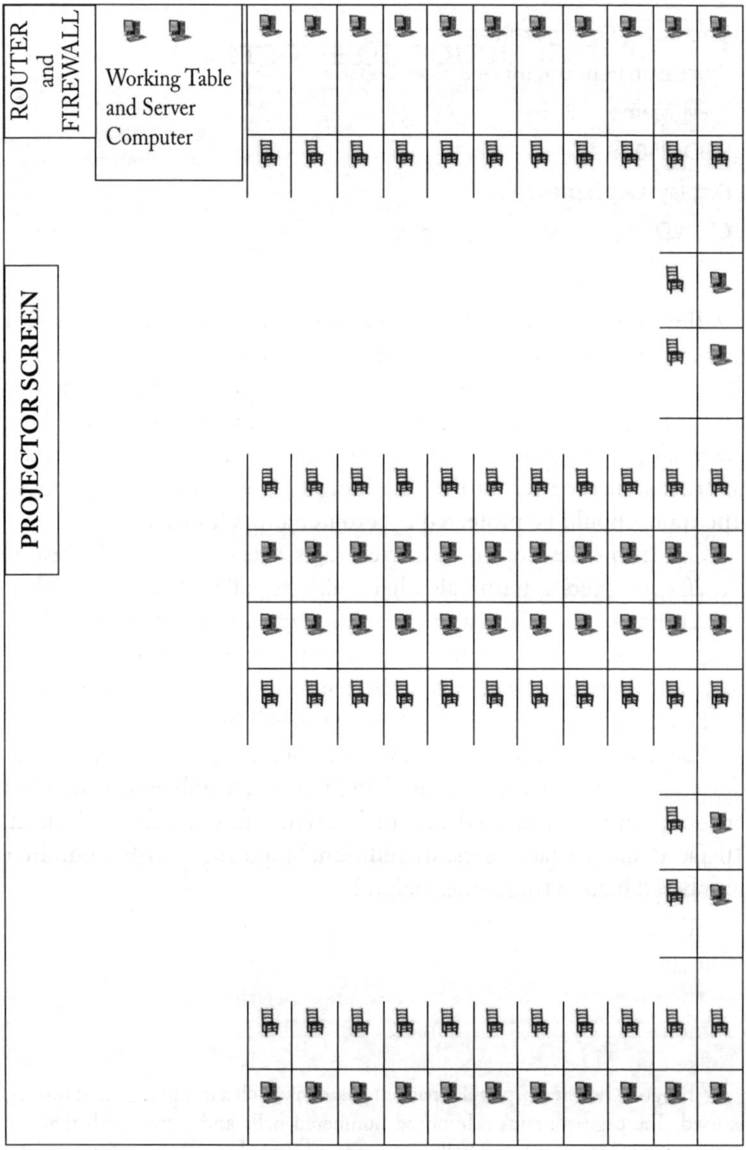

Source: Drawn by the author for this publication.

seven

Introduction to Programming using z-Tree[1]

Zurich Toolbox for Readymade Economic Experiments (z-Tree) was developed in the University of Zurich by Professor Urs Fischbacher for designing and conducting economic experiments in the laboratory. This is an open source software which can be downloaded free of cost. You will, however, need a written permission from Professor Fischbacher before you can use it. Do make sure to acknowledge Professor Fischbacher and z-Tree in all your papers and reports. Like any other programming software, there is scope of entering data, displaying outputs, performing arithmetic and logical operations, running conditional statements and repetition. The network architecture of z-Tree is client-server type with each client connected to the server instead of being connected to each other. The minimum machine configuration is a 486 processor, 16MB RAM and a LAN connection.

z-Tree has two components, the z-Tree as the server program and z-Leaf as the client program. Any one machine in the LAN can be treated as the server (experimenter's PC) and the z-Tree program loaded in it. z-Leafs are loaded in the client machines (subjects PCs) with the IP address of the server noted in the client machines.

Experiments in z-Tree are programmed in a sequence of stages. The stages are designed according to the sequence of activities involved in the experiment. For instance, if an experiment consists of passing some information to the subjects on the basis of which, the subjects make individual decisions, which in turn, leads to some outcome, then the stages would be as shown in Figure 7.1.

[1] Co-authored with Santanu Mitra, Associate Professor, Women's Polytechnic, Kolkata.

Figure 7.1 Stage Sequence for Experiments about Individual Decisions

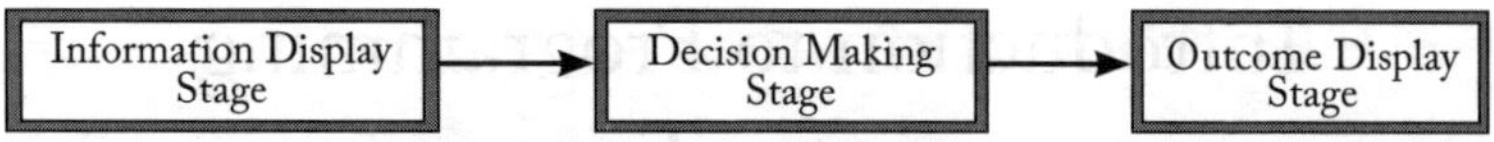

Source: Drawn by the author for this publication.

The control of the program runs sequentially from one stage to the next. This is a default option which is used to design simultaneous move experiments, where all the subjects have to make decisions at the same time. However, you can use the option of omitting stages and this option is used to design sequential move experiments like the UG experiment.

With this elementary background on z-Tree we shall see how simple simultaneous and sequential move experiments can be programmed using z-Tree. Since the purpose of this chapter is to introduce beginners to z-Tree, we shall leave out experiments requiring complicated programming. We should also clarify that we shall be discussing a very small part of the vast options and features available in z-Tree. Those who are interested in pursuing farther may refer to the z-Tree manual (freely downloadable in pdf format at www.ztree.uzh.ch/static/doc/manual.pdf; accessed 9 September 2015).

Programming

The opening screen of z-Tree is shown in Figure 7.2. The basic structure of any z-Tree program is a sequence of stages. Each stage consists of a program and 2 screens, the active screen and the waiting screen. The active screen is used to enter data or display output while the waiting screen is used to request subjects to wait till the experiment continues again. The initial stage of the sequence of stages is called the Background stage and appears as the first entry in the opening screen. To set the general parameters of the experiment you need to double click on Background and a dialog box will appear (as shown in Figure 7.2). Here there is an option to set the numbers of subjects, groups, paying periods, practice periods and exchange rate between

Figure 7.2 The Opening Screen in z-Tree

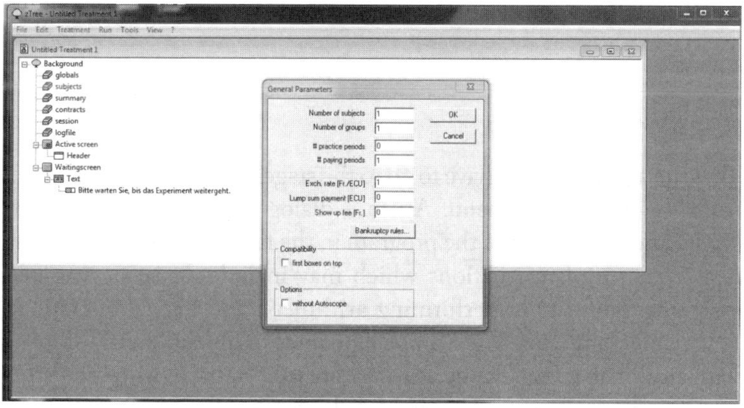

Source: Screenshot from z-Tree. Reproduced by permission of Urs Fischbacher.

actual money and experimental money/points and so on. There is also scope of defining the bankruptcy rule. In the Background stage is a list of tables: globals, subjects, summary and so on.

To insert a program in the Background stage you have to go to the entry just above active screen and select Treatment from the menu bar. From the dropdown menu you should select New Programs. A dialog box will appear and you can write a program or declare values of parameters in the field Program and click OK. The delimiter at the end of any program line is a semi-colon (;).

Adding a New Stage

New stages can be added under the Background stage by going to Background and then selecting New Stage from the Treatment menu. The general rule is to go to the stage under which the new stage is to be added and then select New Stage from the Treatment menu. As soon as New Stage is selected a dialog box appears on the screen where you can insert the name of the stage in the field Name. For the time being, the other options and the default values are not to be changed.

The new stage takes the name given to it and under it you will find the active and waiting screen. Each stage has a provision to write programs which will be executed at that stage.

Declaring Variables

To write a program you have to go to the stage and select New Program from the Treatment menu. Again a dialog box will appear on the screen and you can write the program in the field Program. A program is a sequence of instructions which may include declaring variable, assigning values to it, performing arithmetic and logical operations. A variable name in z-Tree can be alphabets or alphanumeric starting with an alphabet (e.g., *X*, *abc*, *X1*, *abc1* are valid variable names but *1abc* or *3A* are invalid names). No special characters other than underscore (_) are allowed in the variable names and they are case sensitive, that is, *X* and *x* are treated as two separate variables.

Figure 7.3 The Treatment Menu

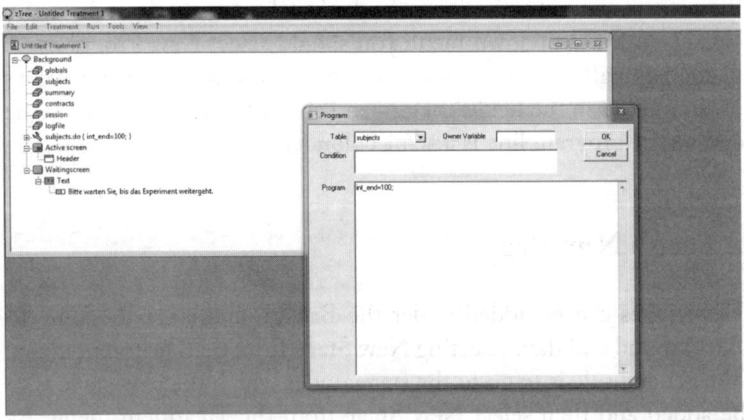

Source: Screenshot from z-Tree. Reproduced by permission of Urs Fischbacher.

The general syntax for writing mathematical expressions is:
Variable = mathematical expression;

This is an assignment statement, that is, the value of the mathematical expression on the right hand side will be assigned to the variable. For example, *X = 5;* implies that *X* is assigned the value 5, or *X = 5 + 3Y;* implies that for a given value of *Y*, the value of the right hand side expression will be assigned to *X*. However, in the latter example, the variable *Y* has to be declared earlier. All basic mathematical operations (addition, subtraction, multiplication and division) are allowed in writing mathematical expressions. There is a long list of pre-defined functions and table functions in z-Tree which can also be used in writing the mathematical expressions. These functions make programming very simple in z-Tree. A short list of commonly used functions is presented at the end of this chapter.

Input and Output

Two other important functions of any programming language are entering data/input and displaying information or outcomes (that is, outputs). In z-Tree both these functions are performed through the Active Screen. The data entry or display is done in pre-designed boxes. To select a box, first go to the Active Screen and then select New Boxes from the Treatment menu. A list of boxes will be displayed. For the time being select Standard Box from the list. A screen with options to set the box dimensions will open, but you should accept the default setting and click the OK button. In the z-Tree screen, just below the Active Screen, the standard box will appear as Standard. After creation of the box you need to enter the information for display or request subjects to enter values of decision variables or display results of the experiment. First, how should the information to the subjects be displayed? Say, to remind them about an important rule of the experimental design. You should go to Standard and select New Items from the Treatment menu. A dialog box called Item will appear on the screen. In the field Label you may write whatever instructions or reminders you want to give to the subjects and click OK. For instance, if you want to remind them of their initial endowment, which you have declared as Rs 100, write *int_end = 100;* in the program at the Background stage, then write **Your initial endowment is** in the field Label and **int_end** in the field Variable. In the next field, Layout you should write **1** (see Figure 7.4) and click OK. When the program is executed **'Your initial endowment is 100'** will be displayed in the standard box.

Now if you want the subjects to enter their decisions, say, their decision to contribute in a public goods experiment, then you should go to the last item under the Standard and select New Item from the Treatment menu. Again the dialog box with the heading Item will appear. In the field Label you may write: **Please enter your contribution**. In the field Variable you can write the variable name, say, **cont**, and in the layout you should again put **1**. The values entered by the subjects will be stored in the variable **cont**. The value 1 in the layout implies that only the integer part of the value entered will be shown. Now since this is an input given by the subjects, click on the check box called Input. Two more fields, Maximum and Minimum, will appear. In the Maximum field you should insert the maximum amount a subject can possibly contribute (100, in our example) and in the Minimum field you need to enter the least amount a subject can contribute (0, in our example). Next, click OK. When the program is executed this will be displayed as **'Please enter your contribution'**, just after the previous items in the Standard Box.

Figure 7.4 Using Labels

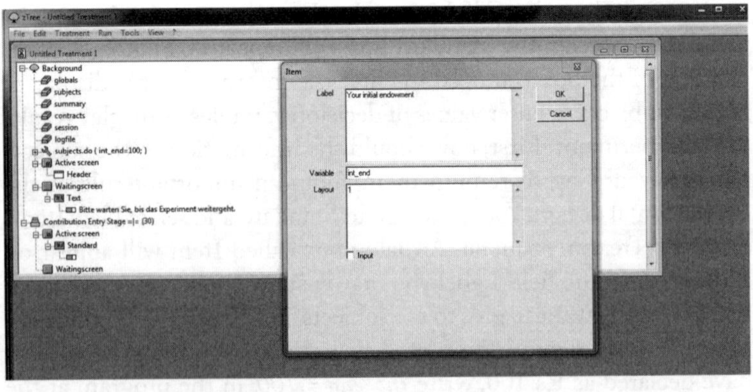

Source: Screenshot from z-Tree. Reproduced by permission of Urs Fischbacher.

Figure 7.5 The Computer Screen before a Subject

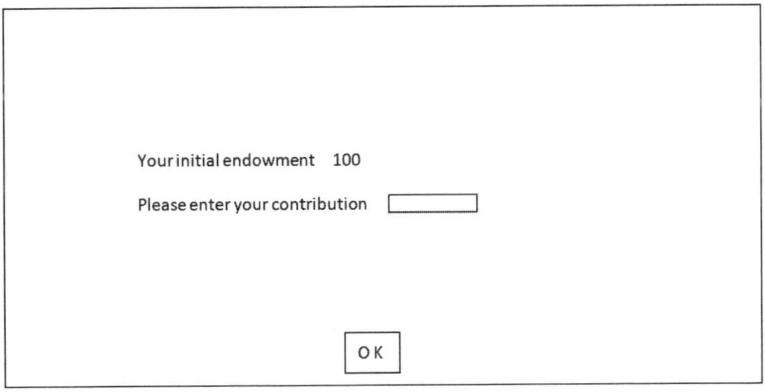

Source: Screenshot from z-Tree. Reproduced by permission of Urs Fischbacher.

When the experiment is run a screen like that in Figure 7.5 will come up on the computer screens of the subjects.

Programming a Public Goods Experiment

Suppose there are 10 subjects and each have been endowed with Rs 50. The experiment will run for 2 periods. At the opening screen of z-Tree double-click on the Background stage and in the dialog box titled General Parameters insert the number of subjects (10), group (1), and number of paying periods (2) and click OK. Next go to the table just above the Active screen and from the dropdown menu Treatment select New Program. Another dialog box titled Program will appear. In the program field of the dialog box write **endowment = 50;** and in the next line **eff_factor = 2;** (*m* in Chapter 3) and click OK. Now the background parameters have been set and the background variables **endowment** and **eff_factor** have been declared. We are now ready to add a new stage. In this stage the subjects will be informed about their endowments and they will then enter their contributions to the common fund. Let us call this stage the Contribution stage.

As discussed in the previous section, to add a new stage you have to go back to the Background stage and select New Stage from the Treatment menu. A dialog box titled Stage will appear and in the field Name you can write thc name of this stage, **Contribution Stage** and click OK. A new stage called Contribution will be created below the Background stage with two screens under it. Next you should go to the active screen of the new stage and select New Box and then Standard Box. In the dialog box titled Standard Box you should accept the default settings and click OK. You will see that just under the active screen the word Standard appears and is highlighted. Now it is time to write items in the Standard Box. While being at the Standard Box you should select New Item from the Treatment menu. Again a new dialog box named Item will appear. In the field Label you can write: **Your endowment in this period is**, and go to the field Variable and write the name of the variable under which the value of the endowment is stored, that is, **endowment**. Then you can insert the value **1** in the Layout field and click OK. This item will be shown under the standard box and from this item you can select another New Item. Again a dialog box appears and in the field Label, you can write: **Please enter your contribution**. In the field Variable you can declare the name of the variable under which the values of the contribution will be stored. Let the name be **contribution**. In the Layout you again put **1**. Since this is an input you have to click the check box. In the new fields that appear you should insert 0 in the Minimum field, 50 in the Maximum field and click OK. After this you should select New Button from the Treatment menu and click OK in the dialog box named Button.

Next you have to create another stage in which the profit (earnings) of the subjects will be calculated and the same will be displayed on the screens of the subject computers. Since this stage will be created under the Contribution stage, you have to go to Contribution stage and from Treatment menu you should select New Stage. In the field Name you can write the name of the stage, **Profit Calculation Stage** and click OK. Next you should select New Program from Treatment menu. In the dialog box you can write the following program and then click OK.

After profit of each subject is calculated it is time to display the result. You can now go to the Active Screen of the **Profit Calculation Stage** and select New Box and then Standard Box from the Treatment

Box 7.1 The Public Goods Game

SumCon = sum (contribution);

n = 10;

*Profit = endowment – contribution + eff_factor * (SumCon)/n;*

menu. In the Standard Box you now need to insert the items to be displayed. As before, you should select New Item from the Treatment menu and in the Label field of the dialog box you write: **Your contribution in this period was**, in the field Variable you can write **contribution**, in the field *Layout* you should put **1** and click OK. To display the profit, you must select New Item once more. In the field Label you can write: **Your Profit in this period is**, in the field Variable you write **Profit**, in the field Layout you enter **1** and click OK. Finally you must insert another button to end the stage. The public goods program should look like Figure 7.6. At this point you should take a break and begin programming a public goods experiment applying what you have learnt till now up to this section.

Figure 7.6 Program for the Public Goods Game

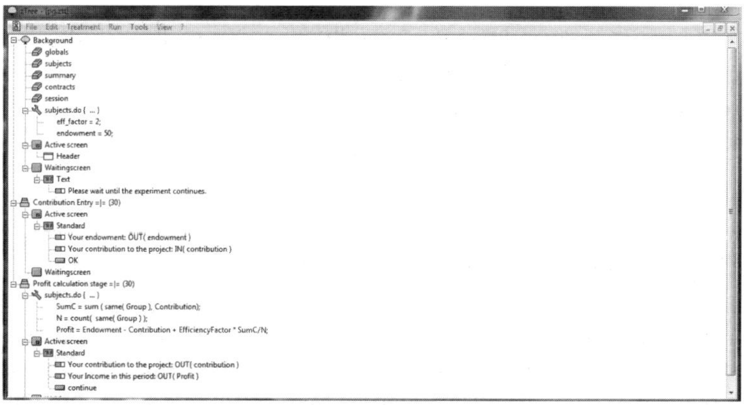

Source: Screenshot from z-Tree. Reproduced by permission of Urs Fischbacher.

Conditional Statements and Sequential Experiments

The public goods experiment was a normal form experiment where all the subjects participated in the decision-making process simultaneously. In this section, programming of sequential move experiments like the UG is discussed. To do this we shall have to first learn the general syntax of conditional statement. The general syntax is:

if(c, x, y);

This is read as *if condition c holds, then event x, else event y.* With this simple statement you can handle almost all types of conditional situations. Suppose there are 3 conditions and 3 events as shown in Table 7.1 below. That is, if condition A holds, then event X; if condition B, then Y; if condition C, then Z. Here a nested conditional statement is written as *if(A, X, if(B, Y, Z));*

Table 7.1 Conditional Statement

Conditions	Events
A	X
B	Y
C	Z

Here, it is assumed that the 3 conditions are mutually exclusive and exhaustive. However, if there are other conditions, but these 3 only are relevant, then you could have written the statement as:

if(A, X, if(B, Y, if(C, Z, 0)));

Programming an Ultimatum Game

With what you have learnt in the previous section about conditional statements, you should now be ready to program the UG. This is a sequential game where a Proposer, say, Type 1, is to distribute an endowment between herself and another subject, called the Responder, say, Type 2. The Responder, in the next stage, can accept or reject the offer made by the Proposer. If she accepts the offer, then she gets the amount offered while the proposer gets (*endowment – offer*) as her profit. But if the offer is rejected then both get nothing.

Suppose the game is played between two subjects. So you should first go to the Background stage and double click on it. In the dialog box that appears you can enter **2** in the field labelled Number of Subjects, **1** in the field labelled Number of Groups and **1** in the field labelled number of paying periods and click OK. While being at the Background stage select Parameter Table from the dropdown menu Treatment. A table is displayed on the screen with row-heading 1 and column-headings S1 and S2. You should double click on the cell just below column heading S1 (subject 1) and a dialog box called Specific Parameter opens. In the field labelled Group you must enter **1**, as there is only one group and both subjects belong to the same group. In the next field Name you may enter **P** (to denote proposer) and in the Program field you should write **Type = 1;** and click OK. Next you double click on the cell just below column heading S2 (subject 2) and make the following entries **1, R** (to denote responder) and **Type = 2;** in the respective fields.

Now to write the background program you must go to the table just above Active Screen and select New Program from the Treatment menu. In the Program field you should write **endowment = 100;** and in the next line **Type = 0;** and click OK. Next you have to create a new stage (say, Offer Stage) where the Proposer (Type = 1) will be informed about her endowment and asked to make an offer to the Responder (Type = 2). Note that the Responder will not participate at this stage. This is done by writing the command **Participate = if (Type == 1, 1, 0);** in the Program field of the new stage. Then you have to go to the active screen and select the Standard Box.

While being on the standard box, you must select New Item and write **Your endowment is** in the Label field, **endowment** in the Variable field and **1** in the Layout field. To write the next item you must select another New Item and write **How much would You Like to Offer R** in the Label field, **offer** in the Variable field, **1** in the Layout field. Since this is an input, you click the check box named Input and set the Minimum and Maximum as **0** and **endowment**, respectively. You can end this stage by selecting New Button from the Treatment menu.

Figure 7.7 The Ultimatum Game Parameters

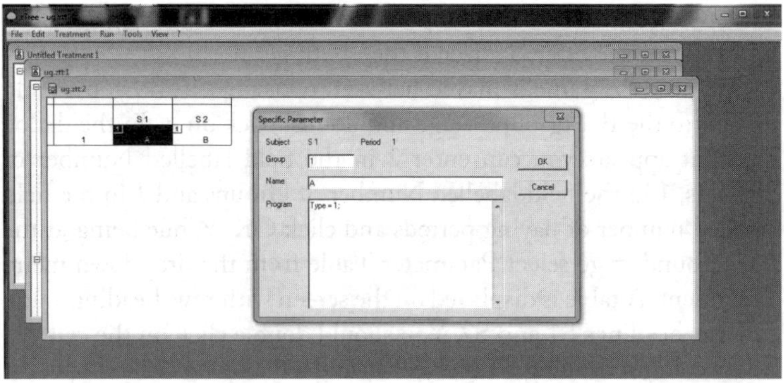

Source: Screenshot from z-Tree. Reproduced by permission of Urs Fischbacher.

Now you need to create another stage for the Responder to accept or reject the offer. You should go to the Offer Stage and create a new stage called Acceptance Stage. Then you must select New Program and write the following program in the Program field and click OK.

Participate = if (Type == 2, 1, 0);

offer = find (same (Group) & Type == 1, offer);

The last line will find the offer made by Type=1 of each group and store it in the variable, Offer. For this particular program, the use of the command same (Group) may be redundant as there is only one group. Next you need to go to active screen and select Standard Box and write the first item as **You have been offered**, in the Label field, **offer**, in the Variable field and **1**, in the Layout field. This item will display the offer made by the Proposer to the Responder. In the second item the Responder will choose to accept or reject the offer. Here you may write: **Do you Accept or Reject the offer?** in the Label field, **accept** in the Variable field. In the Layout field you have to write the following to generate radio switches for acceptance and rejection.

! radio:

1= "accept";

0= "reject" ;

Then you click the check box for Inputs and put 0 and 1 in the Minimum and Maximum fields, respectively. You must end this stage by inserting an OK button.

Now it is time to show the subjects their respective profit in this period. First you arrange to display the Proposer's profit. You need to create a new stage called Proposer's Profit. After creating this stage, you must select New Program from the Treatment menu and write **Participate = if (Type == 1, 1, 0);** in the Program field and click OK. Again you must select New Program and write the following program in the Program field to calculate profit for each subject.

accept = find (same (Group) & Type == 2, accept);
share = if (Type == 1, endowment – offer, offer);
Profit = if (accept == 1, share, 0);

Next you must go to the Active Screen of this stage and create a Standard Box. In this Standard Box you need to select New Item and in the Label field and write: **Your profit in this period is**, in the Variable field **Profit**, and in the Layout field **1.** To end the stage you must include an OK button. The final stage is to display the profit of the Responder. So another new stage is created after the Proposer's Profit Stage and named Responder's Profit. Selecting New Program from the Treatment menu you have to write **Participate = if (Type == 2, 1, 0);** in the Program field. You must now go to the Active Screen and create a Standard Box. You will select New Item from the Treatment menu and write: **Your profit in this period is** in the Label field, **Profit** in the Variable field and **1** in the Layout field. To end the stage you must again include an OK button from the Treatment menu.

Executing a Programme

To execute a programme you must first load the programme in the experimenter's PC and then select *Run* from the menu bar on the top of the opening screen. Next you need to select *Clients' Table* from the drop down menu. A screen like Figure 7.8 appears.

Now the clients are logged in and the clients' table will display the list of client PCs connected. When all the clients are logged in, the programme is reloaded from the File menu and once more you must

Figure 7.8 Connecting Clients to Server

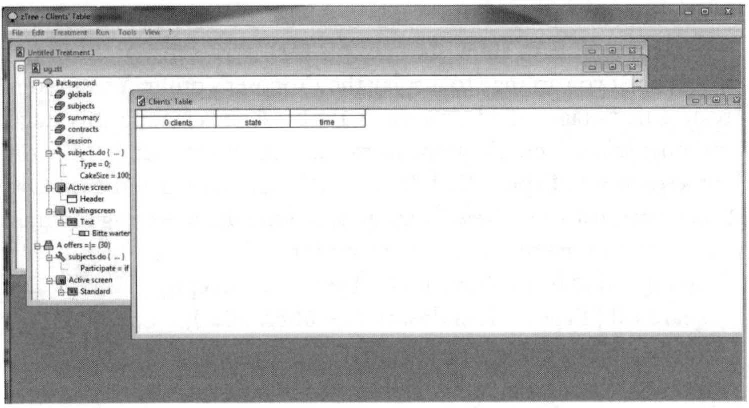

Source: Screenshot from z-Tree. Reproduced by permission of Urs Fischbacher.

go to Run menu and select Start Treatment. Remember, if you have 10 subjects numbered 1 to 10 in an experiment, you must turn on the z-Leaf in the client machines in that numbered sequence 1 to 10 for z-Tree to recognise the first z-Leaf as subject 1, the second z-Leaf as subject 2 and so on.

Weblinks and Programming without z-Tree

Here we present some weblinks (all accessed in September 2015) related to z-Tree which the readers may refer to for better understanding and more complex programming in z-Tree.

1	https://www.uzh.ch/iew/ztree/ssl-dir/wiki/index.php?n=Main.SampleTreatments	Installation, programming language, tips and tricks, sample treatments, question-answers, tutorials and so on.
2	http://www.iew.uzh.ch/ztree/papers.php	Published and working papers using z-Tree.
3	http://www.iew.uzh.ch/ztree/faq/programming.php	Tips and tricks in z-Tree programming

Even though we have devoted this chapter to programming experiments in z-Tree, there is also the option of designing experiments without the knowledge of computer programming. This can be done either by using lab facilities with pre-designed experiments or downloading pre-designed applications. Some of the weblinks are listed below.

1	http://veconlab.econ.virginia.edu/admin.htm	Provides a selection menu of pre-designed experiments on auction, bargaining, decisions, finance, games, information, markets, micro principles
2	http://www.econport.org/econport/request?page=web_experiments	Provides links to experiment application available on EconPort
3	http://www.comlabgames.com/	Comlab helps to design experiments without programming
4	https://www.moblab.com/	Extremely useful for teaching abstract concepts through predesigned experiments which can be customised according to the need of the class

Some Useful Function Commands

1. A short list of commonly used pre-defined functions
   abs(x) returns absolute value of *x*;
   cos(x) returns cosine value of *x*;
   atan(x) returns arc tangent of *x*;
   max(x,y) returns maximum of *x* and *y*;
   min(x,y) returns minimum of *x* and *y*;
   random( ) returns uniformly distributed random number between 0 and 1;
   mod(x,y) returns remainder after *x* is divided by *y*;
   power(x,y) returns value of *x* to the power *y*;

2. A short list of commonly used table functions

Table functions are executed along a particular field of a table for all records. Suppose *x* represents contributions made in a public goods game by different subjects, then

average(x) returns the average value of all *x*;
sum(x) returns the summation of all *x*;
maximum(x) returns the maximum value of all *x*;
minimum(x) returns the minimum value of all *x*;
median(x) returns the median value of all *x*;
product(x) returns the product of all *x*;
find(a,x) returns the value of *x* for condition *a*, e.g. find (Subject == 1, contribution).

Bibiliography

CHAPTER 1

Allais, Maurice. 1953. 'Le Comportement de L'homme Rationnel Devant le Risque: Critique des Postulatset Axiomes de L'ecoleAmericane'. *Econometrica* 21:503–46.

Bentham, J. 1781. *An Introduction to the Principles of Moral and Legislation*. Kitchener: Batoche Books.

Chamberlin, Edward H. 1948. 'An Experimental Imperfect Market'. *Journal of Political Economy* 56 (2): 95–108.

Davidson, Donald and Jacob Marschak. 1959. 'Experimental Tests of a Stochastic Decision Theory' in *Measurement: Definitions and Theories*, edited by C. West Churchman and Philburn Ratoosh, 233–69. New York: Wiley.

Flood, Merrill M. 1952. 'Some Experimental Games', research memorandum RM-789, RAND Corporation. Available at http://www.rand.org/content/dam/rand/pubs/research_memoranda/2008/RM789-1.pdf accessed September 2015.

———. 1958. 'Some Experimental Games', *Management Science* 5 (1): 5–26.

Gneezy, U., K. L. Leonard and J. A. List. 2009. 'Gender Differences in Competition: Evidence from a Matrilineal and a Patriarchal Society'. *Econometrica* 77 (5): 1637–64.

Guala, F. 2005. *The Methodology of Experimental Economics*. Cambridge: Cambridge University Press.

Harrison, G. and J. List. 2004. 'Field Experiments'. *Journal of Economic Literature* 42 (4): 1009–55.

Henrich, Joseph, Steven J. Heine and Ara Norenzayan. 2009. 'The Weirdest People in the World?'. *Behavioral and Brain Sciences* 33:61–135.

Kagel, J. H. and Alvin Roth. 1998. *The Handbook of Experimental Economics*. Princeton: Princeton University Press.

Kahneman, Daniel and Amos Tvresky. 1979. 'An Analysis of Decision Under Risk', *Econometrica* 47 (2): 263–91.

Mabbett, I. W. 1964. 'The Date of the Arthasastra'. *Journal of the American Oriental Society* 84 (2): 162–69.

Marshall, A. 1890. *Principles of Economics*. London: Macmillan.

Marx, K. 1867. *Das Kaapital* 1. Berlin: Verlag

Mill, J. S. 1848. *Principles of Political Economy*. London: John Parker.

Mosteller, F. and P. Nogee. 1951. 'An Experimental Measurement of Utility'. *Journal of Political Economy* 5:371–404.

Pareto, Vilfredo. 1896–97. *Cours d' Économie Politique*, vols 1 and 2. Lausanne: F. Rouge.

Popper, Karl. 1946. 'Why are the Calculuses of Logic and Arithmetic Applicable to Reality?'. *Aristotelian Society, Supplementary* 20:40–60.

Preston, M. G. and P. Baratta. 1948. 'An Experimental Study of the Auction Value of an Uncertain Outcome'. *American Journal of Psychology* 61:183–93.

Ricardo, D. 1817. *The Principles of Political Economy and Taxation*. London: John Murray.

Roth, A. E. 1995. 'Bargaining Experiments' in *Handbook of Experimental Economics*, J. E. Kagel and A. E. Roth (eds.), 253–348. Princeton: Princeton University Press.

Roth, A. E., V. Prasnikar, M. Okuno-Fujiwara and S. Zamir. 1991. 'Bargaining and Market Behavior in Jerusalem, Ljubljana, Pittsburgh, and Tokyo: An Experimental Study'. *American Economic Review* 81 (5): 1068–95.

Rousseas, Stephen W. and Albert G. Hart. 1951. 'Experimental Verification of a Composite Indifference Map'. *Journal of Political Economy* 59:288–318.

Samuelson, Paul A. and William D. Nordhaus. 1985. *Economics*. New York: McGraw-Hill.

Schumpeter, Joseph A. 1954. *History of Economic Analysis*. Oxford: Oxford University Press.

Smith, Adam. 1981 [1776]. *An Inquiry into the Nature and Causes of the Wealth of Nations*, edited by R. H. Campbell and A. S. Skinner. London: Liberty Classics.

Thurstone, L. L. 1931. 'The Indifference Function'. *Journal of Social Psychology* 2:139–67.

Thweatt, W. O. 2000. 'Early Formulation of Say's Law' in *John-Baptiste Say: Critical Assessments of Leading Economists* 5, edited by J. C. Wood and Steven Kates, 78–93. London: Routledge.

von Neumann, John and Oskar Morgenstern. 1944. *Theory of Games and Economic Behavior*. Princeton: Princeton University Press.

Wallis, W. Allen and Milton Friedman. 1942. 'The Empirical Derivation of Indifference Functions' in *Studies in Mathematical Economics and Econometrics in Memory of Henry Schultz*, edited by O. Lange, F. McIntyre and T. O. Yntema, 3–109. Chicago: University of Chicago Press.

Walras, Leon. 1874. *Elements of Pure Economics*. London and New York: Routledge.

Further Reading

Hoffman, E., Kevin McCabe and Vernon Smith. 1996. 'On Expectations and Monetary Stakes in Ultimatum Games'. *International Journal of Game Theory* 25:289–301.

Kagel, John H. and Alvin E. Roth. 1995. *The Handbook of Experimental Economics*. Princeton, N.J.: Princeton University Press.

CHAPTER 2

Andreoni, James. 1990. 'Impure Altruism and Donations to Public Goods: A Theory of Warm-Glow Giving?' *The Economic Journal* 100 (401): 464–77.

Berg, Joyce, John Dickhaut and Kevin McCabe. 1995. 'Trust, Reciprocity, and Social History'. *Games and Economic Behavior* 10:122–42.

Blount, S. 1995. 'When Social Outcomes aren't Fair: The Effect of Causal Attributions on Preferences'. *Organizational Behavior and Human Decision Process* 63:131–44.

Chaudhuri, A. 2009. *Experiments in Economics: Playing Fair with Money*. Oxford: Routledge.

Coase, R. H. 1960. 'The Problem of Social Cost'. *The Journal of Law and Economics* 3:1–44.

Cooper, Russell W., Douglas V. DeJong, Robert Forsythe and Thomas W. Ross. 1991. 'Cooperation without Reputation'. Working paper, University of Iowa, Iowa City.

Davis, Douglas D. and Charles A. Holt. 1993. *Experimental Economics*. Princeton: Princetton University Press.

Falk, A., E. Fehr and U. Fischbacher. 2003. 'On the Nature of Fair Behavior'. *Economic Inquiry* 41 (1): 20–26.

Fehr, Ernst and Klaus M. Schmidt. 2006. 'The Economics of Fairness, Reciprocity and Altruism: Experimental Evidence and New Theories' in *Handbook of the Economics of Giving, Altruism and Reciprocity: Foundations*, vol. 1, edited by Serge-Christophe Kolm and Jean Mercier Ythier, 615–91. Amsterdam: North Holland (Elsevier).

Forsythe, R., J. L. Horowitz, N. E. Savin and M. Sefton. 1994. 'Fairness in Simple Bargaining Experiments'. *Games and Economic Behavior* 6 (3): 347–69.

Giddens, Anthony. 1990. *The Consequences of Modernity*. Stanford: Stanford University Press.

Guth, Werner, Rolf Schmittberger and Bernd Schwarze. 1982. 'An Experimental Analysis of Ultimatum Bargaining'. *Journal of Economic Behavior and Organization* 3 (4): 367–88.

Hoffmann, E. and M. L. Spitzer. 1982. 'The Coase Theorem: Some Experimental Test'. *Journal of Law and Economics* 25:73–98.

———. 1985. 'Entitlements, Rights and Fairness: An Experimental Examination of Subjects' Concepts of Distributive Justice'. *Journal of Legal Studies* 14:259–97.

Hoffman, E., K. A. McCabe and V. L. Smith. 1996a. 'On Expectations and the Monetary Stakes in Ultimatum Games'. *International Journal of Game Theory* 255 (3): 289–301.

———. 1996b. 'Social Distance and Other-Regarding Behavior in Dictator Games'. *American Economic Review* 86 (3): 653–60.

Kolm, Serge-Christophe and Jean Mercier Ythier, eds. 2006. *Handbook of the Economics of Giving, Altruism and Reciprocity: Foundations*, vol. 1. Amsterdam: North Holland (Elsevier).

McKelvey, R. and T. Palfrey. 1991. 'An Experimental Study of the Centipede Game'. *Econometrica* 61:547–73.

Nash, J. F. 1950. 'Equilibrium Points in N Person Games'. *Proceedings of the National Academy of Sciences* 36:48–49.

Pareto, Vilfredo. 1896. *Cours d' Économie Politique* 2. Lausanne: F. Rouge.

Pindyck, Robert and Daniel Rubinfeld. 2013, 'Externalities and Public Goods' in *Microeconomics*, eighth edition, 621–54. New Jersey: Prentice-Hall.

Rabin, Matthew. 1993. 'Incorporating Fairness into Game Theory and Economics'. *American Economic Review* 83:1281–302.

Rosenthal, Robert W. 1982. 'Games of Perfect Information, Predatory Pricing and the Chain Store Paradox'. *Journal of Economic Theory* 25 (1): 92–100.

Selten, R. 1965. 'Spieltheoretische Behandlung eines Oligopolmodells mit Nachfragentragheit'. *Zeitschrift fur die gesamte Staatswissenschaft* 12:201–324.

Smith, Adam. 1759. *The Theory of Moral Sentiments*. First edition. London: A. Millar.

———. 1981 [1776]. *An Inquiry into the Nature and Causes of the Wealth of Nations*, edited by R. H. Campbell and A. S. Skinner, London: Liberty Classics.

Times News Network (*TNN*). 2013. '20 Kumbh pilgrims killed in Allahabad Junction stampede', *The Times of India*, 11 February, available at www.timesofindia.indiatimes.com/india/20-Kumbh-pilgrims-killed-in-Allahabad-Junction-stampede/articleshow/18438964.cms (accessed 2 May 2013).

Walras, Leon. 2013 [1874]. *Elements of Pure Economics*. London and New York: Routledge.

Zak, Paul J. and Stephen Knack. 2001. 'Trust and Growth'. *The Economic Journal* 111 (470): 295–321.

Further Reading

Becker, T. C., Michael Carter and Jörg Naeve. 2005. 'Experts playing the Traveler's Dilemma'. Diskussionspapiere aus dem institute fur volkswirtschaftslehre der Universitat Hohenheim 252/2005, Department of Economics, University of Hohenheim, Germany.

Goeree, Jacob K. and Charles A. Holt. 2000. 'Ten Little Treasures of Game Theory and Ten Intuitive Contradictions'. Virginia Economics Online Papers 333, University of Virginia, Department of Economics.

Blanco, Mariana, Dirk Engelmann, Alexander Koch and Hans-Theo Normann. 2010. 'Belief Elicitation in Experiments: Is there a Hedging Problem?'. *Experimental Economics* 13 (4): 412–38.

Nyarko, Yaw and Andrew Schotter. 2002. 'An Experimental Study of Belief Learning Using Elicited Beliefs'. *Econometrica* 70 (3): 971–1005.

CHAPTER 3

Bochet, O., T. Page and L. Putterman. 2006. 'Communication and Punishment in Voluntary Contribution Experiments'. *Journal of Economic Behavior and Organization* 60 (1): 11–26.

Bohm, P. 1972. 'Estimating the Demand for Public Goods: An Experiment'. *European Economic Review* 3:111–30.

Chakravarty, S., C. Sebi, E. Somanathan and E. Theophilus. 2013. 'The Demographics of Cooperation: Evidence from a Field Experiment in the Gori-Ganga Basin'. *Journal of Economics and Management* 9 (2): 231–69.

Davis, Douglas D. and Charles A. Holt. 1993. *Experimental Economics*. Princeton: Princeton University Press.

Dawes, Robyn M., J. McTavish and H. Shaklee. 1977. 'Behavior, Communication, and Assumptions about other People's Behavior in a Commons Dilemma Situation'. *Journal of Personality and Social Psychology* 35 (1): 1–11.

Fehr, Ernst and Simon Gaechter. 2000. 'Cooperation and Punishment in Public Goods Experiments'. *American Economic Review* 90 (4): 980–94.

———. 2002. 'Altruistic Punishment in Humans'. *Nature* 415:137–40.

Fiorina, Morris P. and Charles R. Plott. 1978. 'Committee Decisions under Majority Rule: An Experimental Study'. *American Political Science Review* 72:575–98.

Ghate, R., S. Ghate and E. Ostrom. 2013. 'Can Communities Plan, Grow and Sustainably Harvest from Forests'. *Economic and Political Weekly* 48 (8): 59–67.

Isaac, R. M., K. McCue and C. Plott. 1985. 'Public Goods Provision in an Experimental Environment'. *Journal of Economics* 26:1–74.

Isaac, R. M. and J. M. Walker. 1988. 'Group Size Effects in Public Goods Provision: The Voluntary Contributions Mechanism'. *Quarterly Journal of Economics* 103:179–200.

Isaac, R. M., J. M. Walker and S. H. Thomas. 1984. 'Divergent Evidence on Free Riding: An Experimental Examination of Possible Explanations'. *Public Choice* 43:2–34.

Kim, O. and J. M. Walker. 1984. 'The Free Rider Problem: Experimental-Evidence'. *Public Choice* 43:113–49.

Ledyard, J. 1995. 'Public Goods: A Survey of Experimental Research' in *The Handbook of Experimental Economics*, edited by J. H. Kagel and A. E. Roth, 111–94. Princeton: Princeton University Press.

Lindahl, E. 1958 [1919]. 'Just Taxation: A Positive Solution', translated from the German by E. Henderson, in *Classics in the Theory of Public Finance*, edited by R. Musgrave and A. Peacock, 168–77. London: Macmillan.

Marwell, Gerald and Ruth E. Ames. 1979. 'Experiments on the Provision of Public Goods: I. Resources, Interest, Group Size, and the Free-Rider Problem'. *American Journal of Sociology* 84:1335–60.

Ostrom, Elinor, James Walker and Roy Gardner. 1992. 'Covenants With and Without a Sword: Self-Governance is Possible'. *American Political Science Review* 86 (2): 404–17.

Palfrey, T., ed. 1991. *Contemporary Laboratory Research in Political Economy*. Ann Arbor: University of Michigan Press.

Pigou, A. C. 1931. *The Theory of Welfare*. London: Macmillan.

Samuelson, P. A. 1954. 'The Pure Theory of Public Expenditure'. *The Review of Economics and Statistics* 36 (4): 387–89.

Solnick, S. 2001. 'Gender Differences in the Ultimatum Game'. *Economic Inquiry* 39 (2): 189–200.

Yamagishi, Toshio. 1986. 'The Provision of a Sanctioning System as a Public Good'. *Journal of Personality and Social Psychology* 51 (1): 110–16.

———. 1988. 'Seriousness of Social Dilemmas and the Provision of a Sanctioning System'. *Social Psychology Quarterly* 51 (1): 32–42.

Further Reading

Erev, Ido and Alvin E. Roth. 1998. 'Predicting How People Play Games: Reinforcement Learning in Experimental Games with Unique, Mixed Strategy Equlibria'. *American Economic Review* 88 (4): 848–81.

Palfrey, Thomas R. and Jeffrey E. Prisbrey. 1997. 'Anamalous Behavior in Public Goods Experiments: How Much and Why?'. *American Economic Review* 87 (5): 829–46.

Bowles, Samuel and Herbert Gintis. 1998. 'The Evolution of Strong Reciprocity'. *Research in Economics* 98-08-073e, Santa Fe Institute

———. 2000. 'The Evolution of Strong Reciprocity'. UMASS Amherst Economics Working Papers 2000–05, Department of Economics, University of Massachusetts Amherst.

Sethi, Rajiv and E. Somanathan. 1996. 'The Evolution of Social Norms in Common Property Resource Use'. *American Economic Review* 86 (4): 766–88.

von Neumann, J. and O. Morgenstern. 1947. *Theory of Games and Economic Behavior*, second edition. Princeton: Princeton University Press.

CHAPTER 4

Allais, M. 1953. 'Le Comportement de l'Homme Rationnel devant le Risque: Critique des Postulats et Axiomesde l'Ecole Americaine'. *Econometrica* 21:503–46.

Ang, James S. and Thomas Schwarz. 1985. 'Risk Aversion and Information Structure: An Experimental Study of Price Volatility in the Security Markets'. *Journal of Finance* 40:824–44.

Battalio, Raymond C., John H. Kagel and Komain Jiranyakul. 1990. 'Testing Between Alternative Models of Choice Under Uncertainty: Some Initial Results'. *Journal of Risk and Uncertainty* 3:25–50.

Camerer, C. F. and Teck-Hua Ho. 1990. 'Isolation Effects in Reduction of Compound Lotteries' draft submitted to *Decision Sciences*, University of Pennsylvania.

Chew, Soo Hong and William Waller. 1986. 'Empirical Test of Weighted Utility Theory'. *Journal of Mathematical Psychology* 30:55–72.

Conlisk, J. 1989. 'Three Variants on the Allais Example'. *American Economic Review* 79 (3): 392–407.

Cox, J. C. and S. Epstein. 1989. 'Preference Reversals without the Independence Axiom'. *American Economic Review* 79 (3): 408–26.

Davis, Douglas D. and Charles A. Holt. 1993. *Experimental Economics*. Princeton: Princeton University Press.

Kahneman, Daniel and Amos Tversky. 1979. 'Prospect Theory: An Analysis of Decision Under Risk'. *Econometrica* 47:263–91.

Luce, R. D. and H. Raiffa. 1957. *Games and Decisions: Introduction and Critical Survey*. New York: Wiley.

Machina, Mark J. 1982. 'Expected Utility: Analysis Without the Independence Axiom'. *Econometrica* 50:277–323.

Marschak, J. 1950. 'Rational Behavior, Uncertain Prospects and Measurable Utility'. *Econometrica* 18:111–41.

Rawls, John. 1971. *A Theory of Justice*. Harvard: Harvard University Press.

Starmer, C. and R. Sugden. 1991. 'Does the Random-Lottery Incentive System Elicit True References? An Experimental Investigation'. *American Economic Review* 81 (4): 971–78.

von Neumann, J. and O. Morgenstern. 1947. *Theory of Games and Economic Behavior*, second edition. Princeton: Princeton University Press.

Further Reading

Cohen, M. and J. Y. Jaffray. 1981. 'Experimental Results on Decision Making Under Uncertainty'. *Methods of Operations Research Proceedings* 44:275–89.

Kunreuther, H. 1976. 'Limited Knowledge and Insurance Protection'. *Public Policy* 24 (2): 227–61.

Slovi, P. 1969. 'Differential Effects of Real v/s Hypothetical Pay-offs on Choices Among Gambles'. *Journal of Experimental Psychology* 79:434–37.

Yaari, M. E. 1965. 'Convexity in the Theory of Choice under Risk'. *Quarterly Journal of Economics* 78:278–90.

CHAPTER 5

Ahmed, Ali M. 2009. 'Are Religious People more Pro-social?: A Quasi-experimental Study with Madrasah Pupils in a Rural Community in India'. *Journal for the Scientific Study of Religion* 48 (2): 368–74.

Ahmed, Ali M. and O. Salas. 2009. 'Is the Hand of God Involved in Human Cooperation?'. *International Journal of Social Economics* 36:70–80.

Akerlof, G. A. and R. E. Kranton. 2000. 'Economics and Identity'. *Quarterly Journal of Economics* 105 (3): 715–53.

Anderson, L. and J. Mellor. 2009. 'Are Risk Preferences Stable? Comparing an Experimental Measure with a Validated Survey-based Measure'. *Journal of Risk and Uncertainty* 39 (2): 137–60.

Anderson, L., J. Mellor, and J. Milyo. 2010. 'Did the Devil Make Them Do It? The Effects of Religion in Public Goods and Trust Games'. *Kyklos* 63 (2): 163–75.

Andreoni, James. 1990. 'Impure Altruism and Donations to Public Goods: A Theory of Warm-Glow Giving?'. *Economic Journal* 100 (401): 464–77.

Andreoni, James and L. Vesterlund. 2001. 'Which is the Fair Sex? Gender Differences in Altruism'. *Quarterly Journal of Economics* 116:293–312.

Arch, Elizabeth C. 1993. 'Risk-taking: A Motivational Basis for Sex Differences'. *Psychological Reports* 73:3–11.

Atkinson, Stanley M., Samantha Boyce Baird and Melissa B. Frye. 2003. 'Do Female Mutual Fund Managers Manage Differently?' *Journal of Financial Research* 26 (1): 1–18.

Basu, S., Santanu Mitra and Gautam Gupta. 2013. 'Wealth Differences in a Centipede Game: Backward Induction in an Experimental Economics Framework'. *International Journal of Humanities and Social Sciences* 3 (10): 127–31.

Benjamin, D., J. Choi and G. Fisher. 2010. 'Religious Identity and Economic Behavior'. NBER working paper no. 15925.

Blanchflower, David G. and Andrew J. Oswald. 2004. 'Well-being Over Time in Britain and the USA'. *Journal of Public Economics* 88 (7–8): 1359–86.

Boarini, Romina, Jean-François Laslier and Stéphane Robin. 2009. 'Interpersonal Comparisons of Utility in Bargaining: Evidence from a Transcontinental Ultimatum Game'. *Theory and Decision* 67 (4): 341–73.

Brooks, Benjamin A., Karla Hoff and Priyanka Pandey. 2015. 'Culture and the Efficiency of Coordination: Experiments with High- and Low-Caste Men in Rural India', working paper. Available at http://www.benjaminbrooks.net/downloads/bhp_culturecoord.pdf (accessed 9 September 2015).

Buchan, N. and R. Croson. 1999. 'Gender and Culture: International Experimental Evidence from Trust Games'. *American Economic Review* 89 (2): 386–91.

Buchan, Nancy R., Rachel T. A. Croson and Sara S. Solnick. 2008. 'Trust and Gender: An Examination of Behavior, Biases, and Beliefs in the Investment Game'. *Journal of Economic Behavior and Organization* 68 (3): 466–76.

Carlsson F., G. Gupta and O. Johansson-Stenman. 2003. 'Choosing from Behind a Veil of Ignorance in India'. *Applied Economics Letters* 10:825–27.

———. 2009. 'Keeping up with the Vaishyas: Caste and Relative Standing'. *Oxford Economic Papers* 61:52–73.

Chattopadhyay, Raghabendra and Esther Duflo. 2004. 'Women as Policy Makers: Evidence from a Randomised Policy Experiment in India'. *Econometrica* 72 (5): 1409–43.

Clark, Andrew E. and Andrew J. Oswald. 1996. 'Satisfaction and Comparison Income'. *Journal of Public Economics* 61 (3): 359–81.

Easterline, R. 1995. 'Will Raising the Incomes of All Increase the Happiness of All?'. *Journal of Economic Behavior and Organization* 27:35–47.

Eckel, Catherine C. and Philip J. Grossman. 1998. 'Are Women Less Selfish than Men: Evidence from Dictator Experiments'. *Economic Journal* 108:726–35.

———. 2001. 'Chivalry and Solidarity in Ultimatum Games'. *Economic Inquiry* 39:171–88.

———. 2002. 'Sex Differences and Statistical Stereotyping in Attitudes toward Financial Risk'.. *Evolution and Human Behavior* 23:281–95.

———. 2004. 'Giving to Secular Causes by the Religious and Nonreligious: An Experimental Test of Responsiveness of Giving to Subsidies'. *Non Profit and Voluntary Sector Quarterly* 33 (2): 271–89.

———. 2008. 'Differences in Economic Decisions of Men and Women: Experimental Evidence' in *Handbook of Experimental Economics Results*, vol. 1, edited by Charles R. Plott and Vernon L. Smith, 509–19. New York: Elsevier Press.

Fehr, E. and S. Gaechter. 2002. 'Altruistic Punishment in Humans'. *Nature* 415:137–40.

Greif, Avner. 1989. 'Reputation and Coalitions in Medieval Trade: Evidence on the Maghribi Traders'. *The Journal of Economic History* 49 (4): 857–82.

Gupta, G., M. Mahmud, P. Maitra, S. Mitra and A. Neelim. 2013. 'Religion, Minority Status and Trust: Evidence from a Field Experiment', technical report, Monash University, Department of Economics. Draft version available at http://www.buseco.monash.edu.au/eco/research/papers/2013/2813religionguptamaitra.pdf (accessed September 2015)

Harrison, Glenn W. and John A. List. 2004. 'Field Experiments'. *Journal of Economic Literature* 42 (4): 1009–55.

Henrich, J., Robert Boyd, Samuel Bowles, Colin Camerer, Ernst Fehr and Herbert Gintis. 2004. *Foundations of Human Society: Economic Experiments and Ethnographic Evidence from Fifteen Small-Scale Societies*. Oxford: Oxford University Press.

Henrich, J., Steven J. Hein and Ara Norenzayan. 2009. 'The Weirdest People in the World?' *Behavioral and Brain Sciences* 33:61–135.

Hoff, Karla, Mayuresh Kshetramade and Ernst Fehr. 2010. 'Caste and Punishment: The Legacy of Caste Culture in Norm Enforcement'. Institute for Empirical Research in Economics, University of Zurich series IEW, working paper number 476.

Hoff, Karla and Priyanka Pandey. 2006. 'Discrimination, Social Identity, and Durable Inequalities'. *American Economic Review* 96 (2): 206–11.

Hoffman, E., Kevin McCabe and Vernon Smith. 1996. 'On Expectations and Monetary Stakes in Ultimatum Games'. *International Journal of Game Theory* 25:289–301.

Holt, Charles A. and Susan K. Laury. 2002. 'Risk Aversion and Incentive Effects'. *American Economic Review* 92 (5): 1644–55.

Huntington, S. 1993. 'The Clash of Civilizations?' *Foreign Affairs* 72 (3): 22–49.

———. 1996. *The Clash of Civilizations and the Remaking of World Order*. New York: Simon & Schuster.

Johansson-Stenman, O., Minhaj Mahmud and Peter Martinsson. 2009. 'Trust and Religion: Experimental Evidence from Rural Bangladesh'. *Economica* 76 (303): 462–85.

Joseph, George, Barry Sopher, Gautam Gupta, Anna O'Donnell, Quentin Wodon. 2014. 'Social and Economic Dimensions of Resource Management: Experiments on Public Goods and Common Pool Resources with Endogenous Risk and Benefits', mimeo, World Bank. Draft version available on request at gautamju@yahoo.com.

Kulkarni, Savita. 2014. 'Economics of Informal Institution and Bargaining: An Experimental Game Theory Approach'. Unpublished PhD dissertation, Department of Economics, University of Mumbai.

List, John A. and D. Lucking-Reiley. 2002. 'The Effects of Seed Money and Refunds on Charitable Giving: Experimental Evidence from a University Capital Campaign'. *Journal of Political Economy* 110 (1): 215–33.

Luttmer, E. 2005. 'Neighbors as Negatives: Relative Earnings and Well-Being'. *The Quarterly Journal of Economics*. 120:963–1002.

Malhotra, D. 2010. 'The Desire to Win: The Effects of Competitive Arousal on Motivation and Behavior'. *Organizational Behavior and Human Decision Processes* 111 (2): 139–46.

Masters, R. and R. Meier. 1988. 'Sex Differences and Risk Taking Propensity of Entrepreneurs'. *Journal of Small Business Management* 26 (1): 31–35.

Mitra. S. and G. Gupta. 2009. 'The Logic of Community Participation: Experimental Evidence from West Bengal'. *Economic and Political Weekly* 44 (20): 51–57.

Roth, A. E., V. Prasnikar, M. Okuno-Fujiwara and S. Zamir. 1991. 'Bargaining and Market Behavior in Jerusalem, Ljubljana, Pittsburgh, and Tokyo: An Experimental Study'. *American Economic Review* 81 (5): 1068–95.

Sundén, Annika E. and Brian J. Surette. 1998. 'Gender Differences in the Allocation of Assets in Retirement Savings Plans'. *American Economic Review* 88:207–11.

Solnick, S. 2001. 'Gender Differences in the Ultimatum Game'. *Economic Inquiry* 39 (2): 189–200.

Further Reading

Ahmed, Ali M. and O. Salas. 2011. 'Implicit Influences of Christian Religious Representation on Dictator and Prisoner's Dilemma Game Decisions'. *The Journal of Socio Economics* 40:242–46.

Akerlof, George A. and Rachel E. Kranton. 2000. 'Economics and Identity'. *The Quarterly Journal of Economics* 65 (3): 715–53.

Azzi, C. and R. G. Ehrenberg. 1975. 'Household Allocation of Time and Church Attendance'. *Journal of Political Economy* 83:27–56.

Benjamin, D. J., J. J. Choi and A. J. Strickland. 2010. 'Social Identity and Preferences'. *American Economic Review* 100:1913–28.

Buchan, N. and R. Croson. 2004. 'The Boundaries of Trust: Own and Others' Actions in the US and China'. *Journal of Economic Behavior and Organization* 55 (4): 485–504.

Chuah, S. H., R. Hoffmann, M. Jones and G. Williams. 2007. 'Do Cultures Clash? Evidence from Cross-National Ultimatum Game Experiments'. *Journal of Economic Behavior and Organization* 64:35–48.

Dudley, R. L. and R. J. Cruise. 1990. 'Measuring Religious Maturity: A Proposed Scale'. *Review of Religious Research* 32:97–109.

Eckel, Catherine C. and Rick K. Wilson. 2004. 'Is Trust a Risky Decision?'. *Journal of Economic Behavior and Organization* 55:447–65.

Fehr, E., K. Hoff and M. Kshetramade. 2005. 'Spite and Development'. *American Economic Review: Papers and Proceedings* 98 (2): 494–99.

John, R. 1971. *A Theory of Justice*. Harvard: Harvard University Press.

Karanikolos, Marina, Philipa Mladovsky, Jonathan Cylus, Sarah Thomson, Sanjay Basu, David Stuckler, Johan P. Mackenbach and Martin McKee. 2013. 'Financial Crisis, Austerity, and Health in Europe'. *The Lancet* 381 (9874): 1325–31.

CHAPTER 6

Chamberlin, Edward. 1933. *The Theory of Monopolistic Competition*, first edition. Boston: Harvard University Press..

———. 1948. 'An Experimental Imperfect Market'. *Journal of Political Economy* 56 (2): 95–108.

Diener, E., E. Suh, H. Smith and L. Shao. 1995. 'National Differences in Reported Subjective Well-being: Why Do They Occur'. *Social Indicators Research* 34 (1): 7–32.

Ghate, Rucha, Suresh Ghate and Elinor Ostrom. 2013. 'Cultural Norms, Cooperation and Communication: Taking Experiments to the Field in Indigenous Communities'. *Economic and Political Weekly* 48 (8): 59–67.

Henrich, Joseph, Steven J. Heine and Ara Norenzayan. 2009. 'The Weirdest People in the World?'. *Behavioral and Brain Sciences* 33:61–135.

Hofstede, Geert. 2001. *Culture's Consequences: Comparing Values, Behaviors, Institutions and Organizations Across Nations*, second edition. Thousand Oaks, CA: Sage Publications.

Inglehart, Ronald, Miguel Basanez and Alejandro Moreno. 1998. *Human Values and Beliefs: A Cross Cultural Sourcebook*. Ann Arbor, Michigan: University of Michigan Press.

Marwell, G. and Ruth E. Ames. 1981. 'Economists Free Ride, Does Anyone else?'. *Journal of Public Economics* 15:295–310.

McCrae, R. R. and A. Terracciano. 2005. 'Personality Profiles of Cultures: Aggregate Personality Traits'. *Journal of Personality and Social Psychology* 89 (3): 407–25.

Roth, Alvin. 1994. 'Let's Keep the Con out of Experimental Econ: A Methodological Note'. *Empirical Economics* 19:279–89.

Schmitt, D. P., J. Allik, R. R. McCrae and Benet-Martínez. 2007. 'Geographic Distribution of Big Five Personality Traits: Patterns And Profiles Of Human Self-Description Across 56 Nations', *Journal of Cross-Cultural Psychology* 38 (2): 173–212.

Schwartz, S. H. and W. Bilsky. 1990. 'Toward a Theory of the Universal Content and Structure of Values: Extensions and Cross Cultural Replications'. *Journal of Personality and Social Psychology* 58 (5): 878–91.

Thursone, L. L. 1931. 'The Indifference Function'. *Journal of Social Pscychology* 2:139–67.

Wallis, W. Allen and Milton Friedman 1942. 'The Empirical Derivation of Indifference Functions' in *Studies in Mathematical Economics and Econometrics in Memory of Henry Schultz*, edited by O. Lange, F. McIntyre and T. O. Yntema, 184–209. Chicago: University of Chicago Press.

Further Reading

Friedman, D. and Shyam Sunder. 1994. *Experimental Methods: A Primer for Economists*. New York: Cambridge University Press.

Smith, Adam. 1759. *The Theory of Moral Sentiments*, first edition. London: A. Millar.

———. [1981] 1776. *An Inquiry into the Nature and Causes of the Wealth of Nations*, edited by R. H. Campbell and A. S. Skinner. Indianapolis: Liberty Classics.

BIG BHISHMA IN MADRAS

BIG BHISHMA IN MADRAS

In Search of the Mahabharata with Peter Brook

Jean-Claude Carrière

Translated from the French by Aruna Vasudev

SPEAKING TIGER

SPEAKING TIGER PUBLISHING PVT. LTD
4381/4, Ansari Road, Daryaganj
New Delhi 110002

First published in French by as *A La Recherche du Mahabharata: Carnets de voyages en Inde avec Peter Brook* in 1997
First published in English as *In Search of the Mahabharata: Notes of Travels in India with Peter Brook 1982-1985*, in 2001

This edition published by Speaking Tiger in hardback in 2018

ISBN: 978-93-88326-18-6
eISBN: 978-93-88326-19-3

10 9 8 7 6 5 4 3 2 1

Typeset in Palatino by SÜRYA, New Delhi
Printed at Sanat Printers, Kundli

CONTENTS

ACKNOWLEDGEMENTS

These notes were made between 1982 and 1985 during our first three travels through India in search of the *Mahabharata*. As my original sketches mysteriously disappeared in the course of their travels, I have made new ones for this edition.

All this is thanks to Peter Brook who knows how to make possible the impossible.

TRANSLATOR'S NOTE

When I met Jean-Claude Carrière at his home in Paris, it was to discuss his coming to Delhi where he was going to do a workshop for us, for my Asian film journal *Cinemaya,* on script writing. It was a major event which was to be held at the Cultural Centre of the French embassy which, in those long-ago days, had a small auditorium where we had shown films and held different workshops over a number of years. Jean-Claude Carrière agreeing to come and do a workshop was a huge achievement.

When we met and discussed this in Paris, he presented me with his book *A La Recherche du Mahabharata*. I had not seen the 9-hour play Carrière had written and Peter Brook had presented in France. The film had not yet been made.

I read the book while I was still in Paris and went back to say to Jean-Claude that it MUST be translated into English. He just laughed and said, 'Why don't you do it, Aruna.'

It was quite a challenge but I thought 'why not. It should be read in India and elsewhere by English-speaking people because it is such an inspiringly

written account of something most people outside India, do not know about.' And within India it gives such a moving insight into the role of the *Mahabharata* in our lives.

I returned to Delhi a few days after meeting Jean-Claude, and started the translation immediately. I finished it within the next couple of months. When Jean-Claude arrived in Delhi a few months later to conduct the workshop we had planned, he read it and said, 'It reads better in English than in French.'

Incorrigible as I am, my response was, 'Of course. I know English better than you know French!' It got published very quickly and launched by the then Ambassador of France in India, Bernard de Montferrand, at a lovely ceremony at the French embassy.

It was a very happy moment for me and the book did get good reviews and good sales.

Now I am delighted a new edition is being published by Speaking Tiger all these years later. Jean-Claude Carrière had done a number of sketches for the first edition but now, he has done new ones for this edition which give a new life to his story and the story of his travels through India with Peter Brooke, in search of the *Mahabharata,* in a very evocative and appealing manner. Hopefully, it will also lead to the film being shown again.

ARUNA VASUDEV

New Delhi, October 2018

FOREWORD

Jean-Claude Carrière was the main reason I stuck out what turned out to be a life-changing five-year adventure for me.

It was April 1984. I was five months pregnant with my first child, and had been in bed with jaundice for four months. That is how Peter Brook, Jean-Claude, Marie-Hélène and the two designers, Chloe and Pippa, first saw me, at my home in Ahmedabad. Two days earlier I had received a telegram from my friend, the cultural attachè at the French embassy in Delhi, saying that they wanted to see me. I was surprised and presumed it was for some minor role. I didn't know Peter's work but had read news reports of his casting quest in India. Within ten minutes of our meeting, Peter asked me to audition for the role of Draupadi. I was flabbergasted. Draupadi had always been my favourite character, feisty, unyielding, vocal. There was a catch, of course, and that was that the play was in French (I didn't know the language) and that the contract would be for two years. I was

about to be a mother, had just started a publishing company with my then husband, and the prospect sounded frightening.

However famous Peter was, I knew that I had to like his work before even considering the offer. In New York a week later I watched his *Carmen*, and was blown away. I told Peter I would audition. I was flown to Paris and made to do an audition at two in the morning at Peter's theatre, the Bouffe du Nord. I was offered the role, three weeks off early rehearsals to have my baby, and that was that.

Moving to France with a tiny baby, setting up home for the first time, not speaking the language, in the midst of the worst winter in years, with frozen piping in my apartment, and a rehearsal space which was an eight-floor walk up, was hard. And I disliked the atmosphere of the rehearsals. Every other actor was a star theatre actor from one country or another. I was a dancer. I was the only Indian and the only one amongst the actors who knew and had read and reread many versions of the *Mahabharata*. I had problems with women being interpreted as shrews. (There are no shrews in the *Mahabharata*, I told Peter, only Shaktis!) I disagreed with the way many scenes were interpreted. And I only had Jean-Claude to turn to, a man in charge, English-speaking, encouraging and understanding of my loneliness and despair.

I learnt French. Began to speak it well, in fact.

I learned to hold my own. I made good friends. I started unpeeling myself like an onion as an actor. I learned to be knowledgeable enough to be able to put up cogent arguments for why I thought certain scenes were wrongly interpreted. Previews started. I found women of all kinds reacting positively to my interpretation of Draupadi. We started touring the world. Then came the English version, then the film. And five years had gone by.

All the performance work I have done since, the work I create to bring about changes in mindsets and attitudes, were born in my experience playing Draupadi to diverse audiences. The confidence I got as a storyteller also comes from there. And through it all Jean-Claude remained a friend to turn to, a shoulder to cry on, and a buddy to celebrate with.

This book has been a fascinating read for me too because it predates my adventures with the troupe. And his squiggles are always a delight, capturing as they do, the prana of the figure he has drawn.

MALLIKA SARABHAI
27 September 2018

WELCOME TO INDIA!
MHB
JCC

Arrivals and Departures

1982

DELHI
JCC

We knew the poem, we wanted to see the country. India. We had read the *Mahabharata* at length, Peter in English, Marie-Hélène Estienne and I in French, in Hippolyte Fauche's version. After listening to Philippe Lavastine's long and marvellous accounts; after one year of reading—in Paris, while travelling, everywhere. Another year of reading together, around a table. Comparing versions, eliminating certain digressions, some preliminary accounts ('Yayati', for example, not without regret).

The *Mahabharata* had been, for eight years, our constant companion. I took it with me to Mexico when I worked with Buňuel (Portolés, the Spanish filmmaker). Always one or two volumes in my suitcase, since the whole work is impossible to carry—sixteen times the size of the Bible! I remember a day in New York in 1983, auditioning tenors for *Carmen*. Seated beside Peter in a theatre. At an audition one knows immediately whether a singer is good or not. Then, out of politeness, one listens for another ten minutes. Peter leaned slightly towards me and whispered something about Karna, 'Don't you think

that?...' I don't remember exactly what it was about. But he could think only of that. I, too.

And the tenor carried on singing.

In India now, together, familiar with the story, the characters. Capable of discussing them with the Indians, even with the specialists.

But needing India. Needing to see how the *Mahabharata* is still acted, danced, sung, lived. During several preparatory journeys, Marie-Hélène had been in touch with a large number of schools, artists who sang, danced and acted in episodes of the poem. And who, indeed, does not do that? And some who even do nothing but that. We were to see plenty of them.

But above all we needed to see and to hear India. Meet, gather *all* the images. Not to have, for the moment, any idea of the spectacle, of the play. To remain open, curious, a little childlike. Go everywhere.

We had the advantage of knowing nothing. No *a priori*. We were not experts.

September 1982. I find myself in India for the first time.

I arrive in Delhi in the middle of the night. I have an address, that of a cultural attaché who is supposed to look after me for a few hours. I have to take a flight at dawn for Bombay where Peter awaits me.

No money, no loose change to make a phone

call. Nobody at the airport. Pay the taxi in dollars (exchange counter closed).

In the long avenues of Delhi, in the dead of night, my first sight of cows, like pale ghosts.

❖

I arrive in Bombay the next day. A small hotel (we are on a tight budget). The *Bhagavad Gita* in my room, so also the Bible.

I find Peter, Marie-Hélène, our music director Toshi, and Simon, Peter's son. We are to travel together, all five of us.

My first newspaper, my first bizarre news item: a factory owner swears before the judge that he did not throw the workers into the river.

The first night, shots of firing wake us up. The next day Peter inquires at the front desk of the hotel. Gunshots? Are you sure? Peter is sure, so am I. But the boss has heard not the slightest sound of any shooting; nor have any of his employees. When Peter insists the man replies, 'It was the storm.'

❖

Saturday, 21 August

The first day in Bombay. Into the swing of things immediately. Plunging into the chaos of the city, encounters with directors and actors, with Girish Karnad, with Vijaya Mehta. Dancers too. We announce

our plans: present the *Mahabharata* on the stage, in French. And why not? First tricky questions. But it is all right, we know the work. It is familiar territory.

In the evening, the popular theatre. Girls dance on the stage, men get up and give them rupees. Like an age-old game of seduction, easy and open, without tourists. A lovely wooden hall.

At night, on foot, in the streets. Vendors sitting in their stalls, surrounded by fruits, dressed in white.

No torpor. On the contrary. A vibrant vitality.

We are told we must not miss Ellora and Ajanta. An obligatory tourist circuit. The plane up to Aurangabad, then chauffeur-driven cars, one day for Ellora, one for Ajanta. But tourism is also a part of travelling. Pointless to deny it.

Images fashioned in stone. Ellora is mixed Hindu and Buddhist. Ajanta only Buddhist. Groups of Japanese on a pilgrimage to these sacred sites. Toshi speaks to them.

Our driver is Muslim and does not hide it. His disdain for Hindu festivities (marriages, processions) which we encounter on the way, and which we want a closer look at. Many stops, which exasperate him.

Ellora, a frieze-like mountain. With the landscape like an ornamental backdrop. Sculpting the earth (the temple of Kailash is entirely cut out of a single piece of rock. But how could anyone know that there was a temple in the mountain?).

❖

A few days in Bombay. Film screenings. The *Mahabharata* in Hindi films adapts itself easily to the modern world: for example, two families of bankers destroy each other. Not for us.

Heat and rain. End of the monsoon. We are leaving for the south. Everyone tells us: 'It is the best season.'

Bombay, Chor Bazaar, an incredible collection of bric-a-brac. It seems that one finds *everything* here.

BOMBAY
JCC

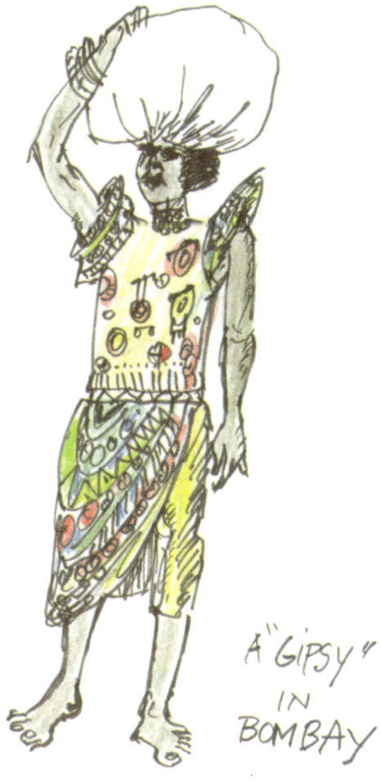
A "GIPSY"
IN
BOMBAY
JCC

BOMBAY
A LAUNDRY
IN A TREE
JCC

Everything is carried, or pulled, by men. People, things, everything everywhere is on the move. It is like a miracle. It feels as if the streets will freeze with the surcharge. But no. A surprising fluidity. The dharma of the masses. The present is sometimes very ancient.

❖

The plane for Bangalore, then another car. And more tourism.

First of all Shravanabelagola, in Karnataka. Twenty-five kilometres away, across the vast plain, one sees the gigantic statue of the Jain saint, Gomateshvara, a very illustrious personality. Every ten or fifteen years he is given a ritual bath; very special ablutions.

We walk six hundred and nineteen steps up to the top of the hill. Toshi arrives first. The towering stone giant stands in the courtyard of a temple. More than seventeen metres high. The gentle hermit is totally naked. Plants sculpted in stone snake up his legs.

His penis is enormous. I imagine it, from time to time, under the effect of certain astral conjunctions and accompanying prayers, swelling and rising,

spraying the audience with semen which impregnates all the women present.

It is time to start inventing Indian myths. The best is that these myths, still very much alive, are open to the imaginings of people faraway.

❖

The next day, inevitably, the temples of Belur and Halebid, also in Karnataka. The usual state of wonder in front of this 'lacework in stone'. Bare feet burn on the stone floor of the courtyard; a puja in Belur; eroticism of the sculpted dancers and, in some places, episodes that we start to recognise. At Halebid, for example, Bhishma on his bed of arrows. And here and there, a little sodomy in between other practices going back to eternity.

And then, Udipi, close to the Indian Ocean, still in Karnataka, for our first visit to a school of dance, the Yakshagana.

Here a tradition going back several centuries has been completely revived and revitalized by a great master. We watch the classes (training starts from the age of six) and, on two successive evenings, performances accompanied by commentaries.

Emotion: suddenly recognising 'our' characters but in the land that gave them birth. Recognising also scenes and episodes, trying to identify the language, the signs. Each dancer here dances the same role all

his or her life, until the dancer and the character become indistinguishable one from the other. Arjuna is over sixty, something that does not seem to upset anyone—especially not him!

Costumes and make-up are lighter than in Kathakali. But the need for *transfiguration* is obvious. The dancer, the actor, is someone else. Long discussions on techniques of gestures, of the eyes. They show us their *Mahabharata*. For us to find ours.

❖

30 August

By car to Kerala, towards the south. Headed for Cannanore.

At first we had planned to take two cars for the five of us. In the end one suffices. It is an Indian Ambassador car. In any case, India has only that. Towards the end of the 1940s, a model had been found which was perfectly suited to the country: slow motor, heavy body, very sturdy. A driver always with us (steering wheel on the right, inherited from the British). Two sit in front with the driver, three at the back. Since the seats in the middle are the least comfortable, we change places now and then. Long distances, frequent stops. A carrier on top of the car for the baggage, Toshi's instruments, our shopping. The driver can stay eight days with the clients. In

the evenings he disappears to eat and sleep, who knows where. It's a secret.

❖

In the car, time to see, time to reflect. All together and each one on his own.

The eroticism of the *Mahabharata*. As soon as a rishi retreats into the forest to do penance, a stunningly sexy woman emerges from the river to distract him. But for that at least two or three beautiful women would be needed. There is something humid and hot in the poem, something primeval. Almost everything starts with a royal hunt, with a king who falls asleep, dreams of his wife and his sperm escapes. Not to be missed. Ganesha might say: 'It is a good beginning.'

The force of destiny, the strength of desire. One often pitted against the other, alas.

❖

In Cannanore for a few days from where we make short trips.

They say it is in Kerala that the traditions of the *Mahabharata*, at least in the performances, are the most faithfully preserved.

First of all in Kathakali, the dance form best known in the West (several visits to the Kathakali centre, several performances). It is perhaps to a Kathakali performance that Peter saw in London

to which we owe our presence in India today. He recollects a particularly striking moment: a strangely dressed creature thrusts his head ferociously into the entrails of another creature and comes up with a red ribbon—the intestines—between his teeth. He wondered what it was all about. Today we know that it was Bhima settling accounts with the terrible Dushasana.

In 1975, an Indian company came to Paris. We went to see their performance and we showed them ours—*Ubu aux Bouffes* (Ubu at the Bouffes Theatre) it was called at that time, then *Ubu Roi* (king), then *Ubu Cocu* (cuckold). Naturally they did not understand a word of French. At the end, we kept them back in the theatre and Peter asked them to tell us in their way, in their language (without make-up or costumes), what they had understood of the play. One of them started, with beautiful hand gestures, 'There was once a powerful king surrounded by courtesans.' He had understood perfectly the idea of a conspiracy against a cruel king. One thing struck them as an obstacle: the fact that an actor could play several characters without—almost—changing his appearance. An impenetrable convention.

In that same period we had started taking some dance lessons from Karuna (Kathakali guru living in Paris, and Peter's brother-in-law). To get used first of all, to bending the knees, the weight on the outside

JCC
KATHAKALI

edge of the feet, the back straight. Learning some hand gestures and movements of the eyes. What the body can express—when one forces it—of another culture and which the mind cannot conceive of![1]

We meet them again. Still amazing. Incredible complexities of appearance—terrifying, melancholy or disdainful, and even burlesque. As if feelings were hidden away, to be expressed only by the eye or a movement of a finger. Sacred dances, bringing alive myths, sometimes the most hallowed ones (the *Gita*). The necessity of sharing at least some elements of a language of sign and gesture. The story told is already familiar to those who watch it unfold. The audience keeps coming back to be reminded of it, or to admire a particular artiste.

A very effective stage design, square, the audience seated on the ground, overshadowed by the living heroes.

A tranquil majesty, sometimes almost clownish (in our eyes). An inexplicable tradition (are not they all?). Here the theatre has a rigorous code. If one takes it, in fact, to be theatre.

And the contemporary perversions: they tell us that certain groups present Kathakali in front of four

---

1. In July 1985, in the courtyard of the Palais Vieux in Avignon, while a play was going on, I was called upon to dance in public with Karuna. I played (but without make-up) Bhima who strangles the wily Kichaka.

or five thousand people, under huge tents, to the raucous music of today. Nothing is spared.

❖

Kerala, home of Theyyam. Another traditional performing art, directly linked to the temple.

Our first encounter with this is in a little temple (name forgotten), by a river. We are allowed to attend a ceremony, the first time for us. Two hundred fervent devotees, incense, prayers, offerings, the Brahmins—young and agile—distributing flower petals to the assembled crowd. One of them, who seems to be about eighteen, has a golden plaque on his forehead.

It is something that has been untouched by time. No tourists, not even Indian. Then comes the head priest, dressed in a strange costume, half-armour, half-flowers. Very odd. Quite astonishing. He carries two silver swords and starts his dance in the middle of the audience, brandishing his arms. Very quickly he seems to go into a trance. But controlled? He charges towards me, raises a sword with both hands, swings it down on my head, stopping two centimetres from my hair.

A sort of 'sacred frenzy'. Words from antiquity come to the lips, words like 'idol-worshippers'. A sense of intoxication, of a contact with something unexpressed, inexpressible. Is it theatre, or not

theatre? We stay about two hours. At the end, a moment of silence beside the river.

❖

Three times, and always at night, we are taken to other temples, to see other dances, this time in the open air—once even with elephants.

First of all, the make-up, very slow, very meticulous. The dancer lies still for about two hours. Minute by minute he becomes a god—or at least the vehicle borrowed by the god through which he manifests himself.

Then his costume is put on, very complicated and weighing up to fifty kilos. They do his hair, put a light wooden trellis frame around his waist, sew on some parts of his costume. Each mask is different, sometimes huge, very elaborate and often frightening—except for the monkey-god Hanuman who makes one laugh. An extraordinary creature, red and black, who comes out of the night from who knows where.

Four or five percussionists, one of whom is a singer, accompanies them. The drums keep going; at times the beat grows louder. Faster. And the dancer follows. It seems as if the god must first enter into the character who awaits him: he shivers, jerks, his helpers rush around, torches are handed to him. Then his movements begin, to the rhythm of the music,

he spins round and round. His face is hidden, you can see only his black eyes.

This is when, they say, he showers his blessings. When he stops, after twenty to thirty minutes, someone else replaces him. Sometime two or three dance together. 'Dance' is perhaps saying too much. The sheer weight of their costumes cannot allow them to actually dance. It is more like heavy, rhythmic steps punctuated with leaps in the air. Truly extraordinary. Once again it is difficult to call it theatre, a play.

Plenty of fire, plenty of brandishing of arms, flurry of movements. It is a veritable sword dance. Constant violence, terrifying at moments. Here there is no language to understand. The effect is direct. Incantations. This world is brutal and bloody. Patently. The gods know it. Besides, they themselves…

The long, red, nights of Kerala. Everywhere.

❖

One day we pass through Mahé, a former French trading post in India. Strange to see wine and liquor shops lining the road. Is this a hangover of the French presence? This our legacy?

❖

First questions. Do we start with the origins? Keep a part of the myth with, for instance, a narrator?

Or, on the contrary, plunge straightaway into the drama as in a tragedy with, for example, a violent scene—of which there are plenty—between the adult Kauravas and the Pandavas.

The second possibility is perhaps too 'Occidental'. Both dimensions must be kept, even if they are self-contradictory: the narrative, like a meandering river covering several generations with their parallel stories, and the concentrated story, the drama, around the *conflict*.

In any case, the conflict is central. Peter wonders whether the heart of the poem is not just that, a grandiose attempt to define the notion of 'conflict'.

Why do we fight? And for what?

What is there within us that fights?

A mystery-conflict.

❖

Three days of rest (alone with Peter) at Kottakkal on the west coast, in a centre of traditional Ayurvedic medicine. We need to look at things in perspective, to talk.

A pleasant place. And the treatments—potions to drink, vigorous massage with warm coconut oil. Two masseurs, one on either side. They go about it gaily. The effect is very good.

Visit the large garden where they grow medicinal plants used in this traditional system all over India.

An air of magic: they show us, for example, the plant which 'solidifies water', and some which keep the demons at bay. Ready to believe everything (living in another world, another mentality). Over here they make 'helmets of herbs' which one must wear all night long for one week (they are changed every day) and which can cure mental illnesses.

Two successive evenings we are invited to dine with the proprietor in his home opposite the clinic. An immense house crawling with servants. Speciality: the large dining room is on four levels, according to the degree of importance of the invitees. Three or four steps between each level. We are on the top level, with the owner. Men only.

The slaves bring us thalis, plates, supervised by a very superior person, an elderly man with white hair, wearing a lungi, whom we immediately call the slave master. Once again it is a journey into the past. It could easily be a patrician home in ancient Rome, with clients received according to their status and, undoubtedly, huddled somewhere at the back of the house, the poor.

As always in India, meals taken rapidly, in silence. In less than ten minutes it is over. The owners eat, naturally, with their fingers, heads bowed, mixing vegetables and sauces with rice placed in the centre of the plate. Rare are the moments when food appears to be a pleasure worthy of appreciation. A balanced

meal, vegetarian, consisting of local, regional products has been found once and for all, and it never varies. In the whole of the south we eat more or less the same thing, twice a day. A foreigner enjoys it the first time, perhaps even the second. The third time, he starts to find it boring. At the end of one week, he forgets that he is eating. For a change, we stop from time to time in a village to have an onion omelette cooked on a charcoal fire out in the open. Always delicious. When we get to a big city (Madras, Calcutta), we will go to a restaurant in a grand hotel to regale ourselves with chicken and lamb and watch the dancers undulating.

ALL VEGETAL
KERALA

JCC

In Kottakkal, evening; end of the day. Peter goes for a walk alone among the palm trees across the rice fields. He comes back marvelling at the peace, the silence, the solitude, at the stone houses of Kerala, the singing of the insects at twilight, the little paths through the already tall rice fields.

The last day, just before leaving, he is told that the rice fields are full of particularly dangerous snakes. Hence the solitude and the peace!

❖

By car to Trichur. Long discussions about energy, its rise and fall. A question that has always fascinated Peter—understandably. What is it that creates the energy, the intensity that one senses at times in the theatre? Only on certain evenings, at certain moments? Can it be measured *scientifically*? Will that ever be possible? When human energy is at its peak does it become one with another which could be called cosmic?

How can one find it? How can one hold on to it?

Three hours of discussion, on a slow drive going from one river to another, through the green hills of Kerala.

❖

Kerala is a delight: Very hot, humid, tropical. Forests of coconut palms. Many meetings with dancers, actors,

musicians. Improvisations, unexpected concerts. An insatiable pleasure in acting, singing.

Houses built of stone, solid, cool. We stay in a hotel by the sea. Quite pleasant but broken down. The roof of the dining room has completely collapsed. I meet a young woman from Delhi who is here alone to work. She is designing textiles.

❖

Must not try to grasp everything, understand everything. Let things flow, at first, without trying to plumb their depths. A quick, superficial first impression is perhaps the best.

We defer all analysis, all categoric judgement. Peter often speaks, even while working, of a 'naive look'. One of our strengths: our ignorance.

❖

We are very active, always ready to take off. Impossible to keep track of everything. In Trivandrum, a festival of martial arts is rather disappointing. Called Kalaripayattu. Lances, swords, bare hands. But the heroes tend to be on the plump side. Gestures uncertain. Indians flatter themselves on having invented these martial techniques, which were Buddhist in the beginning because the use of weapons was forbidden. Toshi turns up his nose.

Nevertheless we have to include them. There are numerous battle scenes and fights in the poem. What is one to do?

We find, and admire, a belt made of sharp steel nearly three metres long, which is tied around the waist and which, properly used, can cut off a head. But of course, say the Buddhists, it is not a weapon, it is a belt.

Peter decides we should have this in the play. It is very dangerous, they warn us. It doesn't matter. Alain (Maratrat) will take charge of it.

❖

3 September

We leave for Madurai by car. It takes a whole day, with a stop at Palani. We go from one end of the continent to the other, and from Kerala to Tamil Nadu (a different culture, a different writing on the signposts and hoardings).

A great shock: the Meenakshi temple at Madurai. We had been warned but all the same...The temple possesses and swallows up the city. Immediately plunged into the past; it is Babylon dreamt up by Cecil B. deMille and directed by an Indian. It is totally, incredibly, full of life. The hall of a thousand columns, the dark statues in every corner, vendors selling everything, the sacred elephant, groups of pilgrims from all over India, specially dressed and

MADURAÏ

TAMIL NADU

made up, like dandified Shivas. The crowd is not too noisy. Some of them carry sackfuls of coconuts on their heads. Some have come like this on foot, covering hundreds of kilometres. The atmosphere is difficult to grasp, even more difficult to describe. Like entering into a dream. Must come back. How to transpose even a whiff of this to the Bouffes du Nord (a theatre in Paris).

A thought for St Jean of the Cross: 'We do not travel to see, but to not see.'

Here, how can one *not* see? At least for a moment.

The elderly, those who have sought renunciation, those who have nothing, seem to compete with each other in the oddness of their appearance. We stand out in the crowd, almost demanding to be noticed. Many come to this temple to ask for a husband or a wife. The offerings are made accordingly. The smell of vegetation is pervasive. All the odours of the vegetal world.

Baroque, tumultuous, chaotic, a torrent, the stuff of fantasy, strange, surcharged: no adjective suffices. We have not seen anything like it anywhere in the world.

❖

And what if, behind this appearance of massive disorder, of this babel of divergent sounds, lay hidden a clandestine dream of unity?

❖

We stop for a few days in Tamil Nadu, in Tiruchirapally (again the feeling of having gone into another time zone), in Thanur, from Kumbakonam to Chidambaram, where we find again the dancers of stone.

Here there is a sensation of being truly in India. In any case, of being *somewhere*.

On to Pondicherry where of course we find France, at least in the names of the streets and restaurants. It's a little Palavas-les-Flots (a small seaside resort in the south of France). Not disagreeable, but, oh well…I stay away from the Mother's ashram.

In the evening we take off for a village. In the car again; it's becoming exhausting, never sleeping before three o'clock in the morning to get up at six without having really slept.

The *Mahabharata* in one of the Terokutu traditions. Superb. In the village square, with strings and pieces of wood, something very poor, very dusty, but with an overpowering vitality. Costumes, nondescript and torn, makeshift weapons and yet, the work breathes through it all. Since we are fairly familiar with the scenes, we begin to feel very close to the peasants present. We laugh at the same points. We sense the same fears.

Dogs and children are asleep. It is night above the tall trees. Feeble lights. Arjuna and Karna challenging each other under the moonlight.

Passing through a street in Pondicherry our driver points to a building and tells us:

'Very good post office.'

A walk in the evening with Toshi. Dozens of children surround us asking him where he comes from. He replies, 'From Japan.' My turn. I also reply that I am Japanese. It is accepted without question. Nationalities, physical differences, all disappear.

Later, one of the children asks me to send him a postcard of the Eiffel Tower. He does not even dream that he could one day leave here, go to Paris. He will never move out of this place, he knows that. But at least the Eiffel Tower can come to him in the form of a postcard.

We are the strangers who pass in the night. We come, we stop and we leave. They stay. They remain where they are.

❖

In a courtyard at the back, in the middle of piles of garbage, an old bicycle has been thrown away. Everything that could be reused, has been removed. All that remains is a carcass, rusty, worn away.

On a pedal an inscription is still visible: 'Life is just a dream.'

Some of the elements of the *mise en scéne*: When Arjuna goes into the mountains, the Himalayas, to do penance to ask Shiva for the boon of a fatal weapon,

he is sometimes shown climbing a very tall pole at least ten or twelve metres high. From on top, wearing a simple loincloth, he speaks to God.

Elsewhere, in the last battle, the one in which Bhima breaks Duryodhana's thigh with a single blow, the two actors start the fight (using clubs) in a temple outside the village. Followed by an increasingly large crowd, they move towards the village, still carrying on their fight. In the central square lies an enormous statue of Duryodhana, fifteen metres long. The two combatants fight on around the clay figure until finally, Bhima breaks the thigh of the statue.

Almost everywhere—in Karnataka, in Kerala, in Tamil Nadu—the actors are behind a simple, cotton curtain, held by two assistants. When all is ready, the assistants lift the curtain and the actors appear.[2]

2. Peter used this twice, with certain modifications—for the appearance, and then the disappearance, of Krishna.

In some places, under a tent, many days are spent making a serpent of flowers. The tent is huge, about sixty square metres, like a gigantic mandala. On the day of the festival, the dancer first dances on the serpent, then rolls frenetically on the petals, destroying the patient masterpiece in a matter of moments.

That is how it is.

❖

Madras. A great centre of music, the capital of Tamil Nadu. A good hotel, at last, and a few days of rest, of relaxation. Fatigue seems to have become our permanent companion.

Several concerts, with Toshi as our guide. He has worked many months in India, especially in Calcutta (his favourite city) where he even has students. He studied the songs of Tagore which have some relation to the *Mahabharata*. To sing them one day? Perhaps. He also plays with Indian musicians; he has a great ability to adapt himself.

We go and visit a very famous flautist (I forget his name) who plays for over an hour; to a temple to hear the chanting of the Brahmins, and to many public concerts. Sometimes we only stay twenty minutes. Arriving late or leaving before the end—no one is bothered. The audience does not seem particularly

attentive (or so it appears); people talk, eat, some fall asleep.

And then, a visit to the centre of Bharata Natyam, the most famous dance of India. A big park with bungalows around a theatre. The director of the centre is Rukmini Devi, the great reformer of Bharata Natyam in the twentieth century. Over here one rarely describes a young woman as beautiful. She is 'pretty', 'nice-looking', 'attractive', but very rarely 'beautiful'. It seems that beauty is a quality reserved for women above fifty, a quality that is acquired. Often, when we were to meet a woman who was director of such and such an organisation, we would ask 'What is she like?', and we would be told 'She is beautiful.'

Before meeting Rukmini Arundale, who had agreed to receive us, I asked a man who knew her, 'What is she like?'

'She is very beautiful,' he answered.

And it is true. She is over eighty and does nothing to hide her age. She walks slowly, leaning on a cane. Dressed in white and light beige. Her long silvery hair hangs down to her waist. When she enters the room where we are waiting for her, it is as if a light had entered.

We watch many rehearsals and many dance classes. Groups of young girls who work hard together. It seems as if the dancer never wants to lose touch with the earth. Contrary to our classical ballet

which seems always to be poised for a flight—an ephemeral flight, repeatedly begun—here the young women dancers return constantly to the earth, beating down hard with their feet, calling upon it to bear witness, drawing energy from it.

This earth which is created as it is destroyed by the dancer in the course of the dance (how can I express it?). Dance of the world whose secrets are constantly sought to be discovered. A Western ballerina dances with the air, always ready to take flight; a dancer here affirms her oneness with the earth which gave her birth. Her body, firmly planted, launches into a thousand movements, sinuous as a plant, like an extraordinary tree, full of flowers, speaking a secret language. The body is divided into three undulating parts in the form of an 'S'. Strictly no straight line.

This dance is called 'graceful', or 'charming'; superficial terms which hide a profound vitality, sexual energy and a certain smiling violence, a pronounced taste for the enigmatic. Even without understanding the meaning of the movements, the poses and postures, I can watch for hours the dancers who come one after the other, here and there (they are everywhere). I am almost hypnotised in the end. Peter is much less sensitive to this. He finds it instead somewhat 'kitsch'.

One evening in Madras, on an Italian-style stage, we see the *Mahabharata* presented in less than two

hours. Expeditiously rendered. Really kitsch, ultra-fast and truly bad. Bhishma is a fat man, pot-bellied and often out of breath. Painted backdrops and little fireworks. Local travesty of Western theatre. Poor operetta, to be quickly forgotten.

❖

Visit to Mahabalipuram; temples by the sea where the Pandavas are celebrated. We return to them as to old friends: the little Draupadi temple, that of Bhima and the big rock where Arjuna (but we're not sure if it was really him) did penance, his long and hard penance on the rock. All the while, a big cat gazed mockingly at him.

❖

First meeting with a saint.

In the countryside, in a temple a few hours from Madras. A dense crowd, as always in such cases, but quite calm. We wait to see him.

Shankaracharya is a one-in-three saint. Since this monastic order (or this brotherhood, this tradition in the heart of Hinduism) was founded, this is how they have been called. They are always three, belonging to different generations—an old man, a mature man and a young man who prepares himself for the succession.

The aged Shankaracharya is a true saint.

MADRAS

BIG BHISHMA IN MADRAS

Apparently a revered person in the history of Hinduism. Perhaps the most venerated in the twentieth century. But now one cannot see him. He does not move out of Kanchipuram, the seat of the order or deviate from his vow of silence. He has not spoken a word for many years.

Around five o'clock in the afternoon, the mature Shankar, a man full of smiles, with a round face and an alert look, receives us on a terrace out in the open. The young Shankar is seated nearby. He listens and looks, without speaking.

A few words are spoken in English, then a translator becomes indispensable.

I ask some questions of the saint (red robe, bare arms, the marks of Vishnu on his forehead, a small topknot and a thin stick of bamboo in his hand). I ask him the reason for Yudhisthira's reticence—whom he considers the central hero of the *Mahabharata* which he calls the Dharmaraj (Dharma-king). Why does he agree to lose his kingdom in the game of dice (a question debated at length among us)? Why this long exile? Why this consistent refusal to fight, to reclaim, if necessary by force, that which is his own by right?

Why, during the battle itself, these perpetual hesitations, these repeated retreats, which sometimes appear like cowardice?

Shankaracharya replies with a big laugh: 'Because

otherwise Arjuna and Bhima would have ended the war too quickly!'

I speak to him also of Krishna, his questionable ruses. I say to him: 'How is it that Krishna, who is a god descended on earth to bring succour in a period of crisis and threats, appears at moments troubled, indecisive? How is it that being himself a god, he does not know what is coming, who is taken unawares, shows surprise and disquiet? Is he really a god, or simply a man?'[3]

Once again the saint laughs full-throatedly and replies: 'That is really a human question!'

Laughter all around.

On a parapet, behind the saint, are seated four young Germans. Blonde hair, blue eyes. They are dressed in white and listen respectfully, immobile. Four angels come from the West, almost translucid against the setting sun.

❖

Calcutta. Meeting with Satyajit Ray. He comes to fetch us from the hotel. We see him from afar: very tall, very handsome, towering above the crowd. Speaks excellent English—remarks Peter.

---

3. Krishna, according to Hindu tradition, is the eighth avatar of Lord Vishnu, the Preserver, who holds the world together.

After lunch he takes us home. A large apartment, somewhat sombre, in a great grey building. Musical instruments. Long conversation about the *Mahabharata*. He had also thought of adapting it for the cinema, for television. But it meant doing it in English, and he did not want that. 'Can you imagine Kirk Douglas as Arjuna?' He is much more positive about our project. The advantage, according to him, of not being Indian. Distanced from it, greater freedom. The famous remote look. He is encouraging. Says he is ready to help us, recommends certain musicians. At the moment he is working with children, something he feels passionately about. And he is selecting music for films other than his own.

We talk of *The Cherry Orchard*, which we have just done, and the connection we found with *The Music Room*. He agrees. We talk a lot about that film. I tell him that the shot of the shimmering chandelier reflected in the glass of wine (presaging the fatal drowning, later on) is to me by far one of the most beautiful in the history of cinema. He thanks me with a smile. Very elegant, very courteous, master of himself.[4]

❖

---

4. We would see him many more times. In Calcutta in 1989, I even watched the first screening of *Branches of the Tree* sitting beside him. For me it is among the three or four best of Ray's films.

Still in Calcutta. We hold a press conference on 13 September. The cultural attaché's name is Jean Racine. Then we spend a whole day, Peter and I, with one of Mother Teresa's nuns. We follow her everywhere. A young Indian, she must be under thirty, dressed in white and blue. Her mission is to go every morning to the overcrowded pavements of the city and collect those without hope, to help them die in dignity.

Her authority is impressive. She finds a man dying and immediately calls some men to help her carry him away. Nobody refuses her. She beckons a rickshaw man with an imperious gesture. The man obeys her, knowing full well he will not be paid.

No room for sentimentality. We help place the dying man in the rickshaw. A ravaged old man, on the threshold of death. A man who has nothing. The young nun directs the operation with very few words. She seems to know exactly what she has to do. No sentimentality, no pity. Very matter-of-fact.

Another time we find ourselves with her in a small train, then at a station. Behind the station, thrown on a heap of garbage, two corpses, barely covered. We look at them for a moment.

We are on our way to the famous 'dying room', filmed by Louis Malle in *Calcutta* in 1968, not without creating a scandal. Nothing seems to have changed. The 'poorest of the poor' are there, dying in silence. There is nothing more to be done for them. They

generally die of dysentery. They are taken care of, eased into death. A process often held against Mother Teresa. But what else can be done? From the Christian point of view this life is not the true one. Important to die well; real life is elsewhere. Even for the Hindus?

We give some money and all the medicines we still have with us.

❖

A meeting in his house, a little way outside the city, with Professor P. Lal who is completing a translation of the *Mahabharata* into English verse. He has been working on it for twenty years, publishing his huge work in a series of elegant volumes. One of those rare men (along with the Frenchman Hippolyte Fauche in the nineteenth century who died without having accomplished his task. It was taken up by another Sanskritist, who died also before completing it) who set out to do a complete translation. It is like spending one's whole life with a single book.

An elegant, handsome man, sixty-five years old. Clearly knows the book perfectly. Very interested by our project, he places himself at our disposal. (We meet him several times.)

He believes it possible to adapt the *whole* work for the theatre.

He is coming to Paris. Soon.

❖

CALCUTTA
LITTERARY COCKTAIL

At least five or six performances in Calcutta, especially (outside the city) by a young theatre group which presents contemporary Bengali plays with a certain energy. We are removed from all vestiges of tradition: no make-up, no costumes. The audience sits all around the room which has nothing of the theatre about it. We understand none of the words but the vibrations are good. No costumes, no 'lighting'. An impression, at moments, of improvisation. Good teamwork. And today's themes.

Some beautiful women in the audience. They sometimes look boldly at us, eyeing us provocatively with an expression that in the West would be taken as an invitation. But that is not the case. Here one makes love only with the eyes. When we leave at the end, the young woman who, a few minutes earlier had been staring at us, turns and leaves with her friends, without once looking back. Something had transpired, but what?

We listen to the singers, the musicians. It is unending. Watch a narrator following a special ritual. He has to kneel on one knee. He has a single accessory, an object which resembles a sort of paddle. In his hands this object becomes all sorts of things: a club, a bow, a lance, a musical instrument, a woman, a tree, a horse.

Three musicians accompany him, seated behind him. He tells the whole story of the *Mahabharata*

(playing the different roles, singing sometimes) in eighteen evenings—eighteen here is a sacred number (the *Bhagavad Gita* has eighteen chapters, for example).

We watch him do an episode from the battle, the death of Drona.

❖

Calcutta, 'City of Compassion'. That is how its inhabitants like to call it. They remember how during the Bangladesh war the city of Calcutta, already overpopulated, nevertheless took in millions of refugees and gave them shelter.

Smell of fresh blood in the early morning, in the Kali temple on the bank of the Ganges. That is where they slaughter the goats. A sombre atmosphere, almost sinister. We look in vain for what we call 'sacred'. In the practice of religion are found poverty, harshness, darkness. And a rapacious greed for money.

After a futile attempt at a modest hotel (our budget put palaces out of our reach), we settled down in the Bengal Chambers, a sort of British-style Indian pension with a common dining table, vast rooms, fans, an Indian lady-proprietor with, naturally, a British manner. Very special. A hybrid place, not without a certain charm and for us, affordable. Peter adores it: an England in disguise, a British masquerade.

❖

One evening, at the home of the Dagar brothers: Indian singing.

Here, among all the instruments of music, the human voice reigns supreme. And one understands why. Nothing left to say, after such singing. To hear it is enough. It is the entire body that listens.

❖

It has been, it still is, very difficult enough to enter into the *Mahabharata*. But how do we get out of it?

What we understand more and more clearly is that the many different levels in the work—multiple, complex, moving from farce (Bhima disguised as a woman in order to choke the life out of Kichaka) to the highest spiritual summit of the *Gita*—are levels that can be found in Indian society, in the Indian mentality. This complexity is all around us. In a society of supposedly sharp distinctions, divided strictly even by caste, it is often the ambiguity which strikes us. Feelings are not always what we think they are. Seriousness, dignity, charm, humour—all present at the same time. With what appears, at least to us, an element of strangeness.

What binds all this together is indisputably a vitality. That is what strikes us most strongly. An incredible energy, everywhere. Unexpected, of course: it is the opposite of the usual image of India.

❖

Still in Calcutta.

We meet a group of Bengali ethnologists who work in India itself. Some have come back from three or four years of study in a village in Rajasthan (different language, different culture). They have just published an inventory they have made (they show it to us) of the stories they collected in this one village. More than seventeen thousand.

Told of our desire to go to Orissa and Bihàr to look for the survivors of the *Mahabharata* among the tribal people (in India there are at least fifty million), two anthropologists decide to join us. They are very interested. In India, they say, it is not necessary to go anywhere else. One can find here itself all the eras of history, all the epochs.

We leave (a Land Rover and an Ambassador).

I get into the Ambassador with one of the anthropologists and some of our stuff. Peter, Toshi, Marie-Hélène and Simon in the Land Rover (more chic).

Plenty of zigzags and wrong turnings on the way. Pass through Purulia. As night falls we arrive in the village of Chau. Our car is the first to arrive. No sign of Peter's. While the anthropologist, who speaks a bit of the language, goes off to try and get some news, I sit in front of the house which belongs to the chief, a short, stocky man, very dark and wearing a lungi, strongly resembling an Australian aborigine.

He offers me some water, which I refuse although I am dying of thirst (the bottles of soda water are in the other car), then something to eat: potatoes in a reddish sauce, atrociously spiced. I eat one or two out of politeness. Then I make signs to indicate I am tired, that I would like to lie down and rest while waiting for the others.

Fine. He has a bed brought out into the open, that is to say a wooden frame with interlaced ropes, and tells me to lie down while he carries on with his evening chores. It must be seven or eight o'clock. Before going he tells one of his daughters, dark like him, to keep an eye on me.

She must be twelve or thirteen. While I lie on the ropes, she sits silently, gracefully, near me. I close my eyes. A moment later I feel the little girl's hand very lightly touching my shoulder. I open my eyes: she has brought me a cushion to place under my head. I do so, and close my eyes again. Another moment, another light touch. I reopen my eyes. Without any words, knowing they would be incomprehensible to me, she makes me understand with signs that I am lying partly under a tree on which there are insects, or caterpillars, which could fall on me and sting me.

I get up. With her help I move the bed a little further away and lie down again. She again sits down in silence near me, fanning me with a small

fan made of peacock feathers. Above us is the sky, the night. Closing my eyes I have the impression that my sleep is protected by a little girl come from far away, from prehistory, at once younger and much older than me.

❖

I have hardly fallen asleep. The second car arrives and the evening—which lasts the whole night—gets going. First a reception in the courtyard of the chief's house, a courtyard which must measure around thirty square metres. He has grasped that Peter is the head of our delegation. He makes Peter sit opposite him and asks first—through one and at times, two interpreters (the anthropologists): 'Where are you from?'

This question is always primordial. It is translated into English as either 'Where from?', or 'Native place?' Peter replies, with great seriousness, 'London.'

Peter, therefore, is from London. The chief, who hasn't the slightest idea where London is to be found, nods satisfied, and asks the second question: 'Do you have a house in London?'

The phrase is translated for Peter who, still very serious, replies, 'Yes.'

The chief again nods his head. Good. Here is a man who has a house in London. Then comes the third question, as important as the first two: 'How many cows in your house in London?'

Peter smiles, tries to answer. The explanations go on.

During this time a feast is being made ready, and a performance. Very beautiful images, very strong, the strongest since the Theyyam in Kerala.

Here also the actors, back from the fields, with the night all around us, allow themselves to be made up for the roles they are to play. They lie down on their backs and close their eyes; two, three or four hours pass by as the others work in silence around them. Little by little, as in Theyyam, in the hands of his friends, of his neighbours, the peasant becomes a god. Or at least a sacred character. The manners of the others towards him become respectful. As if he has been invested with a new power, which the make-up symbolises. Metamorphosis.

When all is ready around eleven at night, in the village square the feast begins. It lasts the whole night. Everyone is there, even the children who at some point fall asleep. Songs and dances with drums. Scenes we recognise: Arjuna in the mountains fighting in vain with the hunter who was no other than Shiva and who would give him the supreme weapon—which he would never use; then a moment from the *Gita,* the beginning; and Bhima's fight with the terrible Rakshasa in the forest. Very beautiful, very strong, full of sound and fury.

Also the death of Abhimanyu, that marvellous

adolescent, son of Arjuna who in his mother's womb, learnt how to break Drona's discus-like formation of war (*Chakravyahu*). Actually, he heard how to enter into the *Chakravyahu* but not how to get out of it because his mother fell asleep while Arjuna was telling the story.

The death of youth in the war (a war for which it had clamoured). 'These heroes have killed a child'.

At times when a character moves while speaking, especially when he is enraged, a drummer follows closely behind him, like a second voice mute, yet articulate, a striking shadow.

We drink it all in avidly. The Bengali anthropologists take notes. Toshi records the rhythms.

It goes on almost until dawn.

In other Chau villages, dancers use masks, painted on a white background. We take one back for the actor who will play Ganesha, the scribe with the elephant head, patron of artists—and of thieves.

❖

Another place the next morning, a well-known centre we have heard about. A performance organised for us, and paid for by us. But everything is different. A French ballet master passed through here towards the end of the eighteenth century. Something of him still remains in the style, in the rhythms. It is as if

they are dancing a minuet, without any sense of conviction, vapidly. (Western dance, English rather than French, only became known at the beginning of the twentieth century.)

In the city now, where a famous guru runs a dance institute. But the guru is absent. Could we still visit the school? We ask the administrator sitting at a desk on a raised platform in the centre of the room. All around him an incredible pile of documents and files thick with dust.

He asks for a translation. Then he thinks about it. Is he authorised to allow us to enter? The effort of thinking shows on his face. He asks a question which is translated for us. We try to answer it. He thinks again. And again. And again. This goes on for more than an hour. The man remains silent for a long while, raises his eyes, asks some more questions. Let us enter the dance school? No. Finally he says no. And we leave.

A palatial building, whitish, pitted by rain, and mysteriously closed.

❖

From time to time, for an hour or two, below a temple, or in the shade of a tree, we sit and read the *Gita*, slowly, with stops and comments.

❖

Return via Benaras, the inevitable stopover, and via Agra where, as the sun sets, we gaze at the dazzling unity of the Taj Mahal. End of exuberance, here is Islam. A perfect work would combine the Taj and the temple of Madurai. But that would be inconceivable.

The visit to Benaras: classic emotion, more or less guaranteed. But everything depends on the order of the voyage. Where one begins, where one stops.

To die in Benaras: the promise, or almost, of *nirvana*. In the streets, a marriage. The bride and groom are decked out like princes. Installed in a sort of horse carriage but pulled by men who carry on their heads, each one of them, a sort of *lighted* neon tubelight. These are actually linked by thick, twisted electric wires to a small generator which follows the procession.

Let each one carry his own light. That is the way it should be.

❖

We have several times slept in the most improbable places. Arrivals in the middle of the night. Nobody, nothing to drink, throats on fire. We were grateful if at times, we found a warm Pepsi-Cola. On two or three occasions I shared a room with Toshi. Bugs, one time, which had to be killed. Noises. Almost all over India a faint, cloying smell of shit.

ORISSA
JCC

BIHAR

ON THE ROAD

JCC

In Delhi, the circle is complete. Physical exhaustion. The shaded charm of the Imperial Hotel. Even a swimming pool.

We stay four very full days. Lots of meetings, films, visits, parties. Finally, even a little shopping. I write a few bits of scenes, I read, I talk. What sort of adventure is it that have we embarked upon?

The tenacious presence of the *Mahabharata*. It is everywhere, in all forms, even in the piles of comic books (in Hindi and in English). It is perhaps the only really common point between different cultures and languages. Very well known, even among the tribals. More than the gods, more than the laws.

A subcontinent identified by a book. The greatest poem in the world. The most complete? A phrase, arrogant in its way, in the middle of the poem goes: 'All that is in the *Mahabharata* exists in the world. What is not in it, does not exist.'

No point then, in looking anywhere else.

The extreme ambition of the work. The physical effects that it implies (to be seen).

Does the complexity of India correspond to the complexity of the poem? And vice versa? Here nothing is simple, but it can all be analysed. The philosophy does not forbid any tunnel, any jungle. To go even towards darkness (necessary). Contradictions even in our own reactions. It could be compressed into one sentence, 'But what horror, what abasement, never seen such filth.... What marvels!'

The *Mahabharata*: it is also a mixture of emotions; of disquiet, with no sign of light; of shocks, of precise and sometimes cynical descriptions—like a prodigiously ambitious pattern that a genius of a poet (or was it several poets?) attempted to apply to the world, the world that he knew, the India of antiquity.

Make of India of the past, the world of today. But how? In juxtaposing scenes of different colours. Or introducing different colours in the same scenes? And how not to abandon the *action* on the way? Is it possible?

In Kerala today, children are still given names from the poem. Avoiding those which bode ill, like Karna, a bastard rejected by his mother although the son of the Sun. Superb warrior with a huge heart, but so uneasy in the shadows.

❖

The plane leaves Delhi for Paris on the night of the 23/24 September. I write a few last words in the plane (very 'intimate diary'). Persistent fatigue. Need time to recuperate. Lost four kilos or more in a month (not a bad thing).

Head whirling. Millions of images, sounds, smells. Impossible to put them into any sort of order. In any case, what would be the point?

What is a foreigner? A country, a land, ceases

to be foreign the moment one puts one's foot on it. And the air one breathes immediately becomes one's own.

Strange, in the plane, to find once again French newspapers, the French language. I am sleepy.

I feel as if this five-week journey began a very long time ago. We metamorphose time, sometimes. I know that in Paris my wife and my friends will be astonished to see us return so soon. We will ask what had been happening in France. Oh, not much, they will reply. As usual. Yet we ourselves are coming back from across several centuries.

India is not necessarily a phantom. A place where everything seems to have been foreseen, from one extreme to the other. Anything that one can do with this or with that. Complete. The least boring in the world, that is certain. A meticulous exploration of reality. Continuity of ancient kingdoms, the only one left. A gigantic anomaly: unless all the other countries are shadows of India.

❖

Proof that everything has been anticipated: one day in Bombay, in the business area, I stop in front of a tree. A rope has been tied around a branch and hangs down along the trunk. The end of the rope is burning slowly.

I am a little surprised at this unknown ritual, in

the middle of the city. All the more because nobody seems to be looking after it.

And then a man arrives, stops, takes a cigarette out of his pocket and lights it with the end of the dangling, smouldering rope.

It is, in fact, a public lighter.

Who said, Civilisation?

❖

I often think of Hippolyte Fauche, this obscure nineteenth-century Sanskritist who gave us the almost complete French version of the poem (the only one in the world, apart from the Indian languages, and English. But the first English translation, before Lal's, was done by Indians in Bombay around 1900, which is to say, after the French).

This man worked through subscriptions. Initially, he had two or three hundred clients who died one by one over the years. Towards the end a few dozen of them were left. Fauche worked everywhere—even under a bridge, at night, during a storm. I can imagine his regret when he knew he was dying without having completed it. For me he has become a hero, on par with those whose exploits he translated.

❖

In Paris in 1983, we meet again Professor Lal from Calcutta who is continuing with his huge translation

in verse. He is giving a lecture at the Kwok On museum and Jacques Pimpaneau asks me to come and translate. With pleasure. In the audience of a few hundred people, arrive suddenly Joyce Mansour (the French-Egyptian poet) and Henri Michaux (also a poet, and a writer and painter), whom I don't know. They sit down in the front row.

Lal has chosen to comment on two lesser-known stories from the *Mahabharata* which are not directly linked to the main flow of the narrative. I translate as best I can, under Michaux's brilliant gaze, so close to me. One of the stories is about a master and his young disciple who sit down one day under the shade of a tree. The master asks the disciple—a very young man—to go and get him some water to drink. The young man goes to a village, meets a beautiful young woman near a well, falls in love with her, follows her home, asks her parents for her hand, marries her, lives there with her, brings up several children, lives out his life. When his hair has turned grey he suddenly remembers his master, takes up a pot of water, goes running back to the tree. There he finds his master who says to him: 'I was waiting.'

The flexibility, the inconsistence of time. A story, a game. With resonances.

At the end, after many exchanges and comments, Michaux came to me and said smilingly, that I had translated 'with the casualness of a naughty boy'. He did not seem disapproving.

Up to what point can this casualness be pushed? Two dangers always threaten every adaptation: a systematic lack of respect which treats the original work like a springboard to who knows not what interpretation and which disfigures and transforms everything—or absolute respect which holds the original as sacrosanct, to the minutest detail.

Somewhere between the two. Yes, but easy to say.

❖

I start to write. Nine years earlier, from 1974, after listening to Lavastine's stories, I tried to write a play. Just to see. Depending heavily on a narrator. Obviously, everything has to start afresh.

The auditions also begin. Because a date has been fixed for the first performances: Avignon, in July 1985. Before that we will do some performances at the Bouffes. This meant starting rehearsals around August or September 1984. Just as well if the play were written before that.

Peter quite frequently asked me to take part in the auditions, talk with the actors, who had come sometimes from the other ends of the world. The scene would often be just written, which meant a double audition—for the actor as much as for the scene. For me it meant seeing whether it worked, whether something stirred, came to life.

All that one discovers—the weaknesses above all—while acting.

The Search Continues

1984

DELHI
MYSTERIOUS
OCCUPATION

Second trip. Departure 31 March. Work well advanced in the past eighteen months. A tryout for one week in November 1982, at the Bouffes theatre, with actors, musicians (particularly the violinist Subramaniam from Madras). Looking for a common factor, archaic sounds, rhythms—also words. And other long sessions of work during the whole of 1983 (among other writings and travels). And the auditions which carried on. Casting very difficult: sixteen principal roles.

It was time to return to India. A felt need.

Delhi, first of all, for just one night.

What were we looking for? As usual, we had no idea.

This time Chloé Obolensky came with us (she was to do the sets, the costumes); so did Kim Menzel, the Danish musician whom we were to meet in Madras where he was finally able to extract some sounds (after a month of trying) from Indian wind instruments.

We drive down towards the south, from Bangalore towards Mysore.

Still looking out for atmosphere, images, sounds, gestures, perfumes, colour.

Stopping every thirty kilometres, or twenty. Always wanting to stop, always looking for an excuse to stop.

Life along the way: grains spread out to dry, vegetables just asking to be squashed by passing cars, animals roaming around, countless pedestrians, birds chased away.

Driving at around thirty kilometres an hour. Surprises all the time.

Extravagant hotel near Mysore, on the top of a hill full of monkeys. The former palace of a maharaja. Each room is different, with amazing furniture of the 1920s. We are the only clients which means that we can each have two rooms—and go from one to the other in the middle of the night. Can't sleep (the heat, a little fever). Dozens of servants dressed in white in a colossal, red-draped dining room.

Just below the hotel, a noisy temple, full of life, fairly primitive. Throngs of women pressed together, screaming. It is said to be a gypsy temple. As sometimes happens, Peter is not allowed to enter, except into the courtyard, because of his light-coloured hair and blue eyes. Since I have very short hair and a bronzed skin, they let me in. I sometimes pretend I am from Kashmir, even pronouncing a few words in some strange lingo. Usually it works. One time I picked up a young child (they are everywhere) and entered into the sanctum sanctorum

carrying the child in my arms. No one said anything to me.

Coming out of the temple I put him back where I had found him.

❖

I have started to write, without haste. I try to find the tone, the vocabulary. I make lists of words strictly forbidden to me, all those which carry in them something Occidental, parasitical (no word is neutral or innocent). Such as the word 'noble', the word 'knight', which is connected with our folklore, our history. Impossible to use 'javelin' (inseparable, for some, from images of the Roman legionaries). Even 'lance' or 'sword' are suspect, 'sabre' is banished. A horse cannot be a 'mount' because it seems that the cavalry did not exist. 'Unseat' is unsuitable, 'prophet' too Biblical. Every little phrase poses a problem. Certain concepts such as that of 'dharma' are impossible to translate. It has to be explained (as it is in the heart of the book), undoubtedly by inventing a scene. Vyasa, the legendary author of the poem, says that the aim of the *Mahabharata* is 'to inscribe the dharma in the heart of man'. No question of leaving that out. It is a complex notion that everyone talks about. There is an individual dharma which each one must know and follow, and also a collective, universal, cosmic dharma which

one could call the world order. And one depends on the other. If a great number of people respect their individual dharmas, the cosmic dharma will be maintained. That is where our responsibility (and it is a great responsibility) lies, that on which depends the survival of the universe.

According to Lavastine, this sense of menace, of an imminent rupture, of a tragic rejection of dharma, is the centre of the work. This is why the grass is afraid during the battle. Fearful that the dharma might be forgotten by the fault of men, by their arrogance and greed. Impossible to leave this out. That would be a real betrayal. Lavastine says that for him the most important sentence of the book is: 'The dharma, when it is protected, protects. When it is destroyed, it destroys.'

Certain scenes are a must. They cannot bc avoided. For example, the scene where Kunti reveals to Karna that he is her son, her illegitimate and rejected son, and that the Pandavas against whom he was making war, were his brothers. Perhaps the positioning of the scene needed to be changed, brought in earlier (than in the poem), into the first days of the battle. But I already have enough elements to start writing. Start with that, maybe. Then go back to the beginning, as in a patchwork. The possibilities—and the task—seem unlimited. The months pass, more travels, a play to be done—and I still don't have the courage to write.

In other, more obvious, cases, one can invent scenes which do not exist in the poem. Introduce characters, imagine relationships, new situations. Indispensable: when Karna receives the ultimate weapon from the hands of the hermit Parasurama (himself an avatar of Vishnu)—another ineluctable scene—in the poem all that is said is: 'He gave him a weapon.' A way must be found of visualising this redoubtable gift. Invent today, if not Indian myths, at least some mythological details unknown or ignored up to now.

A few words, generally monosyllabic, traverse centuries and cultures without being affected. Words which have a certain radiance, a certain resonance, which are open to several meanings, like *blood, heart, flesh, life, breath.*

A Sanskrit expression which we today call (without any sexual connotation) the subconsoncious speaks of 'the secrets movements of the atman'. How can that be translated? I struggled a long time with it. Then I found in the works of Amadou Hampâté-Bâ, specifically in *L'etrange destin de Wangrin* (The Fortunes of Wangrin) the expression 'the depth of your being'. I jumped on it immediately. It seemed very well suited to the characters in the poem. As when Krishna, seemingly suspicious of the moral integrity of Bhishma when he decides to take part (despite his reluctance) in the war, says to him,

'Are you sure in the depth of your being, that it is not your supremacy which you want to demonstrate?[5]

❖

In Madras, to Peter, Kim, Toshi and Marie-Hélène, I read out a possible beginning. About twenty minutes. Just to gauge their reactions—which were not bad. But it is not quite there yet. The beginning is decisive and unquestionably there must be a child (as in the poem, which is recited to an adolescent).

I imagined a temple with people lying down, apparently asleep. A child enters, looks around him. One of the people (it is Vyasa) speaks to him in the shade, 'Do you know how to write?'

This sentence should be the very first one. It prepares the arrival of Ganesha, the celestial scribe sent by Brahma himself. Because Vyasa who had composed it, did not know how to write. He needed someone to do so.

The other actors could get up one by one,

---

5. This sentence would finally be modified but the expression 'the depth of the heart' reappears many times in the narrative. Later I found the same expression being used by Claude Lèvi-Strauss to translate the words of the Amerindians (in *The Jealous Potter*). Had he also read Hampâté-Bâ? Strange, and interesting, triangle.

according to their order of appearance in the story.[6]

I write all over the place, at airports waiting for planes which would not arrive. In a traffic jam in Madras I read out a scene to Peter. The story, the characters, are now constantly with us. It is about time. We start rehearsals in September.

❖

The *Mahabharata* is in a way, a long poem about forgetfulness. Beauty forgotten, the harmony of the earth forgotten, forgotten by man his origins and his place in the scheme of things. They are all born through divine relations and find themselves enmeshed in problems down here. As if the puppet's strings were broken. On many occasions the characters must be asking themselves, 'But what has happened?'

A *reminder*. Imperative to be vigilant. We are responsible for everything, and first of all for ourselves. Must not forget anything (forgetting is easy, alluring). The poem promises to those who read it, good health and a long life. The most potent talisman in the world. Who we are. Vyasa decided to tell us, without flattery. 'You are that' (and nothing else; pointless to look further).

---

6. This beginning would be modified. The first sentence remains, but Vyasa is alone with the child in the wilderness, beside a little lake.

I remember a short passage from Cioran: 'Man is a deceitful animal. History is his punishment.'

❖

Chloé shows us textiles or rather teaches us how to see them, touch them, feel them.

Is there a secret relationship with writing? Fabrics have a woof and a weft, some are tightly knit, others are lighter, heavier, coarser, impalpable; they have their own smell. In the same manner should there be some tightly constructed scenes, some looser, more roughly sketched? The very *stuff* of a scene. A scene made of jute, a scene made of silk.

❖

Two ravishingly beautiful young women—their mother as well—in Madras. Exquisite, of great refinement, slightly haughty, or anyway, distant. They are in the dyeing and block-printing business. One of the daughters—who speaks fluent French—is super-elegant. She takes me to visit her factory where an indistinguishable mass of slaves splashes around in a sort of brown mud. I ask her: 'Is this an old Indian technique?'

'Yes,' she tells me. 'But I attended a three-week workshop in the Ardèche (in the south of France).'

❖

By car up to Cannanore, with a breakdown on the way, in a forest.

As it becomes night, we are taken to a village feast. A long walk along a beaten path, across a wood. Slightly worrying. But a light weaves through the trees. A peasant, warned of our arrival, has come to meet us with a lantern.

He guides us to the village. We hear a distant music.

It is the feast of the patron-hero, present as an effigy, whose exploits are sung this evening. A group of musicians, among them an albino whom we recognise, having met him in 1982. We had called him 'the missionary's son'.

The *Mahabharata* is here also, in this little village. It is everywhere. Tired, we lie down on the ground, on a bed of leaves. A sense of well-being. Children are asleep. I also fall asleep, despite the insistent beat of the drums.

Awakening at dawn.

The next day, meetings at Cannanore. In the evening, the small temple we love so much. Then a Theyyam, for Chloé to see.

❖

In Kerala, towards the end of the 1960s, men started to emigrate to find work in the Emirates across the way. Directly transported from an agricultural, ancestral

culture into modern, petrol-driven salaries, they come back in their holidays loaded with transistors, electric mixers and other objects of civilisation. At this sudden contact with electrical appliances, their wives are immediately stricken with a new sort of depression which has in fact been given a name—*the Kerala depression*.

Specialists from all over the world come here, to study this on the spot. After which they write papers and speak about it in seminars.

❖

In the car to Mangalore, then a plane up to Ahmedabad, much further up, in Gujarat.

❖

10 April

Visit the city, an important textile centre. Fabulous textile museum, run by the Sarabhai family who seem to own the whole city. One member of the family, Mrinalini Sarabhai, is a very well-known dancer. She also runs a dance school. Her daughter Mallika who, it seems, speaks French, could be—so they tell us—a possible Draupadi (we had not found anyone for that role). Unfortunately, she is ill. We cannot meet her.

Draupadi, the 'star of women'.

The next morning we have to drive to Rajasthan.

Before leaving the hotel, without knowing why, I suggest that we phone this Mallika. Marie-Hélène calls. Yes, Mallika is feeling better. Her house is, in fact, on the way to the road north. Hardly a detour.

Peter hesitates a little, then he gives in to destiny. In her superb house we find Mallika, pregnant, recovering from hepatitis. Superb (to me) and yes, French-speaking.

We spend some time with her. An Indian Sophia Loren. A strong woman, intelligent, decisive. She listens smiling, to our project.

We stay hardly twenty minutes.[7]

❖

They say that India is 'structured' according to pure and impure. Usual point of view, very probably false, in any case limited. Peter, anyway, pretends that he only loves impure theatre. Pitilessly distrustful of purity, because pity is of necessity impure.

---

7. Without realising it, we had found Draupadi. Mallika Sarabhai would come to Paris two months later (from New York) to read a few scenes for us. Entering the Bouffes theatre, she bent down to touch the ground. She would stay with us—a precious personal presence as much as the presence of India—throughout the whole adventure. Her son was born just before rehearsals began at the end of August. Because of his birth she arrived a little late in Paris. She acted in French, in English, in the film. Impossible, today, to imagine the *Mahabharata* without her.

Here also things appear less simple than one would expect. In fact, all through the journey or rather our moving around, we hardly notice the separations, the castes. Perhaps because we are ourselves distinct and separate. In the streets one cannot miss seeing the slaves, sweepers, cart-pullers, dark and dried-out, spades in hand, unsmiling, no doubt untouchables. We also see the rich—hidden away, much more idle. But between the two the social texture, in our brief impressions, appears incredibly complicated, often even contradictory.

Who can pretend to understand it clearly? Each time we think we have found the thread, and when we pull on it, it becomes unending; it takes on ramifications, changes colour. The feeling of an inexhaustible world. Of a universe in constant expansion.

❖

It is the dry season. The season of heat and dust.

Along the course of a dried-up riverbed which passes through Ahmedabad, thousands of men and women who come from four hundred kilometres away in the north, to stay for six or seven months. They dig deep trenches, build mud huts and cultivate vegetables which they sell in the city.

From the garden of his sumptuous house, a man dressed in white, part of the Sarabhai family, a glass

of fruit juice in his hand, says, pointing to the human ants: 'They make a very good living.'

When the first rains fall from the sky in the month of June, the river flows again, sometimes only for a few hours, and carries away fields, trenches, houses. The migratory peasants leave on foot for their mountains in the north. They will return next year.

❖

A stroll, at night, with Peter. Very hot. Lots of men sleep outside, on beds made of ropes.

One man has set up an open-air cinema. It is a bicycle, or rather a tricycle (the man riding it creates the required electricity by pedalling) which is linked to a sort of coffin-like box with tiny holes pierced in the sides. The 'film' (in fact pieces of ad films stolen from here and there), is projected into the inside of the box. The smallest cinema in the world. The interior is painted like a minuscule theatre with a curtain and even seats. The spectators, not more than five or six at a time, keep standing, looking through the holes. The projectionist pedals. The film (silent) lasts four or five minutes, no more; a hotchpotch of images—karate, a singer who sings without anyone hearing him, some love, some dance. A glimpse of Indian cinema in a few moments.

❖

After the meeting with Mallika, we leave Gujarat for Rajasthan, towards the north. Everything is bone dry. Police checks on the way.

Jodhpur, then Udaipur, then Jaipur. The classic circuit. It is a different country, too Muslim for the *Mahabharata* to have made any special mark. But a very beautiful concert in Jodhpur where an Indian musicologist has brought together some excellent instrumentalists in the open air. Among them a child who plays Indian castanets, his eyes raised to the sky. Evening falls. We are served mango juice and the sound of the kamanche traces designs in the evening air.

Two restful days in the Lake Palace at Udaipur. Everyone tells us that it was here that the James Bond film was shot. But none of us has seen it.

High fever. But I carry on working, and I read some scenes to the others. Reading has become almost a daily ritual.

Here the women wear pants, the men wear robes. Jaipur, the dream of Orientalists. Palaces, hotels, an observatory. And everything is pink.

❖

Half a day in a Rajasthan village. To listen to songs, look at very beautiful costumes and jewellery worn by the women. The inhabitants respect all life, like the Jains. Avoid killing snakes, or swallowing mosquitoes. Very poisonous snakes here.

Noticed the presence of a large number of peacocks in the village. I ask if, by chance, peacocks didn't kill snakes. Oh yes, they reply, it is quite possible.

❖

14 April

Back to Delhi by plane.

One short night at the Imperial and off again the next day to Kathmandu, very early in the morning.

Somebody told us that the Pandavas, in the course of their exile, had retreated to Nepal. So let us go and see if any vestiges remain of that.

No, nothing. A disastrous impression. From Kathmandu to Bhakhtapur (the town restored by the Germans), all the men we meet appear drunk, or drugged. Beaten down, an air of defeat. Among buildings restored are men destroyed. It is a festival day.

Everything depresses us, even the sight of the young virgin-goddess at her window, even the visit to the great Buddhist monastery (where I buy some Bhutanese cloth). Ninety-five per cent of Nepal's resources come from foreign aid.

Everything that can be designed to keep a people down. Never forget forgetfulness.

In the evening a dreary walk through the streets.

Sadness. Not even the heart to rebel. The Indian rupee which is not convertible and which no one outside India seems to want, is much sought after here.

Decide to leave the next day.

❖

A plane for Benaras. Arrival into a furnace. The impression, on leaving the plane, of breathing something hotter than oneself. Immobile in the taxi which takes us to a hotel, we are drenched in sweat. It is 41 degrees in the shade. I think I have never, not even in the Sahara, felt so hot.

Yet, the pleasure of getting back to the vitality of India. You feel it everywhere. That day, a hundred marriages were celebrated in Benaras.

Chloé gets to know Benaras. Flight back to Delhi the next day. A big rat, unmoving, awaits me right in the middle of my room at the Imperial Hotel. I ask him what he is doing there; I explain to him that this is no longer his room, that it is mine, I have the key to it. He turns his back to me and goes tranquilly away, towards the hole in the wall through which he had entered.

In the evening of 18 April, a last reading in the hotel, with discussions as always. Peter, Marie-Hélène, Chloé: the first audience. Some scenes already exist.

In the very beginning, in 1974, when the decision

was first made (late one night after an evening at Lavastine's, on the pavement of Saint-André-des-Arts street), Peter said to me: 'We'll stage it when it is ready. And it will take as long as it takes.' The stories, to us, seemed magnificently mysterious. And unknown, in that marketplace far away.

Bit by bit it became clear that the play would be divided into three parts. The last would be called 'The War'. Naturally. Long and difficult (more than three hours), but it would hold. Plenty of action. Difficult comings and goings from one camp to the other. After which it would be necessary to move rapidly between the war and paradise (the audience would be completely worn out, that much was certain).

The second part would be 'The Exile in the Forest', with the return from the forest, and the embassies, just before the war. With all Krishna's efforts to avoid war, knowing full well that it was inevitable. This is the most varied part and also the most attractive; plenty of parallel stories such as Arjuna confronting Shiva in the Himalayas, the disguises in the court of King Virata, the battle of the cows.

The most difficult: the first part. It would have to include the game of dice, a scene lasting almost one hour. But the rest? The origins, the births, childhood, the tournament, marriage, different fights, Krishna's entrance on the stage—how to make all that hold

VARANASI
JCC

HEAT
JCC

together? For the moment it seems impossible, unless one were to simply speed up the rhythm and let everything pass by like a film clip—which would be a real betrayal.

Long discussions. Continued the next day.

❖

What becomes clearer, little by little: the need to find our own path. Tradition here is very strong, with an energy that is constantly renewed. How is it that such ancient heroes, with their stories so well-known (we have seen 'The Death of Abhimanyu' seventeen times!) retain such power, almost primeval, after so many centuries?

We cannot hope for anything to equal it. In the West we will, on the contrary, present an *unknown* story. Therein lies the danger of exoticism, of picturesqueness. We must establish from the start that it interests us directly, that it is written for us, that it is in no way a cultural duty.

On the other hand, in India, this all-powerful and omnipresent tradition must have a paralysing effect on contemporary expression. And even beyond that: to continue a tradition does it not mean, in a way, that the order of things is good as it is, that the caste system is excellent and that nothing must be touched? The first wish of an angry young author today must be to throw everything out, including the theatrical conventions.

I know perfectly well that our problem does not lie there, but all the same. It is at least worth thinking about.

Journey's End—And a Beginning

1985

EVERYWHERE

JCC

On 29 January, after four months of rehearsals, we leave for India with the whole group of actors (without Mallika, who knows the story) and some of our technicians.

Plunge the actors—who already know their roles—into the heat, noise, pulsating energy of India.

Great excitement.

From Paris to Bombay and, without stopping, directly from Bombay on to Mangalore, from Mangalore to Udipi. Difficult to imagine a more radical change.

The whole of the 31st at the Yakshagana school to which we return with pleasure. The next day by bus to Cannanore, to the still crumbling Seaside Hotel. In the evening, Theyyam. The next day Kalamandalam, lunch at a temple in Calicut, off banana leaves on the floor. Then, after the Kathakali, to Trichur. Reunion with known roads, familiar smells. But this time very rapidly.

❖

In the evening, we are allowed in to the Koodiyattam (or Kutiyattam) centre; a different school, the oldest and to some the most authentic, the best preserved.

It is late evening. A big dilapidated building. It is very dark, as everywhere in India when night descends. We had learnt of the existence of a very great guru, old and tired. We are permitted to see him for a minute.

We enter a room and sit on the floor. Ten minutes later, literally, they bring him to us. He can no longer walk. Heavy, fat, very old. A simple white lungi. His assistants set him down (with a hundred marks of respect) into an armchair opposite us. A man who has danced his whole life long. Someone explains to him who we are and what we are looking for in India. He keeps his eyes shut, he listens, breathes fast. We can hear his difficult breathing.

Then he says something in a low voice. They translate for us: the master will offer you a sample of his art. He will show us 'the young girl who goes to her first rendezvous with love.'

And he actually shows us. His eyelids lift open, his eyes become animated, he blinks, the hint of a smile plays on his lips, he raises one of his hands, sketches a gesture.

For a few minutes, he is no longer himself. This very old man, at death's door, becomes a young girl, ardent and expectant. He shows us, and how; with no props, nothing.

Then, suddenly, it is all over. And they carry him away.

❖

3 February

Very early departure by bus for Madurai. First elephant on the way: everyone rushing to the door, photos, etc.

Twenty kilometres before Palani, we start overtaking people walking down the road carrying strange, light wooden structures more or less in the form of houses.

Quite accidentally we have chanced upon the day of a great pilgrimage. An immense crowd at Palani. We stop. It lasts more than three hours. Millions of pilgrims are conducted through streets cordoned off with ropes held by students.

The temple is on the top of a high, rocky hill. One goes up on a big cableway, or on foot for the more energetic ones. At the top, visitors are led into the sanctuary by vociferous and agitated Brahmins. Absolutely nothing sacred about it. Naturally, it is a Shiva temple.

We descend on foot, some down the hillside, others by the steps. Almost at every step, holding out his bowl, a monster. Some of them are quite extraordinary. One might well believe that all the sick beggars of India have come together here. Long garland of what humanity could be, could have been. Their looks, as we pass by.

Their hands held out. The absence of hands.

And from place to place, in their midst, a very beautiful child-god, made-up and indifferent.

❖

Sixteen different nationalities, in our group. Cohesion of colours. Mirror, my beautiful mirror. How well one feels with others. Like a little world within the world, doing at his level what the whole wide world does not. There is here (and vice versa?).

❖

The play is written, naturally, since we have been rehearsing it for four months. But anything is still possible.

It has been a stupendous job (everyone admits that), but Peter knows how to give the impression, to me, to the actors, that he works without actually working. It is a path always full of surprises. We learn martial arts, shoot with bows and arrows, travel around India, watch performances; and the work gets done through all that. As if the moments of solitude indispensable for a writer (moments which last many hours) were also a part of this pleasure.

Without speaking of the invisible work, the most precious of all.

❖

Return to Madurai (3 February) and to the great temple. Vittorio (Mezzogiorno) stops for a moment near some women selling objects spread out on the ground. He knows he is to play Arjuna, he is preparing for that. During a year of exile, Arjuna, the great warrior, in order not to be recognised, chose to disguise himself as a woman and become a dance teacher to a king's daughters.

There, at the entrance to the temple, he picks some ankle bells and has them tied to his ankles. He even tries them out. Great astonishment all around at this blue-eyed European who beats the ground with his bare feet.

Arriving from Italy, Vittorio came to see me one day in Paris, at the very beginning of the rehearsals (another actor had dropped out of playing the role). Not knowing anything about the poem, he asked me to tell him about it. Both of us in the kitchen. After five or six minutes he interrupted me to say: 'If I understand correctly, what you are asking me is much more than acting.'[8]

In the evening, as it happened, a big festival. The

---

8. It was much more, and he felt it. For him it became a total involvement. Quite magnificent. He acted in the play and in the film, in both versions. Five years altogether. Everyone loved him. Cancer carried him off despite his courage, in 1994. The third one of the group to leave, after Duta Seck and Ryszard Cieslak.

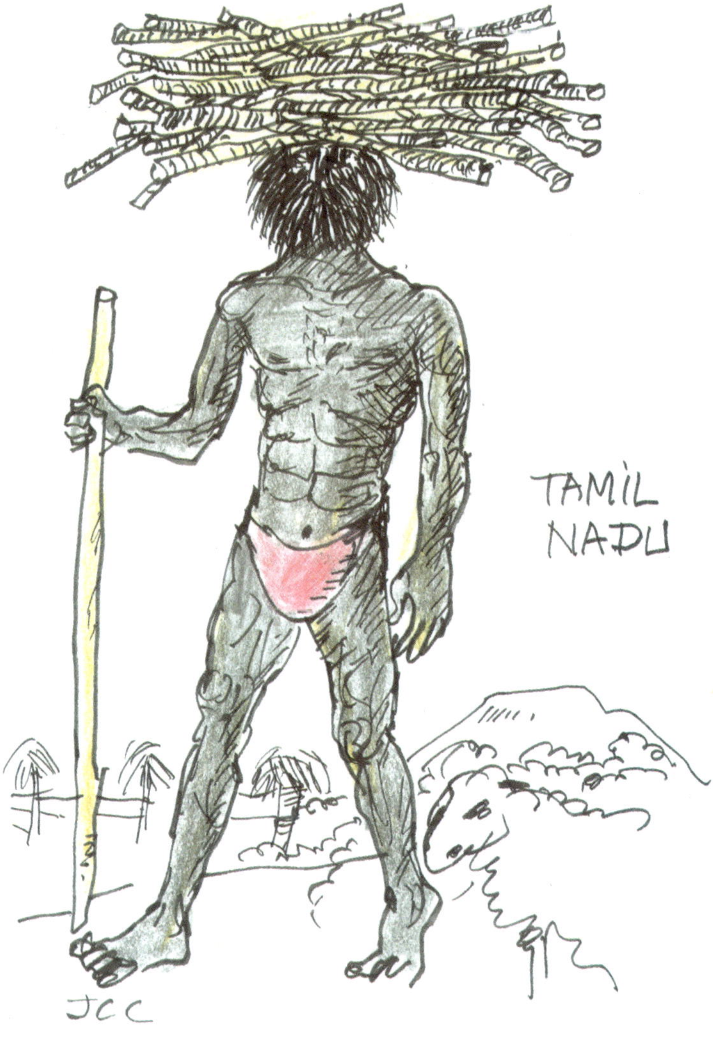
TAMIL
NADU
JCC

day when the great idols (three tall, golden statues, one of them a horse) are taken out of the temple and carried to the lake. A colossal crowd. A million strong. We quickly get separated. I literally allow myself to be carried off by the crowd which presses tightly against me, though without any problem. Quite the opposite. I go where the crowd goes, I don't take any initiative, I do nothing, I follow the movement. Almost intoxicating.

After going around the lake, the splendid idols are taken back to the temple until the next year. The crowd parts. Some of us find ourselves in front of the main entrance and we reassemble to enter together. They allow us to go up to the sanctum sanctorum, a room carpeted with sculpted golden plaques. It is late, past midnight. Barely a few dozen of the faithful. We copy them. We pass the palms of both hands across the bowl of flames which is presented before us and press them, still warm, against our faces. The last ritual before getting to the hotel. We will go to bed purified.

❖

We all leave Madurai on 5 February for a morning in the forest. Still the same quest: see, feel, listen, to an Indian forest. Many scenes during the exile of the Pandavas, take place in a forest, the place of exile and apparently of solitude.

Visit to a small temple on a mountain. Full of life. Meet a child-god, made-up, decked out in peacock feathers. He suddenly appears in front of us, at a bend in the forest trail. Not a word. Face calm, a distant look in his eyes. All he wants is a rupee or two. Young divinity who begs in the forest.

In the middle of the forest we find a small temple in ruins. A platform, six by four metres, is surrounded by a sort of terrace where one can sit.

A brief pause. Peter asks each one of us to go into the forest for twenty or so minutes, and bring back an object that we find particularly striking.

No sooner said than done. We go and we come back, with a pebble, a leaf, a branch, a handful of earth, a long palm frond, a dead insect.

We pile up all these objects in the middle of our terrace. And we start our daily exercises: first the vocal then the physical. We must present a strange spectacle: twenty-five people, Europeans, Africans, a Japanese, a Balinese, most of them in odd costumes, singing at the top of our voices in the thick of the forest, signalling, gesticulating, improvising, reading out pieces of the text.

No Indian forest is completely deserted. Peasants, woodcutters pass us by, looking at our group with curiosity, with astonishment. And there is something to be astonished about, even in India.

All of a sudden a woman, a peasant, approaches.

Without any hesitation, she walks the few steps up to our terrace and, without casting a glance at us, lies down flat on the ground with both arms outstretched, hands folded, towards the heap of objects we have collected from the forest.

She has seen what looks like an offering; she has come spontaneously to pay homage to it.

We watch in silence, holding our breath.

Simplicity, omnipresence of fervour. Like a very special welcome.

She stays about a minute, stretched out on the ground. Then gets up, leaves the group (still without a word being spoken) and goes off into the forest.

We remain silent a long time. That day we do not go back to our exercises.

❖

The African actors who are part of the journey, four of them, are Tamsir Niane, called Fifi: witty and lively; the great Sotigui Kouyaté who is getting on for fifty and will play the impeccable Bhishma; the strong Mamadou Dioume who will be Bhima, and the odd Clement Masdongar, originally from Chad, a trained dancer, handsome, brilliant, endearing and slightly unstable.

They all find themselves in India for the first time and their reactions are similar: everything reminds them of Africa. They keep saying: this is like at home,

it is like in Africa. Direct and profound links, even with the landscapes. But most of all in the way of thinking, the rituals, the rhythms.

One evening, having got a splinter in my foot, I knock at Sotigui's door as his room is next to mine. I ask him to take out the splinter. He takes my foot between his hands and first of all murmurs something in Bambara.

Then he puts on his glasses, takes a needle and removes the splinter.

❖

From Madurai to Madras by plane. On 6 February, the whole day in Kanchipuram.

We find Shankaracharya, this time in a sanctuary in Kanchipuram, a vast maze, rather strange, in the centre of the sacred city (the Benaras of the South). The rooms are like a labyrinth full of scribes, visitors, devotees carrying offerings, well-dressed men walking by briskly in animated discussion. Papers, odours.

Four servants (slaves?) struggle to push a big elephant through a doorway. It had strayed in there and now could not get out. That is certainly going to take time.

Our group is received first of all by the person we had met three years earlier; the middle-aged Shankar. Long and interesting conversations with the actors.

Each of them wants to learn something special about his character. Here too, we are on a terrace.

I have to submit to a sort of test. The Brahmins place before me a large parcel of paintings, of ex-votos, all representing mythological scenes. As I am a 'writer', the Ganesha, the one who dares to write the story of the poem, I ought to know these scenes, be able to say who is who. They show them to me one by one. I don't do too badly (not an easy test because the bearded men all look alike in the paintings, and all the women are the same).

After this we are admitted into the presence of the saint himself, the very famous, very old Shankaracharya, who has not opened his mouth for close to eight years.

We are led into a small courtyard. They ask us to sit on the ground, which we do. It is morning. We wait in silence for a good hour, facing a small, closed door. A modest building, worn-out. Peeling walls. A few hens moving around us; a little further away, the crows.

Nothing solemn, nothing special. Sainthood suffices. Quite something.

Finally the door opens. A very old man, wearing a lungi, appears. A closed face, almost severe. A squint in one eye.

He stops in the doorway and barely glances at us. He seems to be in a bad mood (disturbed?). He

nods his head, first to the left then to the right. A Brahmin comes running and, without a word, brings him the day's newspaper.

The old saint—one of the most revered men in the world who is known to have performed miracles—stays a long while on the doorstep, looking a little sullen—or distracted. He looks without looking, newspaper in hand. To the right, then to the left. This lasts six or seven minutes. We don't stir.

Finally, he makes a sign with his hand (a benediction? For us?), goes back inside and closes the door behind him.

It is over.

We leave in silence.

A little later Maurice Bénichou (preparing to be the first Western actor to play Krishna) does us an excellent imitation of the old saint.[9]

❖

---

9. We saw him four years later, during a series of theatre workshops which we conducted in India in 1989. He was nothing more than a very old man, lying on the ground. The crowd pressed together in front of a curtain. Then the Brahmins pulled the curtain and we could see him, curled up on the floor, wearing a pair of large spectacles, very emaciated. He no longer moved at all. They showed him for an instant, still alive, and then let the curtain fall again.

After this we are received by the young Shankaracharya whom I have now known for several years but without ever having heard him speak.

He seems more dry, more reserved, more stern, more 'fundamentalist' than the middle-aged man. But as soon as he starts to speak he comes alive, even smiles. He shows a profound knowledge of the work, the *Gita* especially, and has some personal interpretations. The idea of a performance in the West, in France, is surprising to him but he accepts it ('the *Mahabharata* is good for you', a sentence we heard often). He tries to imagine how such a performance could be possible, outside Indian traditions and technique. Peter tells him that is precisely our problem.

What part, ultimately, should India play in our work? The manner of telling, the *mise en scéne*, the manner of acting, the costumes, the music: all pose problems. Quite obviously we cannot offer an Indian presentation. We are incapable of it. It would be ridiculous, absurd. Nor could we appropriate the poem, transport it to the West in our own style, ignoring on the way its culture of origin. Impossible, certainly, to write it in the form of a *tragedy*, of a *dramatic* work. I accepted that a long time ago. A part of the storytelling has to stay. Peter told the actors: 'You have to be storytellers with twenty-five faces.'

Could we, for example, keep the names as

they are? Is it even conceivable to present in Paris, in Avignon, a play where the actors are called Yudhisthira, or Dhrishtadyumna?

Too late to change, in any case.

In Kanchipuram, at the end of the day, they let a sacred elephant out from one of the temples and allow him to roam about freely in the town.

I saw him, one evening, going towards the market street, in the middle of fruit and vegetable sellers. He delicately picked a lettuce here, a banana there, with the tip of his trunk. And nothing was refused to him.[10]

❖

A sentence of Henri Michaux which could be applied to the *Mahabharata*: 'You tell this story to an old stick; it will sprout leaves and take root.'

❖

The plane from Madras to Calcutta.

The day of 7 December in Calcutta. Many meetings with actors and storytellers, who already

---

10. During our trip in 1989, we learnt that the middle-aged Shankaracharya, that kind and smiling man, apparently quite worldly, had suddenly gone into retreat. He had taken refuge in solitude, somewhere in the Himalayas. No further news from him. Another young man has been called upon. He is seventeen. The baton is passed.

knew us. Accompanied, naturally, by the cultural attaché.

In a group, they say, one individual never belongs but remains a loner. This was the case with Georges Corraface. The bus hardly stopped somewhere and he disappeared. When it was time to leave we looked for him. A phrase constantly on Marie-Hélène's lips, 'Where is Georges?'

❖

Night train from Calcutta to Benaras.

A mass of people at the station. The usual apparent disorder so secretly ordered. Sotigui, ill, vomits on the platform.

The windows of the trains are barred. We are told that thieves at night, at the stations, do not hesitate to cut off the hands of the sleeping travellers to steal their rings and watches.

Peter and I are in a sleeper with two others, one Muslim, the other Sikh. They get up several times, each in his turn, to perform their devotions.

I don't get a wink of sleep. But that is how it is: one sleeps very little in India, at least in our case.

Benaras at dawn. Peter, Marie-Hélène and I—and also Maurice Bénichou who came once in between—can now become guides for others. We recognise places, sometimes even shortcuts, shops.

All of us on a big boat. Slowly, in silence. Towards

evening, as we move towards the cremation fires, Kudsi, our Turkish musician, takes up his flute and plays a little. *Apropos*, he has to find out what Krishna played on his flute. Not easy.

Meditation in front of the pyres. One gets the impression that that's all there is to it. A burnt leg and a foot stick out. One of the men in charge breaks the leg with one blow and pushes it back into the fire.

After this, I get lost in the small streets of the town, along with Maurice (Bénichou). Everything reminds him of the *souks* of his childhood in North Africa. We pass in front of a bas-relief where Krishna saves Draupadi from being disrobed at the end of the game of dice by lengthening her sari indefinitely. One of the rare ancient representations of this episode.

Then we really get lost. It takes us good hour to find the others back at the hotel.

❖

Between Marie-Hélène, Peter and me, the *Mahabharata* is like a code. We see someone: it is a Shakuni, or a Kunti. The poem constantly comes between us and the world. We also speak of our dharma, which sometimes creates zones of incomprehension. We understand the contemporary political games in the light of Krishna's.

'Krishna' signifies black. And it is true. The work is full of darkness; it accepts it and sometimes demands it.

Everything is dark. We light a candle; it confines itself to a circle of light surrounded by darkness. A second candle: the circle gets enlarged. Ten, a hundred, candles. One sun, ten suns, a million suns: the circle of light is gigantic, it seems infinite. But it is always encircled by the dark arms of Krishna.

'What can cover the earth completely?' the lake asks Yudhisthira. The reply: 'Darkness'.

❖

For the scene where the lake questions Yudhisthira (a true test because the lake is his hidden father), I need other questions than those posed in the poem. I reread Plutarch, especially, in his *Life of Alexander*, the part about the meeting between the young conqueror surrounded by Greek philosophers and the Indian sages come to greet them.

The Greeks ask, the Indians reply. For example, 'What came first, the day or the night?' The Indians reply, 'The day, but it only preceded the night by one day.'

Another question: 'Which is the cleverest animal?' The Indian response: 'The one that man has not yet managed to find.'

I feel like putting some of these question-answers into the play. Have I the right? I phone Georges Dumézil who has become interested in our project.

I ask him if I can mix Plutarch with the *Mahabharata* for some exchanges.

'But of course,' he replies. 'They belong to the same era! And in any case, everything belongs to everybody.'

Last trip to Agra. Inevitable. But this time we won't go to Rajasthan.

❖

Delhi, at last, on 9 December.

It all ends with an open-air feast to which we are invited by Rajeev Sethi, our elegant adviser, our friend from the very beginning. In a beautiful, ruined old fort, outside the city. Dancers, puppeteers, magicians (with, at every turn, the unforgettable words: '*Begui, begui* and ... gingerly')! Peter goes on for a long time about the word 'gingerly'.

Half reclining on carpets with cushions, drinks—and a buffet. Very pleasant, without a shadow of doubt.

❖

The *Mahabharata* awaits us in Paris. It is the end of the last holidays. End also of my notes (in the plane on the return journey) and the beginning of anxiety. Each one of us feels it: this obligation to *play*. What has India given us? Impossible to say. A secret dimension that will remain probably always

secret, beyond wonder, charm, irritation, repulsion. The pulsating energy, above all else, and the mixture of things. The closeness that one only finds when working together and which no one can define. To travel in order not to see, travel to do, or to be.

The play opens in three months.

AFTERWORD

Naturally, our relationship with India did not end there. I myself have returned frequently in the past ten years, either with Peter or for other reasons. In 1994, I even spent two weeks in Dharamshala in the Himalayas, with the Dalai Lama, and we co-published a book, *Violence and Compassion*. Today I have plans for a film with Mani Kaul, a longtime friend. An Indian film, to be produced by Suresh Jindal and shot in India (in 1998?), an adaptation of an episode in the *Mahabharata* (again!) and entitled *The Dicing*. I have been accepted officially as an Indian scriptwriter, the first non-Indian. I am very proud of it.

One does not separate oneself from the *Mahabharata*. It is a work one gets 'attached' to, one which puts into question all other writing. It is also a new vocabulary, another aspect of our always difficult relations with the world.

An unexplored territory which we carry within ourselves without knowing it. I have often been called upon to speak in public, even in India, on the poem,

on the *Gita*, our work, the film that was shown (the play could never be performed in India). I have often written on it, articles and prefaces. I have published, in the form of a narrative, a *Mahabharata* which has been translated into fifteen or so languages. And so on. It will never leave me. And nor have I any desire for a separation, a divorce. 'The *Mahabharata* is good for you.'

Sometimes everything turns upside down. As much as India helped me to write the *Mahabharata* in the form of a play, so now it helps me to live in India, to feel at home there. A poem and a continent; two continents, in fact. Reunited with a place that is multiple, yet one. As Krishna said to Vyasa, the god to the man: 'Which one of us invented the other?'

ALSO FROM SPEAKING TIGER

TRAVELS ON MY ELEPHANT

AN INDIAN JOURNEY

Mark Shand

'I enjoyed this book immensely. Shand is the most engaging adventurer I have come across.'—Imran Khan

When Mark Shand, an aristocratic playboy and travel writer, decided that what he needed was an elephant, it wasn't long before he started getting phone calls from India, offering elephants for sale. With the help of a Maratha nobleman, he purchased Tara, a young, scrawny female, and travelled with her—and a retinue of friends, old and new—for more than 800 kilometres across India, from Konark to the Sonepur Mela—the world's oldest elephant market.

From Bhim, a drink-racked mahout, he learnt the skills of elephant driving. From his friend Aditya Patankar, he learnt about the culture and attitudes of India. And with Tara, his new companion, he fell in love. So much so, that decades after their travelling days were over, Mark Shand was still fund-raising and campaigning on behalf of Indian elephants, becoming one of the most high-profile conservationists in the world.

Travels On My Elephant is the story of an epic journey across the dusty back roads of India, as Mark Shand and his party astound, amuse and puzzle all those they encounter on the way. It is also a vivid portrayal of a cheerfully chaotic India and the memorable, touching account of Tara's transformation from a sad beggar to the star attraction, and Mark Shand's loyal companion.

Page Extent: 208 pp **Price: ₹299**